PRAISE FOR *WALKING HOME*

"If you have ever wanted to become a hiker or a long-distance walker, there is no better way to begin your journey than by joining Celia in *Walking Home*. On her 59th birthday, after taking stock of her life, she sets her priorities. A lifelong hiker, she decides to join her love of nature with her love of Vermont, where she spends many months of the year. The Long Trail, a grueling 273-mile hike stretching the length of Vermont from Massachusetts to the Canadian border, known as the LT, is waiting for her.

Celia was a walking child who fearlessly explored woods on her own, a small, self-taught naturalist. Throughout her life she had hiked many trails; but nothing like the one ahead of her. She admits that she had never owned a backpack nor slept in a tent. She persuades a friend to join her and is delighted when she accepts. There is much to be done. She and Sandy begin their planning, down to the smallest detail. After seven months, they are ready. This is the story of that walk, its struggles and glories. It is also a goldmine of information for anyone willing to take this journey."

—Felicity Vaughan Swayze, author of *War Torn: A Family Story*

"Celia Ryker hiked 272 miles along Vermont's Green Mountains from the Massachusetts border to Canada, following the Long Trail, the oldest long-distance hiking trail in the United States. Through it all she details her interactions with the land, the fellow hikers she meets, and the memories it evokes.

Accompanied by a good friend for much of the trail, she also hiked solo, overcame her trepidations and achieved her goal while along the way she sees a bull moose, finds her 'trail legs' and sees glorious vistas.

Reaching heights of 4,394 feet at Mount Mansfield, she describes the scenic beauty of the land while also providing practical guidance. Duct tape applied to her walking sticks served as hand grips when walking uphill. She notes the value of putting most of her gear in a sealed plastic pack liner and provides cautionary advice about hypothermia.

A fascinating narrative."

—Jennifer Belton, former White House Library Director

"Reading *Walking Home*, my astonishment that a woman who had never slept in a tent and had balance issues would undertake an almost 300-mile backpacking trek on one of the toughest trails in North America matured into something deeper: an appreciation that being in touch with nature helps us be in touch with ourselves. I think you'll enjoy this book. It's great."

—D.W. Allen, author of *Dappled Psychiatric*

There is a bigger difference between taking a hike, which almost everyone can do, and thru hiking. Thru hiking, tackling an entire long-distance trail over a period of months, takes a special kind of hiker. Celia Ryker is just that, one with dedication, perseverance, curiosity, and a sense of humor. *Walking Home* is a memoir of her epic experience hiking the 279-mile Long Trail from the Massachusetts border through Vermont to Canada. Along the way she entertains us with childhood memories and reflections on her life off the trail, interspersed with poetic references to the transforming experience of being in the woods."

—Anne Richter, journalist/writer

Walking Home

Trail Stories

Walking Home

Home

Trail Stories

CELIA RYKER

Rootstock Publishing

Montpelier, VT

First Printing: June 2021

WALKING HOME Copyright © 2020 by Celia Ryker

Release Date: June 22, 2021
Softcover ISBN: 978-1-57869-053-4
eBook ISBN: 978-1-57869-057-2

LCCN: 2021902968

Published by Rootstock Publishing
an imprint of Multicultural Media, Inc.
27 Main Street, Suite 6
Montpelier, VT 05602 USA

www.rootstockpublishing.com

info@rootstockpublishing.com

Interior and cover design by Eddie Vincent ENC Graphic Services (ed.vincent@encirclepub.com)

Author photograph courtesy of Celia Ryker.

Cover art by Peter N. Fritsch, "*Path on the Way Up to Camel's Hump*"
www.peternfritsch.com

Printed in the USA

Dedicated to my parents Bud and Bertha,
and my paternal grandmother, Augusta.

Their encouraging words have filled my life.

TABLE OF CONTENTS

I went to the woods because I wished to live deliberately,
to front only the essential facts of life . . .

Henry David Thoreau

INTRODUCTION

It was my fifty-ninth birthday and as my waking brain realized what day it was, my mind jumped to a childish declaration made over a cake illuminated by ten candles: "I am halfway to twenty."

Aunt June turned from ice cream scooping and said, "Don't even say something like that."

I guess she didn't want to think about children growing up because that would mean she would age as well, but to me, being halfway to twenty was cool. Why do I remember that moment so vividly and yet yesterday I spent hours looking for my shoes?

I know that getting old is what happens if you don't die young, but the idea of running out of time was both inspiring and sobering.

On my fifty-ninth birthday, I made a list of the things I'd hoped to accomplish by then and had either failed or not attempted at all. I was alarmed by the length of that inventory. To keep from being depressed, I made a second catalog of achievements I had realized and was pleased with those numbers—but I'm not done yet.

I took the first list and prioritized it. Two projects vied for the top spot: My love of nature and the Long Trail had been calling me since my first visit to Vermont. And then there was my love for writing. I'd written short stories, journal entries, and poetry since I'd learned to hold a pencil, and had two unfinished books in literary limbo. Weighing these challenges, I decided I could write when I was no longer able to walk— but distance hiking could not wait.

I was halfway to one hundred and eighteen years old when I made the decision to hike the Long Trail.

1

CHAPTER ONE

GREENWALL

The woods can be a bit strange.
It takes a long time to feel you belong there
and then you never again really belong in town.
It's a choice made for you by your brain
at a moment you don't notice.

Jim Harrison, "The Woman Lit by Fireflies"[1]

S andy and I were ten days and seventy miles into the Long Trail when we reached Greenwall. We were way behind our plan to hike ten to fifteen miles a day, but we were getting used to it. Sandy was eight inches taller and twenty years younger than me, but neither of us was setting a land-speed record. We generally enjoyed chatting with fellow hikers at the end of our hiking day, but at Greenwall we were listening.

The Greenwall Shelter was a three-sided wooden structure with a wooden floor that served as a sleeping deck for up to twelve people. There were no windows, tables, or benches and the unpainted walls were bedecked with nails of every size, at varying heights, for hikers to hang gear to dry. The roof slanted front to back and the two-by-twelve header across the open front of the building held a row of heavy cords looped around it, six feet from the floor. Each had a sturdy six-inch-long stick tied to its end, and an upside-down tuna can with a hole poked in its center a few feet above each stick. The sturdy little stick could be slipped through the loop at the top of a backpack, as three

3

now were, with the tin cans preventing mice from using the cords as access to the packs from the ceiling.

"I've hiked the Appalachian, Pacific Crest, and North Country Trails, and I think the Long Trail is the toughest in the United States." Moose Jaw spoke from experience. He was thirteen hundred miles into his second tour of the Appalachian Trail.

Five of us sat in a row along the front edge of Greenwall's sleeping deck, like birds on a wire. We gazed across the open area in front of the shelter, past an unlit campfire ring, watching the afternoon sun slant through the forest that surrounded us.

The guy next to me, Duck Tape, spoke through a scruffy gray beard. "I've done the AT, PC, and Great Divide Trails and I agree, the LT is tough and gets worse the closer you get to Canada."

Most hikers call trails by their initials—except the Great Divide Trail. GD sounds like an editorial comment.

Duck Tape added, "I've hiked all over Canada and Mexico and I think the LT is not just the toughest in the United States but the toughest in North America."

I leaned toward Sandy. "Is he trying to scare us?"

Moose Jaw named daunting trails in Canada and Mexico that he'd heard about, but Duck Tape had walked them and he shook his head. "The LT is harder."

They digressed into a dispute over the merits of their backpack and boot choices, sharing strong feelings about both. Sandy nodded along for a while before she said, "I did weekend hikes in Tennessee with friends who told me I'd picked one tough number for my first distance hike."

I wanted to think that Moose Jaw and Duck Tape were messing with us, but Sandy's friends hadn't been joking. "I didn't realize how difficult this trail was. And we're still on the easy part," I said.

Sandy leaned against her backpack. "We're in it now."

Gazing into the darkening forest, I wondered: What have I gotten us into?

A fit young hiker with long braids poking from her baseball cap walked into Greenwall as darkness neared. She was hiking the AT, NOBO (northbound in trail speak), on a break between high school and college. Her trail name was Phoebe; maybe that was her real name, or perhaps her name was Sue or Jane and she had always wanted it to be Phoebe.

Almost every hiker had a trail name, and if you didn't pick one for yourself, someone else would. Duck Tape got his name when he threw a roll of duct tape to a fellow hiker, who ducked as it sailed over his head. Sandy had chosen the name Sweet T. The T could stand for tea, which she did like sweet, or Tennessee, where she lived. My Michigan trail name had been Yogi, but on the LT Yogi is a name applied to a mooch, based on the cartoon character Yogi Bear. I chose the name Oven Bird, but when I told people my name they said it reminded them of roast turkey or chicken, not the woodland bird whose nest is shaped like a Dutch oven. Patty-O dubbed me Bent Bike. I wasn't fond of it, but hadn't come up with a better one yet.

Phoebe had hiked that day from Peru Peak. Jelly Bean, Moose Jaw's buddy, was blown away. "You hiked over fifteen miles today? We put down a couple fifteen-mile days further south on easier ground, and I thought I was gonna die. You don't even look tired."

She looked up while changing from boots to crocks. "I average sixteen-mile days, but I must say that coming down to the shelter from the AT was the longest two-tenths of a mile I can remember."

"OK, I feel a little better now," Jelly Bean said. "If someone who can hike like you noticed it, then I don't feel so bad about wondering if we'd ever get to this damned shelter."

Sandy and I kept quiet. We didn't want anyone to know that we'd hiked from the Lula Tye Shelter, just five and a half miles south. Everyone else at Greenwall was hiking NOBO on the AT, over twenty-one hundred miles from Georgia to Maine. Sandy and I were NOBO on the LT, a distance of 279 miles from Vermont's Massachusetts border to Canada. There's no shame in hiking a shorter trail, but a five-and-a-half-mile day was something to keep to yourself in that company.

Hiker's-midnight is 9 p.m., and Sandy and I wandered back to our tents before it was fully dark. Moose Jaw and Jelly Bean had tents a few yards away and we could hear them ending their day. We'd looked at their campsite before they arrived, but decided the best spot was the soft level area next to an abandoned privy lying on its side. We sniffed around to be sure it hadn't been used recently, and then employed nails protruding from its aging wooden sides to hang our gear to dry.

I crawled into my tent as inky darkness descended, and lay atop my sleeping bag reminiscing about how I'd roped Sandy into this.

My birthday had been in September and by December I was researching and planning my hike. Over the Christmas holiday, Sandy stopped in to see my husband Don and I. She'd come back to Michigan to visit family and friends, from her new home in Tennessee. We talked about my Long Trail plan and I showed her maps and what little equipment I'd acquired. I shared the fact that I would probably be hiking alone, since I couldn't find anyone willing to join me.

Sandy was surprised that Don supported my plan but had no interest in hiking with me; she seemed enthusiastic, but said little else. A few weeks later, I received an e-mail asking if I'd like company on my trek, and we began to plan our adventure together.

Neither Sandy nor I had ever done a distance hike, and I'd never owned a backpack (a daypack does not count). I had never slept in a tent, unless you count the blankets my sisters and I had draped between chairs as children. I brought new meaning to the term *novice*, and Sandy was only a half-step ahead of me.

The night I received Sandy's e-mail, I lay awake long after Don drifted off. When it was clear that sleep was not coming, I eased out of bed, grabbed yesterday's clothes from the chair by the door, and tiptoed downstairs. I dressed warmly and slipped outside under a nearly-full moon, leaving the dogs in. I wandered into the woods, observing the shadows of leafless trees against the snow. This is really going to happen, I thought. I have someone to hike with—I have to get serious about this.

I mulled over training ideas as the shadows of tree branches trembled in the slight breeze, and imagined branch-shaped fingers scratching into the snow toward the soil beneath. I was lost in such thoughts when the shadow of a huge bird pulled my eyes to its silent flight.

The winged silhouette of a Great Horned Owl riffled through the forest shadows splayed across the ground's uneven white surface. The sight left me with goose bumps. It felt like a positive omen.

Now here it was the following summer, and I was camping next to a fallen privy, wide awake and listening to the snoring coming from Sandy's tent. She'd fallen asleep quickly and I should've done the same but that didn't happen. I imagined Mickey Mouse counting cartoon sheep jumping over his cartoon bed. That didn't help. A barred owl called in the distance and I laughed to myself, thinking maybe I should be counting owls: Number one was my very first owl sighting. I never got to number two, because number one brought its own story to mind:

My twelve-year-old legs didn't have to go far to find wooded areas to search for wildlife; Clarkston was less developed in the early 1960s. Where a sprawling medical center now stands, there'd been an open field, the result of an abandoned building site. This flat area was used by the traveling circus when it came to town, and we hurried out after it left to see if we could find elephant poop or tiger fur where their cages had been. I walked this area often, going to and from the store.

Evening was approaching as I strolled home with the small bag of groceries Mom was waiting for. Midway across the open lot edged by woodland, I stopped in my tracks. An enormous silhouette loomed in a tree a few yards away. It looked like someone had chopped off Batman's head and plopped it on a branch.

I don't know how long I stood there waiting for that bird to move. The owl sat, huge and foreboding in the twilight, and I waited, hoping to see it fly while wishing it would stay there as long as I stood still. Finally, I had to move—it was nearly dark and being home before dark was a must. I was walking sideways and nearly fell over when Batman's head lifted itself into the air and flew into the forest.

Sandy's snoring grew faint and my owl memories faded to black.

In the morning, Sandy and I ate breakfast sitting on chair-sized rocks near our tents, discussing how many miles we hoped to put down and where we'd be sleeping that night.

Sandy looked up from her oatmeal. "Do you remember our first day on the LT?"

I slid to the soft ground and leaned against my rock-chair. "I remember picking you up at the airport, the ride to the trailhead, and the rain. I remember the rain."

Sandy took a more comfortable seat on the ground, leaning on her rock. "It rained every day."

"And it didn't dampen our spirits." I looked up at a brightening sky.

Sandy scraped up the last of her oatmeal. "We'd been planning for so long, I was excited to finally be hiking."

"I was so geeked when I left Michigan," I told her, "I hardly slept the night before. I should have been tired after driving for eleven hours alone, but thinking of what lay ahead kept my mind jumping."

CHAPTER TWO

A FOOTPATH
IN THE
WILDERNESS

*It is not so much for its beauty that the forest makes a
claim upon men's hearts, as for that subtle something,
that quality of air that emanation from old trees, that so
wonderfully changes and renews a weary spirit.*
Robert Louis Stevenson

After seven months of preparation, the Long Trail was at hand and I was driving solo because Don and Sandy's schedules conflicted. My plan was to spend the next day mowing the lawn and cleaning up our house in Vermont, then pick Sandy up at 11:59 p.m. at the airport in Manchester, New Hampshire.

When the lawn was mowed and the house tidied, I drove to a road crossing at the halfway point of our hike. I found a gas station/deli within a quarter mile of where our trail crossed Route 11, and asked the man behind the counter if I could leave a drop-box: a hefty little package containing food and stove fuel. I drove away feeling like I'd left a food cache for an arctic expedition.

Driving toward the airport that night, I could see a starry sky out my driver's side window, but straight ahead where the airport lay, there was a brilliant lightning display. A few large drops of rain began to fall, then more, then a deluge. I could hardly see the road, and had both hands clamped on the wheel. The rain would occasionally let up, then hammer the windshield again and again. My GPS was in charge.

At the terminal, Sandy's flight was listed as en route, which I assumed meant they were waiting for the weather to clear. Flights that had arrived were waiting for luggage that could not be off-loaded, due to lightning. Sandy arrived after the storm rolled through, and by the time we'd picked up her luggage, gotten back to the house, and were ready for bed, it was 3:30 a.m. I should have gone to sleep quickly, but my mind whirled with anticipation and thoughts of my father.

When I told my dad about my hair-brained plan to hike the Long Trail, he didn't scoff or warn me of dangers. He leaned across the table and his eyes, dim with age, sparkled when he said, "You will remember this trip for the rest of your life."

On my next visit, he asked about my plans. I showed him my map and explained that I would be hiking almost three hundred miles. On later visits, I brought the equipment I'd acquired and showed him how I would purify drinking water and prepare food. During one of those sessions, he laughed and said, "This reminds me of when you were a kid and you would take off with your friends and we weren't sure where you were going or why."

I reminded him of the time my friend Cheryl and I walked so far we didn't think we could get home before dark, and called home for a ride. "You sent Arnie out to get us. He wasn't thrilled to be sent to fetch his little sister, but when he couldn't find us he was downright mad."

Cheryl and I managed to walk home that day. Our adventure had taken us to a small farm where we'd seen two spotted horses we thought we should explore. The horses' gray-haired owner had been happy to answer our questions, explaining that the dark mare was the mother of the younger, light-colored horse that he called Benny. Benny had been taught to bow and count out answers to simple math questions, and the owner was pleased to have an enthusiastic audience. It had been worth our time and effort, and Arnie would get over his anger eventually.

Dad said, "Your mother was worried that you had called from a stranger's house, and that you might be too brave for your own good."

I nodded. "I assured her it was no problem because the people owned horses. Somehow, I thought that was good enough. Mom asked me to be more careful and not to do that again, and I agreed."

Dad smiled and shook his head. "You've always been a walker."

When I shared my Long Trail plan with Arnie, he laughed and said, "So, you're reverting to your childhood." He was so much older; when I was nine, he was fourteen and I didn't think he noticed me most of the time. Had Arnie seen me riding imaginary horses when I was old enough to know better? He'd know we were off on one of our hikes when he saw us filling our pockets with what he called "crap", as we prepared to set out for the day. I guess he noticed me more than I'd realized.

I stayed awake with those memories, but was up before six and we were loading packs into Wib's truck shortly after seven. Audrey and Wib (short for Wilber) are our nearest Vermont neighbors. They watch over our property when we're away, and over the years have become dear friends. They'd agreed to drop us off and pick us up when we came off-trail. Getting to the trailhead meant an early morning drive into Massachusetts to put us on the Appalachian Trail, south of the Vermont state line.

As we drove along, chatting about our impending adventure, anticipation was taking its toll. It wasn't fear or trepidation, but excitement—the kind I could remember from my youth. On the first day of second grade, I was so excited that I threw up. Aunt Dorothy thought I was ill, but my mother knew better. She changed my dress and sent me on my way.

Driving toward an unknown trailhead on that bright morning, I felt no fear of losing my breakfast, but I was excited in an old, familiar way. Wib and Audrey told us that it had rained every day for the past two weeks. We were hoping the rain was over and we'd have good hiking weather.

When I pulled my pack out of Wib's truck, it felt heavy. It hadn't seemed that heavy when I'd loaded it. I'd done three weekend training hikes to prepare for the Long Trail, and Ewa (pronounced Eva) had led them all. She'd shared a story about hiking with a cousin when she was young, and how she put rocks in his pack as a joke. Ewa's spirit was with me that morning as I hauled my pack full of rocks into place on my back.

As Sandy pulled out her gear, I discovered that she was a two-trekking-pole hiker, while I used a single pole. I wondered what other differences we would find. Although we'd been planning for months, exchanging e-mails and talking on the phone, we'd never hiked together.

After a three-hour drive, Sandy and I started walking at 10 a.m. Our picture, taken at the head of the Pine Cobble Trail, was in bright sunshine. It felt good to get dirt under our boots. My pack lightened and my stomach tightness disappeared as we walked into the forest.

Our plan was to hike from the Pine Cobble Trail to the Seth Warner Shelter for a late lunch, and then on to the Congden Shelter. My hike times had steadily improved on my weekend hikes. I knew I wouldn't be able to make a three-mile-an-hour pace on the Long Trail, but I thought we could put down two miles an hour without much difficulty.

We weren't on the trail long before we found the first Appalachian Trail sign. The unpainted wood, etched with a router, read: VT Border & Long Trail 3.4 miles. My pack felt even lighter as we passed that sign.

Pine Cobble meets the Appalachian Trail after a steep ascent of thirteen hundred feet. The *Long Trail Guide* described the ascent as being along steps. To call what we walked up steps would have made me laugh if I hadn't been struggling up rocks that required the use of my pole and a substantial reach with almost every stride. On some steps, I had to crawl on my hands and knees and then use the next step to pull myself to my feet. I called to Sandy, "These are steps?"

We heard thunder in the distance and hiked in a drizzle that turned into a downpour. The trail went from difficult to challenging. The soil was soaked from weeks of rain and the irregular steps became a series of miniature waterfalls. It took three hours to hike 3.2 miles to the Vermont-Massachusetts border.

Although we were hiking slower than we'd expected and our pant legs were heavy with mud, our happiness at seeing the Massachusetts border sign was surpassed only by our joy at posing for a photo in front of the first official Long Trail sign. We were smiling in that picture, in spite of the rain. It was where I'd planned to be, back in September, when the Long Trail pushed itself to the top of my list.

THE LONG TRAIL
A SCENIC HIKING TRAIL THAT STARTS HERE
AND FOLLOWS THE GREEN MTN. RANGE FOR

APPROX 263 MILES NORTH TO
THE CANADIAN BORDER.

Those words etched into a wooden sign mark the trail's beginning, but the LT is so much more: It is a path through miles of forest so dense that hikers call it The Green Tunnel. It is a carpet of needles beneath an evergreen forest. It is rocky crags oozing moisture, year-round. The LT is low damp forests where streams flow freely and mountain summits where the wind rarely dies.

James Taylor (not *that* James Taylor) envisioned the Long Trail over one hundred years ago. He planned a hiking trail along the crest of the Green Mountains, from the Massachusetts border to Canada. I had never heard of the Long Trail, or that James Taylor, when my husband Don introduced me to his family's Vermont vacation property.

Don and I were newly married when I discovered Vermont. It was to become my second home and walking in the wooded mountains would become my passion, but I had no inkling of the significance of that relationship upon my introduction to the Green Mountains. Don and I had traveled from Michigan to spend Thanksgiving with his family in Connecticut, and we took a side trip to spend a few days in Vermont.

I feel closer to America's history when I visit New England. There's an old-world feel to the stone walls standing rigid sentry around properties that may have been settled under British rule. Michigan's early farmers had only rounded fieldstone to work with, and the walls that bounded their properties, made of heaps of fist-sized stones accented by a few larger rocks and the occasional boulder, slump and dribble over time, until they disappear. In New England, I'm impressed when I see straight walls formed from stone that may have been pulled from the ground over two hundred years ago. The flat gray slabs sit precisely, without use of mortar, as if they'd been set yesterday but for the moss and lichen growing over them. On my first view of Don's childhood home in Woodbridge, Connecticut, I was pleased to see the classic stone boundary marking the front of their property.

I felt fine rolling down the driveway at the end of our visit, but by the time we were on Vermont's twisting mountain roadways two hours later, I was not well. I'm not sure which family member introduced the stomach bug that moved rapidly through the household, but experiencing its early symptoms on an undulating highway was no treat.

I tried not to dampen Don's enthusiasm; there were things he wanted me to see. Quechee Gorge is always impressive, but my first view into the yawning ravine was dulled by the fear that I might lose my lunch.

We stopped several times along Route 4's winding path as the nausea began to settle in. I took little note of Woodstock's quaint charm, but I was impressed by the steep driveway to our house in the woods. As the car came to a stop, the thing I most wanted to see was a bed in close proximity to a fully-functioning bathroom.

I was feeling better in a couple of days, and Don experienced only a hint of stomach discomfort, so we did get to enjoy our vacation. We visited Bridgewater's Mill Mall, explored Woodstock, and shopped quaint general stores and art galleries. For lunch, we walked to the deli counter at the Bridgewater Corners Country Store and hiked back up the hill to dine on our porch with a view across the valley to Richmond Hill. It's not much of a view by Vermont standards, but it was impressive to me and I was beginning to fall in love with the place.

Beyond shopping and visiting lovely little towns, we walked on our side of Bald Mountain. I was already calling it ours. I knew it was not ours, as in Don and I, but as a member of his family I was feeling proprietary as I shuffled through the fallen leaves. We sat on huge rock outcroppings, found a boulder the size of a semitruck snapped cleanly in half, walked old logging trails identifying various trees and shrubs, and noted marshy areas, often after the water was seeping into our boots. A highlight for me was the stone wall that marked parts of the property. Those aged boundary markers remained tidy and exact, rippling across the uneven forest floor. We roamed the woods listening and watching for signs of wildlife, reveling in the beauty around us. I was hooked.

I learned later, in books about the history of Bridgewater, that our stone walls had been set by the Josselyn family during the years between British rule and 1791, when Vermont became the fourteenth state. To encourage settlement, King George III offered colonists the opportunity to acquire one hundred acres if they built a house on it. After the American Revolution, the Territory of Vermont continued that offer and the Josselyns built their home down the road from where ours now stands. They built a second house for their son, which is now Wib and Audrey's home, and received a second hundred-acre parcel for that effort. Their original homestead is currently a Mennonite church, and our 136 acres falls somewhere within their ancestral property.

I loved the thought of people farming our land years ago. Did they plant the twisted apple trees that still stand along the trail we call The Swamp Stomp? I've visited the Josselyn family cemetery in the woods behind the Mennonite church, and wondered what they looked like, what their voices sounded like, and what they saw when they looked into the forest or down the river. Were they happy in their lives or sorry to have placed themselves in this harsh new land?

I often sat on the wall they built, imagining gnarled hands lifting stones from the soil, adjusting this one, replacing that one with another that is the perfect size and shape to hold its place for centuries. I was awed by the skill that created my stone seat. I watched butterflies flitting from one spring bloom to the next and wondered if ancestors of that particular butterfly danced along this wall when the stone was still damp, having been freshly pulled from the soil.

After our first visit, Don and I planned annual vacations in Vermont. We started to explore further afield from our property, and that is how I first discovered the Long Trail.

At Lincoln Gap, I saw my first Long Trail sign. On the north side of the road, the sign read: Lincoln Gap – Elevation 2424. Below that was an arrow next to the words, Long Trail North. Another arrow pointed toward Battell Shelter 1.8 MI, and a third arrow indicated Mt. Abraham Summit 2.6 MI.

On the south side of the road, another sign pointed to Long Trail South. There were arrows to Sunset Ledge 1.1 MI and Cooley Glen Shelter 4.7 MI. The signs intrigued me—how long would it take to hike to Mt. Abraham and back? What was Cooley Glen Shelter like?

After seeing those signs, I began watching for trail markers and noticed the trail crossing my path as I drove to the store or to visit friends. Trails were everywhere and I wanted to know where they went.

Those memories stumbled through my head as Sandy and I walked a more even path for several miles. It was muddy and deep, but easy compared to the Pine Cobble Trail.

My weekend hikes in Michigan had offered few stream crossings, but when they had, I was forced to deal with vertigo issues. The moving water made each stone appear to be in motion, like whack-a-moles. When I extended my foot toward the next stone step, it would appear to move, leaving me faltering. I often walked in the mud to avoid the whack-a-mole stones that other hikers used with ease. On the LT, stream crossings were everywhere and my boots were caked with mud.

Sandy and I often stopped to take pictures. One of the first images on my camera was a huge rock outcropping encased in lichen. The next was of an oddly shaped boulder resembling the skull of a Cro-Magnon man. I wondered if that rock had been sitting there when Cro-Magnons walked the Earth. Did one of our ancestors recognize its resemblance to their own cranium?

Through the rain, I watched the foliage change with our elevation. The color pallet was limited to shades of green and gray, but the variety in hue, leaf size, and shape were vibrant under an overcast sky. Blue-green lichen and emerald-green mosses draped a smoke-gray boulder and bright green sedge nestled among deep, soft ferns beneath an overhanging canopy of dripping hemlock, making me feel like I was walking through nature's art gallery. Each vignette I viewed through the raindrops was so beautiful that I wished I could stop and observe it all more closely.

The LT and AT share the same trail from the Massachusetts border to Route 4, about halfway up the state of Vermont. On that part of the trail, when we passed other hikers, the common question was, "Are you hiking the AT or LT?"

If the person being asked were resting and you couldn't tell their direction of travel, the next question was, "NOBO or SOBO?" That equates to "North-bound or south-bound?"

Three men passed us during our first break of the day, NOBO on the AT. We'd heard them coming from a ways off, as one called out, "Blaze...Blaze ... Blaze," over and over. The LT is marked by white blazes (two-by-six-inch markers painted on tree trunks), to assure us that we're on the correct path. The hikers stopped briefly in the rain to ask our destination and commiserate about the weather. Their backpacks were disappearing into the forest when I heard the refrain begin again: "Blaze ..."

When they were out of earshot, I told Sandy, "One guy calls out every blaze he sees? If I had to travel with him I might come up with a new use for my duct tape."

We set off a few minutes later and Sandy took the lead, calling out "Blaze" as she passed the first white marker. By blaze number three I was ready with a small stick, and when it bounced off the top of her pack our hike became quiet again. She'd been waiting for my response and we both laughed.

We ate lunch beside a beautiful stream during a break in the rain. The water rushed among huge boulders, and a smooth bit of ground along the bank glistened in the filtered sunlight. The forest was telling us: "Stop here and rest. There is magic present."

It felt good to be rain-free for a few moments. Sandy and I were silent during much of our meal, not due to fatigue or lack of things to say, but because we'd materialized in an oil painting and become a tiny piece of a grand work of art.

We were putting on our packs when the rain began to fall, and Sandy asked to see the map. I reached into my pocket with confidence, but the pocket was empty. It was our trail map, waterproof and detailed, regarding distances and elevations, and I had put it in a large pocket to make it easy to get to. It must have fallen out—but where?

As we walked back for the map, with Sandy marching ahead of me, I felt like a fool. I wondered how far back we'd have to go. Would we make it to Seth Warner Shelter before dark? A few hundred yards back, our map lay along the trail, waiting to be retrieved. Seeing it in Sandy's hand as she walked back toward me was a huge relief. Note to self: Do not put anything of value—like your map—into a pocket that does not have a zip or Velcro closure. Sandy decided that she should carry the map.

CHAPTER THREE

A SLOW GO

After a day's walk everything has twice its usual value.
G. M. Trevelyan

Sandy and I stumbled into Seth Warner Shelter having traveled seven miles in as many hours. We were wet, muddy, and disappointed in ourselves. In my backcountry first aid class, I'd learned you should allow for three hours per mile to get an injured hiker to the nearest road. We were doing better than a hiker with a broken leg, but not by much.

We left the rain behind as we caught sight of a sign with an arrow telling us we were almost at Seth Warner Shelter. We walked faster, eagerly watching for a building in the woods. The shelter was three-sided, with a slanted roof; the wooden floor was the sleeping deck and there was a picnic table and campfire ring in front of it. Judging by the number of packs hanging along the shelter's open front, all sleeping spaces were taken for the night, and three tents stood nearby. We didn't waste time chatting—we were eager to find a soft flat space to pitch our tents.

We set camp near the shelter, under a bright sky. Some shelters have no designated tenting areas and others provide hard wooden platforms, so we were relieved to find two soft grassy tent sites. There were more people arriving and not much flat ground left. We followed signs indicating the water source and privy locations as we began what would become our camp arrival routine: set up tents, restock water supply, nap for a bit, visit with fellow hikers, have dinner, and go to sleep.

I had backpacked in rain on my first training hike in Michigan, but it was nothing like the downpour of our first day on the LT. Sandy and I were both wearing what Don and I call *zippies*: lightweight, fast-drying hiking pants that have many zippered or Velcro pockets and legs that zip off to become shorts. When I zipped my pant legs off at the end of that day, the feather-light fabric sagged beneath a layer of black mud. The mountain trail cools quickly as the sun goes down and my fleece jacket was the first item I unpacked. My crocks were pulled out next, as my boots came off and my camp shoes gave my feet a break.

Blue Jay was sitting on the shelter's sleeping deck when we came to the picnic table for dinner. He assured us that the next two days would be easier. We hadn't told him our goal, but he volunteered that we'd be able to get to Route 4 in nine days, which had been our plan originally. We felt better as we ate dinner and discussed the next day's route while Blue Jay and other hikers shared their insights. They agreed that hiking long-distance in week-long increments was harder than hiking start-to-finish.

"It takes three or four days to get your trail-legs," Blue Jay said. "You'll just be feeling good when your hike ends, then you'll start all over again when you resume, weeks or months later."

Sandy did not have three or four weeks to hike the LT end-to-end; we were hiking in sections that we could cover in a week. The AT thru-hikers would be on the trail for six or seven months, walking from Georgia to Maine. I'd gone from being a day hiker to a weekend hiker to a section hiker. Someday, I would like to be an end-to-end or thru-hiker.

We were handed the shelter's logbook and encouraged to sign in. Most people signed their trail names, but some also commented, adding things like, *more rain!!!!!* after their names. This informal notebook becomes important if someone goes missing; being able to track stops and dates on the trail could assist in efforts to find them. We had already signed in at logbooks kept in wooden boxes at the Pine Cobble trailhead when we reached the AT, and at the Vermont-Massachusetts state line.

Blue Jay knew what he was talking about—he had one day left on the LT, SOBO to the Massachusetts border. He'd been hiking in sections that his work and family schedule allowed, and it had taken him seven years to finish the trail. Sandy and I were confident that we'd get to Canada in two or three summers, but then again, we'd hoped to spend our first night at the Goddard Shelter, which was still more than seven miles away.

We shared the picnic table and makeshift benches in front of the shelter with fourteen other travelers that night. We heard stories about hiking, food, New Yorkers, Bulgaria, rain—all the important news of the day. Several people talked about an older hiker who wasn't much bigger than her pack. She was making a slow go of the AT, but she persisted. Quick Toes said, "I haven't seen or heard about Baggins in a couple of days. I wonder what's going on."

Bench Butt volunteered, "She went into Manchester to restock. She should be back on the trail tomorrow."

Limping Louie relayed a story that day hikers had shared about finding a person wrapped in a foil blanket lying next to the trail with their feet sticking out. It was Baggins taking a break wherever she could, but the day hikers thought they'd found a body. When Blue Jay said that Baggins was only doing three or four miles a day, I thought he was trying to make us feel better. It did help to hear of another slow hiker, and it was good to know that people along our footpath were watching out for one another.

A variety of cookstoves roared warmth under different dinner choices while people chatted back and forth. With bellies full, conversation lagged as hikers readied themselves for their sleeping bags. I looked down the trail that we would leave camp on in the morning and wondered what lay ahead. My intrigue with woodland paths took me back to memories of my youth.

When I was four, Saturday morning meant a special breakfast, and French toast was my favorite. But when Dad announced that we were going to the zoo, I set my fork down—I was ready to go. Mom put the fork back in my hand. "You have to eat your breakfast first."

I looked at her finger pointing at my plate. "But . . ."

Her hand didn't move and I knew she meant business. The plate of French toast with the perfect balance of butter, syrup, and powdered sugar had filled my morning until it became an obstacle between me and the zoo. I had two pieces in my mouth with a third on the way when Mom stopped me. "One piece at a time," she said.

I lowered the fork to my plate and through a mouthful said, "Buuu . . ."

My brothers were laughing. Dad leaned over and touched my nose, saying, "Silly, the zoo isn't open yet. Take your time, there's no rush."

With less food in my mouth, I blurted, "But!"

Now everyone was laughing and after a minute, I joined in.

When the longest breakfast in history was over, Mom wiped the syrup from my face and hands, and we were ready to get serious about the zoo. We lived on Detroit's east side, so the zoo wasn't far away, but Dad drove slower when important events were at hand. Sitting between my two brothers, without a child safety seat or seat belts of any kind, I began to fidget when I spotted the water tower that loomed over the park's entrance. As the car came to a stop, Howard and Arnie jumped out. Mom helped me from the back seat and when my feet hit the ground, they headed for the gate, but she held my hand tightly. Dad slipped the camera's strap around his neck, took my other hand, and we started moving with me straining to drag them forward. "Come on, come on!"

I could see it as we walked through the turnstiles; the zoo's best feature was right there. "Come on!"

The rest of the zoo could wait—there was a forest of huge dark trees and I could see the path, but I couldn't see where it was going and I had to find out. "Come—on!"

I knew where that path would lead; I had been on it many times. I'd been carried into that forest before I could walk, but each time we came I hoped to find something new, a turtle in the creek or a new path leading to places unknown.

When my feet stepped onto the earthen footpath, everything dimmed, life slowed, my parents could let go of my hand because I wasn't going anywhere. I was looking—looking for squirrels, chipmunks, snakes or snails; looking for animals not kept in cages, but wild and living right there. Often, Mom and I were alone because the boys wanted to see the lions, tigers, and other good stuff. We could hear people blindly walking past the best part of the zoo without giving it a glance, their sounds muted by leaf cover. The people who ventured onto our path were subdued by a woodland embrace and spoke in soft tones, if they spoke at all.

I liked it best when it was just Mom and me. We could dawdle on the footbridge where we might see a frog in the water below, or look at a tree, counting the birds in its branches. Mom pointed to a large crested bird. "What's that?"

"Boojay."

"What color is it?"

"Boo."

Mom and I crouched near the fence that edged our path to search for animals among the leaves blanketing the forest floor. We often saw chipmunks and squirrels, but it took patience to see the smaller creatures. Mom pointed to a quivering leaf. "Something's under there."

We watched and waited; I was about to give up when it moved again and a tongue licked the air as a snake slithered into view. When I reached forward, Mom touched my arm. "This is the zoo. You're not allowed to touch the animals here."

The longer we stared into the forest, the more we saw. Butterflies were easy to spot, but the elusive walking stick bug was impossible to see—until it moved. Its body and legs looked just like tiny sticks bent into the shape of a praying mantis, like circus balloons twisted to form a dog. Watching a collection of sticks walk along a branch was magical.

As an adult, my friends and I have reminisced about childhood visits to that zoo. They all spoke of the tigers, lions, elephants, monkeys, even the cotton candy, and they were surprised that my favorite part of the zoo was a clump of trees they'd barely noticed. One friend said, "You mean that cluster of six trees with a couple of shrubs behind a sign calling it a 'nature trail'? I went in there once, but there was nothing there."

I spoke in passionate defense of the first forest in my life. "There were more than six trees, and it may have been nothing to you but it was a wilderness to me."

My blond hair is gray now, but I still look at a forest path and wonder where it might lead.

"Celia? Are you in there?"

Sandy's hand was waving in front of my face. "Earth to Celia."

I shook my head. "I was just wondering what we might see tomorrow."

"I don't know about tomorrow," Sandy said, "but my sleeping bag is calling."

Back at our tents, Dragonfly asked if we were going to hang our food because a bear had been seen in camp the night before. When I replied that keeping food out of reach for a bear meant it had to be hung high, at least ten feet from a tree or building, which was nearly impossible, her reply was, "Just getting it off the ground is better than nothing."

I'd gotten advice from my friend Janine, who was an experienced hiker. She'd been a park ranger and said she always kept her food closed up tightly in her tent.

To avoid conflict, Sandy and I decided not to broadcast our in-tent food-storage method, which Sandy had also heard from her hiking mentors in Tennessee. I noticed that those staying in the shelter hung their packs—with food inside—along the open front of the shelter, hanging at eye level next to where they slept and no one seemed worried about it.

Nanny Goat sang the praises of her fourteen-ounce tent as she proudly showed me her ground cloth that was the consistency of Saran Wrap. She used a trekking pole as a tent prop, and draped a sheer rainfly over that. She was sleeping under a paper-thin tent, accessible to anything that wanted to wander or slither through as she slept. A critter was going to have to work a little to get into my tent. I couldn't imagine that Nanny Goat's tent would be comfortable in a high wind or heavy rain, either.

Years ago, I slept under a poncho stretched between trees while canoeing the Rifle River in Michigan. I woke in the night to see four little eyes looking at me from three feet away. It was a pair of skunks; there was a hint of their scent in the air but not nearly the strength I knew they were capable of. I didn't move while they looked at one another, looked at me, looked at one another again and turned to waddle away. They bumped into one another several times and squiggled their tails, but did not spray. I imagined the music from old Laurel and Hardy movies as they waddled, bumped, and squiggled away into the darkness.

Sandy hiked with two sticks; I hiked with one. She wore a rain coat; I wore a poncho. My stove was a Jetboil; hers a PocketRocket. But we both wore zippy pants, carried CamelBak water bladders, and were kind of slow. We took brief breaks every few hours, even in the rain. When we arrived at Seth Warner, we weren't exhausted physically but we were saddened by our slow pace.

In my tent that night, I read in my trail journal of my first weekend hike in Michigan, and it made me laugh.

CHAPTER FOUR

BACKPACKING 101

Backpacking offers instruction about the
difference between needs and wants.
John de Graaf [2]

The Manistee River Trail was my very first backpacking experience. I knew that a weekend with Sierra Club members who knew what they were doing would be enlightening. Ewa, our leader, had given specific instructions on where to meet and what to bring. When I arrived at Red Bridge, I called her cell number. We'd never met, so I wasn't sure if she was already there, unrecognizable to me.

Ewa and the rest of my group had stopped for dinner. I was invited to join them, but I declined. I wanted privacy as I awkwardly set up my tent for the second time, then sorted through the contents of my backpack—for the ninety-third time.

When Ewa and the troop arrived, each person set up their tent and arranged their gear independent of one another, with little conversation. I didn't know any of them and hesitated before asking Nancy to inspect my tent to be sure I'd set it up correctly. The review was good, except that I needed to stretch my rainfly fully over the tent body. The tent was not waterproof, and leaving edges exposed would result in a wet tent.

Several people had recommended keeping a hiking journal, so I'd bought a Top Flight Composition Book that lived in a Ziploc baggie tucked into my backpack, nestled against my spine. The first page contained Nancy's important tent-assembly advice, however, my very first note-to-self was: *Get out headlamp* before *it gets dark.*

I heard others settling in for the night and hoped I didn't sound as inept as I felt, groping in the darkness for my only light source. I was surprised by how easily sound carried between tents; they provided visual privacy but offered no sound buffer.

With the light on, my tent became a lantern silhouetting its contents, and I was aware that others could see me as I penned my first journal entry. Then it was time to turn off my headlamp and settle back for my first night in the wild—well, sort-of wild.

The campsite was situated between a little-used paved road and the Manistee River. The rushing water created a soothing backdrop and there was no traffic, so we had the illusion of an isolated woodland camp.

I rearranged my gear several times, trying to determine just the right place for everything within my tent. I placed my pack near my feet on the right side of my tent, below the vestibule that I decided to use as my entrance. My tent had a vestibule on both sides, to allow two occupants access without climbing over one another. I slept with my back to the unused door. I put my boots near my head; in one sat my can of bear spray with my watch hung from its glow-in-the-dark trigger, and the other held my knife, wallet, and phone.

I wasn't sleepy yet, so I read the label on the bear spray: *Not for use on humans.* It sounded like pepper spray on steroids. Next it said: *Do not seek out encounters with bears.* That seemed like sound advice. It had a range of up to thirty feet, but stated that it may not be effective in all situations—that was not reassuring.

That first journal entry closed with a feeling of comfort in my woodland abode, along with a note about listening to the pleasant river sounds as I checked my watch and allowed myself to drift off to sleep under the forest canopy, which was exactly the feeling I'd been hoping for.

When I woke in the night, I was happy to hear the sound of rain against my tent flap and grateful for Nancy's advice. I looked around my tent, checked my watch (2 a.m.), then rolled over, glad to be warm and dry.

At 4:30, I awoke strangled by my sleeping bag, whose zipper, formerly located smoothly along my left side, was twisted, its top now near my right ear. My pillow, a.k.a. stuff sack full of spare clothing, was nowhere to be found and I could barely move. As I struggled to free myself, trying not to make any noise, I found my stuff-sack pillow spilling its contents into my sleeping bag.

Managing to extricate myself and realign the sleeping mat, bag, and pillow without my headlamp wasn't easy, but I didn't want any witnesses to the fact that I'd snared myself in my gear. By the time I slid back into my comfy cocoon, it was nearly 5 a.m.

As I lay there waiting for everyone to wake and begin their day, I mulled over how the next two days might go, wondering if I had the gear I would need.

Back in January, when I started preparing for the Long Trail, my friend Janine loaned me her backpack and some equipment, but she suggested I get my own tent before my first weekend hike. She was protective of her tent—not in a stingy way, but more like *I love this tent*. She'd lived in it during stints as a park ranger in Washington, California, and Florida. So I made my first trip to Recreation Equipment International, a retail corporation organized as a consumer cooperative. My advisors recommended it because of quality equipment, excellent return policies, and 10% refunds on eligible purchases.

I became an REI member and wandered into their April sale. Based on advice and research, I had a long shopping list. I told the salesman I wanted a lightweight two-person tent, and he recommended the REI Quarter Dome Ultralight. Janine advised that the one-person tent barely allowed room for a tiny person, but a two-person tent was perfect for one person plus gear.

I also needed a three-season sleeping bag and inflatable sleeping mat. I bought protein bars, freeze-dried meals, and trail mix, a Jetboil cookstove, headlamp, matches, and a collapsible walking stick, a spork, wool-blend socks, a couple of lightweight moisture-wicking shirts, and hiking pants.

My criteria for worthy gear included:

• Buy lightweight equipment; if it is one ounce lighter and does the same thing, buy that one.

• If an item can serve more than one purpose, it is a better choice.

• The prepared dried meals are expensive, but they are light, filling, and tasty.

I found differing opinions on everything from stoves to pack covers to water bottles. With Janine as my base source, along with online advisors and several books, I thought I'd made good choices. My first weekend hike would reveal the truth.

We broke camp in the rain. While still snug inside my sleeping bag, I contemplated the best way to get my tent down and my pack filled without getting soaked. Everyone was already busy with their own gear, so I went with my best guess. I stowed my gear inside of or attached to my pack, and stretched the pack's rain cover into place before stepping out of my tent and into the rain.

Wearing my rain poncho, I went to work on the tent. The stakes popped up and stowed easily; I loosened the rainfly and shook it out, but the effort was futile in the downpour. I pressed it into its stuff sack while draping my poncho over my tent to keep it as dry as I could; this meant awkwardly hovering over my tent while I broke down the poles. I gave some thought to how strange I must look, but didn't have time to dwell on that. The tent was still relatively dry when I balled it under one arm and picked up my ground cloth with my other hand. I shook the ground cloth a couple of times and stuffed it in with my wet rainfly. I stowed my dry tent on top of the grimy ground cloth and cinched the stuff sack. Lifting the rain cover off my pack, I lashed my tent in place and pulled the rain cover back down. I looked around thinking everyone else would be waiting for me, but they were finishing at about the same time. Breaking camp for the first time in a steady rain was not as bad as I'd imagined. Low expectations are not difficult to exceed.

The rain let up as Ewa set off up the trail at a pace I would've had trouble keeping up with on a sidewalk. Sheila shared with me that most hikers with a full pack walk at about two miles an hour over rough terrain. Ewa usually hiked at about three miles an hour. Most of the day, Ewa and Nancy took the lead, Joe and Sheila followed them, and I lagged behind everyone. Following my fellow hikers through a forest of tree trunks, I felt good just being able to keep up.

The first uphill surprised me. Walking up real hills over wet rocks and tree roots with a full pack put a strain on my legs that I hadn't felt while training on road or park hikes. I could feel the tension in my thighs as we moved up steeply. Slipping on wet roots and leaf litter on the downhill slopes, my calves felt the strain and my walking stick was a welcome aid.

I'd attached my water bottles to my pack with carabiners, thinking they'd be easy to get to, but they were not easy to reach and their constant motion was beyond annoying. I wondered if the CamelBak water bladders that other hikers used gave a plastic taste to the water. The idea of a plastic bag of water on my back with a tiny hose to drink from had not appealed to me while browsing the aisles at REI—but it did now.

Two hours into our day, Ewa took a short break. We removed our packs and sat down for a snack. This was standard procedure for Ewa on a long day's hike, and I learned some hiker lingo. I hadn't realized, for instance, that I was eating GORP (Good Old Raisins and Peanuts). I'd thought I was just eating trail mix, but apparently, GORP is trail-speak for any combination of sweet and salty snack food. I hadn't realized I needed a break, but afterward I felt refreshed.

There were a lot of hills on the Manistee Trail—a good start for someone planning to hike the Green Mountains. My walking stick came in handy on the hills, but I found its presence bothersome on flat ground. I tried folding it down to stash in my pack when I didn't need it, but the process was time consuming. I hadn't noticed how irritating the stick had been as it hung from my pack, until I removed the irksome water bottles. I'd been so annoyed at the bottles, I hadn't noticed the stick. Ewa and Nancy used no stick, and Sheila and Joe each used two trekking poles. I had only one and, so far, it was driving me nuts.

Hiking the sandy bluffs alongside the river was hard on my lungs. I'd never needed my rescue inhaler for hiking or any other purpose, but it had been prescribed when I was diagnosed with asthma and emphysema. I get a new one every year, just in case I have an attack, but it makes my heart race and I'd rather wheeze than feel that, if it's not an emergency. I was slowed by my breathing on those steep hills, but didn't yet feel the need for medication.

When we began the descents, I was glad to be able to breathe more easily, but my knees and calves strained for grip in the steep, soft footing. The walking stick was a huge help, but on the flats I was still swearing at it under my breath.

The bluffs high above the river provided a spectacular view, where I could see the enormity of the river's ecosystem. Loons and mergansers floated on the current, while a pair of marsh hawks flew along the river bank. Looking down on birds in flight was mesmerizing. I was surprised by their dark coloring; I'd only ever seen their almost-white chests as they flew over me.

When we descended from the bluffs to walk the river's edge, the perspective changed. The river seemed smaller, its ecosystem broken into pieces, and I could see its intricacies. The birds flew overhead and the water fowl paddled away from us. Huge fish were suspended, motionless in the icy water. They made no discernable movements, but they had to be swimming, or the current would have carried them away. In addition to fighting the things dangling from my pack, my boots were working against me as well. My new hiking boots still needed more break-in time, so I was wearing the work boots I'd been training in, but I hadn't realized how little tread remained on their soles. On wet clay areas, I felt like I was skiing on icy snow with a bale of hay strapped to my back—my walking stick kept me from falling into the muddy slop more than once. I was grateful that I hadn't dropped it into the trash can we passed at the last road crossing . . . I had considered it.

I had so much trouble slipping and sliding down a particular clay slope, Nancy instructed me to take off my pack, and then she carried it down to Ewa who conveyed it up the opposite bank with ease. I was impressed—how did they do that while wearing their own packs. Would I ever be that strong? I pegged my stick into the mud as I slid down one bank and slithered up the other side, vowing to have my boots properly broken in before my next hike.

By midday, I felt like I was on a forced march. The faces of the other hikers reflected a degree of determination I hadn't seen earlier; they were getting tired. My eyes were glued to Sheila's pack like a target, and my mind wandered.

I imagined being in boot camp and marching to an unknown destination, watched over and directed by our drill sergeant. I pictured combat boots stirring up a long dusty line in desert sands. My boots looked a bit like combat boots and if I let my eyes soften on Sheila's pack, it morphed into the shoulders of one of my platoon members. The flat woodland dissolved into desert and I wondered how far Sarge was going to push us today.

Why am I doing this to myself?

Then we came to a bluff, and with the sun on my face, the breeze in my hair, and a fabulous view before me, all forced-marching-through-the-desert thoughts disappeared.

During our lunch break everyone leaned against their packs, resting. Was Sheila asleep? I let my mind wander to reminisce about my youthful love of the outdoors.

A memory: I move through darkness, measuring each step in a pathless jungle alive with branches tugging at my sleeves and scratching my face. I travel in search of something I cannot define yet know I must attain. Being alone in the night doesn't frighten me, but when lights appear I duck behind a fallen tree. The lights are from a vehicle, but how could it find a way through this harsh terrain and what is it doing here? I crouch lower as it bumps past and do not rise until the lights fade in the distance.

A panther I'd been observing earlier from what I thought was a safe distance, has been shadowing me. I'm not sure whether she is following or stalking, and her presence worries me, but not enough to pull out the weapon tucked into my belt. She walked when I walked, and laid low as we watched the mysterious vehicle approach and depart. This baffling feline behavior is other-worldly, and the two of us move from dense jungle onto a broad savannah, yards apart, yet moving in unison. When the lights reappear we freeze and my mind races; if we run we will surely be seen. Our only hope is to lie flat against the ground and blend in with the sparse plant material. Who is this and what do they want? Are they looking for me? But why? Are they hunting this great cat who crouches so near I can hear her breathing?

The vehicle slows. Did they see us? It crawls to a stop, then moves again, but stops once more. I hold my breath as the lights inch forward and abruptly turn, aiming directly at us, then halt completely.

The driver's side door opens and a man steps out. He looks my way but must not see me as he moves across the light beams toward a native hut. I hear him tapping, then knocking, then pounding to awaken the sleeping natives within. This could only mean trouble for these innocent people and my eyes are glued to the events about to transpire. Within my sparse camouflage, I await impending disaster.

What is that bright light? This stranger has lured these primitive people from their sleep to wash them in a brilliant, unnatural light. I hear a voice, then another. They mumble softly, then louder—and now they are calling into the darkness.

"Cecelia Deborah, what are you doing out there?"

As I rise, the jungle transforms to an unmown field, the savannah is our close-cropped lawn, and the natives are my parents standing in their bathrobes beneath the porch light, Mom with hands on hips, awaiting my response.

"Vena needed to go outside," I say. Our dog could be a panther . . . in the right light.

As I trudge toward them, Mr. Kenyon laughs, gets back in his car, and heads off to work. Why does our neighbor go to work at this hour?

Mom holds the door open for me. "Leave that stick out here." I shake my head as I unsheathe my weapon. Mom can't tell a stick from a dagger.

My parents shuffle me off to bed, saying, "We will talk about this in the morning."

I might not have remembered that event so clearly if it hadn't been retold so many times as I grew up. I am told that I was six years old when my parents discovered I didn't require as much sleep as most children my age.

In the morning, Mom asked, "What were you doing out there in the dark all alone?"

"I wasn't alone, Vena was with me. If I make noise in the house you send me back to bed, so Vena and I play outside until we get tired." They knew now that I'd done this before.

My parents laughed when they told the story, because I'd been wearing a white sailor cap that glowed like a reflector in the headlight beams. I remember when Mr. Kenyon gave me that cap. I was in the Kenyons' garage with Mom while they sorted through boxes that smelled of storage. When that sailor cap dropped into the garbage can, I grabbed it before a pea coat, reeking of age, could bury it.

"Are you throwing this away?" I asked. Mr. Kenyon stood in suspended animation with a moldering blue rag swaying above the galvanized can.

"Do you want it?"

"Can I?"

I plopped it on my head and it almost fit. I loved that cap. It went with everything: shorts, dungarees, the dresses Mom made me wear, even my pajamas. I wore it until it fell apart. When Mom pointed out how frayed it was and recommended I throw it away, I fought back tears as I declared, "It looks fine and it doesn't smell anymore—I washed it myself in the sink."

A few days later I had to admit our time together was nearing its end. The cap was torn nearly in half, and I was trying to balance what was left of it on my head. Mrs. Kenyon noticed how sad I was, and a few hours later, Mr. Kenyon came striding across the lawn with a smile. He produced another cap from behind his back and said he'd been saving it for me. He lifted the tattered remnant from my head. Seeing them side by side, I had to admit that my old hat looked awful. Mr. Kenyon concluded, "You got your money's-worth out of this one."

31

When Mom saw my gleaming new cap her expression did not reflect the joy I'd expected. She looked past me to Mr. Kenyon. He gave her a sheepish smile, and with palms turned up, lifted his shoulders and cocked his head. They'd discussed that cap and Mom had implored him not to give it to me. She was afraid I'd insist on wearing an ill-fitting sailor cap to my high school, or possibly college graduation—she wanted more for me.

I don't recall the demise of my second cap, but Mom didn't have to worry. I outgrew that obsession and replaced it with a series of others, my taste improving over the years. At least I think it's been improving.

When lunch was over, everyone stowed their gear and put on their packs. Soothed by memories of my old sailor cap, I put on my baseball hat, still wet with perspiration.

CHAPTER FIVE

LESSONS

Hiking is just walking where it's okay to pee.
Demetri Martin[3]

Late in the day I felt ill. While Ewa and Nancy scouted ahead to be sure we were on the correct trail, Joe, Sheila, and I took a break. As soon as I sat down, I felt nauseous and headachy. Joe thought maybe I wasn't drinking enough water. I got out my water bottle, realizing that I'd been hiking for seven hours and had not urinated. After drinking half a bottle of water, I got up—with a little help, feeling better. Another lesson learned: Drink more water.

Somehow, we'd gotten off-trail; in some areas, the blazes were few and far between, and trails forked off from the path we traveled without blaze or signage. Ewa and Nancy had done the extra walking to double-check our location, but if Sandy and I lost track of where we were when we hiked the Long Trail, it could mean not getting to our shelter and a water source for the night.

Earlier that spring, I addressed the possibilities of getting lost by taking a class with the Green Mountain Club, called Land Navigation Basics. Don strongly recommended it. He often called me Celia 'Lost-In-The-Woods' Ryker. There'd been many times, hiking or driving in unfamiliar territory, when I'd made the wrong choice at a fork. On most occasions, I stopped to consider where I thought I was on this huge planet and after serious consideration, turned the wrong way. Even when I did not overthink and allowed my instincts to take the reins—I still made the wrong choice. How was it possible to go in the wrong direction so consistently?

One time, I was at the wheel as Don and I approached a five-way intersection on a road he was familiar with but I was not. Don said, "You have four choices—three will get us to our destination, one will not; choose wisely."

Knowing that three out of four choices would work, I chose one of the two middle roads before me. I moved with confidence, but as I made my turn Don leaned forward, looking at me. "Are you sure about this?"

I thought he was joking. Eyes ahead, chin firm, I said, "Yes, I am sure."

He dropped his head into his hands, his voice muffled through his palms. "Turn around and take any other road but this and the one we came in on. You do remember which one we came in on, don't you?"

He wasn't being unkind. He was worried that I would truly become Lost-In-The-Woods. That was one of the reasons he didn't care to distance hike with me. He said, "I have this fear of getting lost in a huge forest. I think you should take that class."

So I did.

The classroom applications were simple, but then we had to go out and find a marker in the forest using what we'd learned. I knew how to use a compass and read a map, and I did well on our first exercise, but not on the second. I assumed when I got to a footbridge that I knew where I was. The map, however, was not correct, because there was a second footbridge that was not on the map. Or was it the first bridge that was not on the map? We had to determine where the map error was before we could continue. I appreciated the class, but hoped I would never have to use its information.

Closely watching trail signs and blazes became more important, in light of what I'd learned.

Two summers later, Don and I were day-hiking with friends on a trail we hadn't hiked before. We had a map, but there were features on the map we couldn't find, and others in the woods that were not noted on the map. Don wanted to go back the way we'd come, but I took out my compass and determined that we should continue on the trail ahead and to the right. Knowing my track record, Don wanted to stick with his plan. One of our hiking friends thought I was right, so he and I set off for the parking area with compass in hand, while Don and the rest of our group turned back. We were not far from town, so neither group was in danger of being lost for long.

I was correct; Ken and I were back at the car in minutes. I called to let Don know where we were—he was impressed.

Ewa and Nancy found our trail markers and we hiked on to stop for the night on a river bluff. We camped above the water with an amazing vista, but there were no privies and getting to our water source was a long, steep walk. The morning's breeze had increased throughout the day, and by the time we set camp, our jackets were snapping in the wind. Setting my tent up was a challenge. I'd packed my tent in the rain and was surprised by how dry it was when I pulled it out of its stuff sack. The rainfly and ground cloth were still wet, but in the wind that threatened to pull the fabric from my hands, they dried as I worked.

I stood on one corner of the ground cloth as I set the tent in place and staked that corner, then unfurled and secured the opposite corner, diagonally. When all four corners were solidly in place, I could snap together the tent poles and set the outer frame in place, connect tent to frame, then wrangle the rainfly over the whole thing.

When I stepped back to observe my results, my tent stood trembling like a giant butterfly about to take flight.

Everyone but Ewa melted into their tents as soon as they were set up. Sheila estimated that we'd walked about fifteen miles and I was feeling it. I lay on top of my sleeping bag, but sleep did not come and my thoughts turned to one of my training day hikes.

A month before, on a beautiful Saturday, I arranged to meet some local Sierra Club members for a day hike, but when I arrived at the park I had difficulty finding the correct park entrance, and by the time I reached our proposed meeting place I was a half-hour late and the other hikers had already left. I went to the park office, got a trail map, and decided to put in a good long walk on my own. I threw on my pack and headed for the trail, happy to walk in a new area and hoping for some steep hills.

There were groups of people in the parking lot preparing for a walk in the woods, but one man stood out. He was wearing blue jeans and a knit shirt, which is common day-hiking apparel, but his shoes were wrong. No one hikes—or even goes for short walks in the woods, wearing freshly-polished black dress shoes that would have looked appropriate with a three-piece suit. I thought it a little odd, but there are some odd people out there, so I shook my head and set off for a few hours in the woods.

I stopped to read the signs at the trailhead and noticed Mr. Dress Shoes, not far behind me, stopping to tie one of his shiny shoes. I read the trail signs and notices, and began to walk. I was a aware of Mr. Dress Shoes, but not worried. I could still hear the people in the parking lot, and if he tried something funny, help would be nearby. I slid my fingers over the bear spray canister in my pocket and tapped the other pocket, that held my knife, for reassurance.

At the first trail junction, I stopped to make sure I was on the correct path and noticed Dress Shoes behind me again—stopped to tie the same shiny shoe. That was enough for me to change my plan. I didn't want to walk into the woods with that guy behind me, so I took the left-hand loop that would return me to the parking area.

When I walked, Dress Shoes walked, and when I stopped to see what he would do, he stopped. This had gone from odd to weird to creepy. I tapped my knife and bear spray again, glad to walk back into the busy parking area.

Dress Shoes did not follow me directly, but he was behind me even in the parking lot. I wasn't sure I wanted him to know where my car was, so I walked up to a group of strangers and struck up a conversation. They were getting ready for a day hike, so I asked them what trail they were taking. It was the one I'd hoped to hike earlier, before Dress Shoes intervened. After a brief chat, they asked me to join them and I had a nice long walk, in spite of a late arrival and false start. When I set off with my new friends, Dress Shoes showed no interest.

I've had people ask me why I'm not afraid to hike alone. They usually ask in reference to wild animals, but it's the human animal that more often concerns me. I've had more disconcerting experiences, like the one with Mr. Dress Shoes, in parks than on distance trails. The truth is, there are things out there that can get you—both animal and human. I keep an eye out for both and try to avoid trouble, but the beauty and wonder I find when walking in the forest is well worth the risk.

I crawled from my tent and saw that Ewa had started a fire. My first dinner on the trail surprised me. Wearing my headlamp as a necklace, I fired up my Jetboil and poured in a packet of mulled cider for a warm drink, which I drank while preparing my main course. I thought I would be starving after hours of hiking, but I had to force myself to finish the single serving of chicken teriyaki. Nancy said, "I often feel that way. I'm always thirsty at the end of the day, but not very hungry."

Everyone agreed that I should force myself to eat as much as I could, but that packet of food seemed bottomless. I flattened and zipped my almost-empty food bag shut and tucked it into the gallon Ziploc baggie that served as my trash bag. Was my lack of hunger the result of dehydration?

It was fully dark when I needed to make my first serious visit to the forest restroom. I wouldn't have to go far, because once my headlamp was off I disappeared into the darkness. I went down into a small ravine for privacy. The steep downhill in the trees by headlamp was a new experience. The ground and twigs were distorted in the jostling glow, and I wished I had my walking stick.

I found an appropriate stick to dig the requisite hole, made my deposit, and then realized that I had no tissue. It was in my pocket a few minutes ago—perhaps I put it in another pocket. With the numerous pockets of my hiking attire, it took a few minutes, still crouching over my toilet, before I gave up and figured I must have left my tissue in the tent. What is a camper to do? Leaves—leaves could work. There were no soft green leaves at hand, so I reached down for a large wad of dead leaves to alleviate my problem. Dead leaves were not the best choice; they crumbled easily and added a sandpaper-like grit to the original issue. Soft green leaves would make the correction, but to be certain I wasn't using poison ivy, I had to turn on my headlamp. It was May, with trees and shrubs just beginning to leaf out, and there were no green leaves nearby.

With my pants around my ankles, I waddle-waddle-waddled to the nearest green leafy something: a viburnum made the sacrifice. Several large green leaves later, the job was done and sandpaper-cheeks eliminated, but then I had to find and cover the hole I'd made. Fully clothed, with headlamp on, I could not find my deposit site. It should be right *here*. I kicked some leaves toward the estimated location and headed back up the hill.

I took my place on one of the logs around the campfire, but there was a smell. Somebody had stepped in something—and I knew who it was—and I knew what it was.

Back to the forest to wipe my boot clean. I'd been close to the mark, because it was my leaf-kicking boot that was contaminated. I should've used a stick to push the leaves, instead of my boot—note taken. The boot's smooth sole cleaned up easily and I returned to the fireside, shuffling my feet just in case.

Did they notice? How could they not? But nobody said a word. And I'd learned another valuable lesson: Always carry tissue or have soft green leaves available. Always!

Sandy called from her tent, "What are you laughing at."

I read her that note from my trail journal and we both had a giggle.

Ewa and her crew were soon retiring to their tents. I entered the space that I already thought of as my forest home and began to understand Janine's feelings for her precious tent. After double-checking my boots, I set them in their place between my head and the tent wall, with insoles upright for drying. As always, one boot contained my wallet, knife, and phone, and the other my bear spray and watch.

I kept my watch handy because I knew I'd wake up in the night and want to know what time it was. At home, I'd glance at the digital clock on my bed-side table; on the trail, my watch in my boot served the same purpose. After noting the time, I could then go back to sleep. If I couldn't determine what time it was, I'd lie there wishing I knew and it would take longer for me to fall back to sleep.

An old-time Vermonter once told me, in regard to a possible black bear attack in Vermont: "You got a better chance a bein' struck by lightnin' on a sunny day."[2] He added, "I think all women should have bear spray and a knife

---

2. *I read that the last unprovoked bear attack in Vermont was in 1863.*

handy in the woods. You're more likely to need it against some guy, an' it could come in handy against a rabid raccoon or somethin'."

I carried bear spray on all hikes, usually keeping it close by but hidden, because I took a ribbing when other hikers saw it. Most backpackers don't feel the need for it and say that it weighs too much. But the canister fits nicely in my pack pocket, weighs eight ounces, and has stayed with my pack when other items were cast aside as unnecessary or too heavy.

I called to Sandy's tent, "I've got another one for you. Do you want to hear it?" Sandy replied, "Ready and waiting."

Overnight, the temperature on our windy bluff dropped dramatically. I'd brought a pair of sweat pants that were not recommended layering, but they were what I had. I'd thought about putting them on when I got into my tent for the night, but didn't want to get even colder during the changing process.

When I unzipped my tent door in the morning, ice crystals fell from it like snow. I was happy my tent had not blown away to Oz—the wind during the night had been fierce. I was chilly at 11 p.m., and by midnight I was cold. Within the sleeping bag, I was warm enough, but I had to pull my head down into the bag. I'd read and been advised by others that I should carry a knit cap in case of cool weather, but I'd ignored that recommendation. Note to self: Pack a damn hat.

In the wee hours, I dug my sweat pants out of my pillow and wore the tightened waist band around my head like a hat, wrapping the legs around my neck to form a scarf, and drifted off to sleep in clownish comfort.

When I finished reading, Sandy was laughing and I could hear chuckles from the other tents. I called out, "How many people were listening to this?"

There were answers from several directions, and I responded, "If I'd known that, I would have kept the dried leaf story to myself."

A male voice broke through the multiple responses. "Oh no, man, that was rich." Another male voice called out, "I haven't heard a bedtime story that good since I was a kid."

I reviewed the rest of my first hike in silence.

Breaking camp that icy morning, I wasn't sore or achy. The hours of training under my pack had paid off. Other people breaking camp were smiling and nodding and I didn't know why, until Blood Blister said, "Your stories went into my trail journal."

That explained the smiley nods.

"Glad you all enjoyed them." Was I blushing?

The morning was dry and the wind had died, so I relaxed and observed the others as we prepped for our day. Nancy lifted her tent, with frame attached and door opening unzipped, and held it up, shaking bits of sand and leaf litter out the door. When she saw me watching, she said, "This is the tent dweller's vacuum system."

I vacuumed my tent before I packed it.

Sunday's hike was easier, but I was still working to keep up. I discovered another use for my watch—I could read the signs along the trail that told how far we were from campsites, roads, and trail junctions, and use my watch to calculate that our group was averaging three miles an hour. Sheila thought that had been our average speed on Saturday, as well.

I could then track my speed on different terrain, estimate where a nice spot would be for a lunch break, based on icons on the map indicating a view, and determine how long it would take to travel between campsites. My watch could also serve as a compass: Pointing the hour hand at the sun's location, due south would be halfway between the number twelve and the hour hand. During daylight savings, south is halfway between the one and the hour hand, pointing at the sun.

I was relieved as we descended to the parking area mid-afternoon, and aware of how much work I had to do before embarking on the Long Trail.

My first day back home, the weather was perfect to set up my tent in the sunlight, vacuum it one more time, and air it out. I also cleaned the mud from tent stakes, boots, and other equipment. I draped my rainfly over the picnic table and hung sleeping bag, sleeping mat, and rain gear over lawn chairs to air before being stored until the next hike.

Indoors, I washed clothing and cleaned and disinfected water bottles and cooking gear. I spread out and reviewed the rest of the contents of my pack on the picnic table, leaving the pack wide open in the sunshine to air it. I emptied my Sea to Summit food bag and set it in the sunshine inside out, inspecting my remaining food to make sure there was nothing that would go bad.

By the end of my first day on Vermont's Long Trail, my outlook on distance hiking had changed. I'd thought I was hiking difficult terrain on my hikes in Michigan, but after a few hours on the LT, I had a new scale to measure trail-difficulty by. But with nothing hanging from it, my pack felt tight, like it was part of my back, my boots fit well, and my walking stick was my friend.

Chapter Six

THE RAIN FOREST

Walking is man's best medicine.
Hippocrates

Our plan for our second day on the LT was to get to the Congden Shelter, 7.2 miles away. How could we have thought we could hike fourteen miles on our first day?

We were up at 6 a.m. and it was not raining, but we could feel it lurking as we ate breakfast. The other people at the Seth Warner Shelter area were up early. Some hit the trail before 6:30, others left at around seven. There were three or four hikers still in camp when we struck out at eight. The sun was shining, but progress was slowed by a trail that had not seen a dry day in weeks.

I was picking my way along a sloppy area when a group of NOBO hikers passed me, stepping as though the slop and deep water were not there. Sandy and I paused to survey the best places to step and which side of the trail might be less deep, often ending up in deeper water and muck than appearance had indicated. But if we marched along without thought to the best track, we would accidently pick the better path half the time. New Motto: Mud be damned, just walk.

I'd ripped out the pages from the Long Trail Guide that applied to the part of the trail we'd be hiking, and kept them in a Ziploc bag—within a zippered pocket. Our waterproof map gave us most of the information we needed, but the guidebook provided a description of what we'd be hiking, such as rock scrambles, where to expect ladders, or which way to turn when we came to a road. In populated areas, side trails were numerous and signs might be removed or altered, making the guidebook's information vital. Sandy allowed me to keep the guidebook pages, but she would not relinquish the map.

I made a discovery that day: when I looked up at the next hillside or mountain, I should look for the highest, darkest area and know that was our goal. If there was a light patch to the right or left, indicating sunlight filtering through less-dense trees that would allow us to bypass that highest point, it was *not* where we were bound. Our target was the highest, darkest area before us. That knowledge made it less surprising when an ascent seemed endless.

When I could see a glint of light through the forest around me, I knew we were at or near the summit and our descent would soon begin. Getting to the summit without the reward of a view was disappointing, but a level area, however small, allowed us to stretch our legs and adjust. Moving up-slope was tough on my lungs, but going down a similar grade challenged my legs. I backed down the steeper descents, which meant stepping blindly backwards.

Then there were the PUDs—pointless ups and downs. When I knew our goal was the summit, but on our way there the pitch sloped down, we were losing ground already gained and would be forced to make it up soon. I was especially sad when I saw rock ahead and realized that the make-up steps would be even more difficult. Once I came to terms with the PUDs, though, it made the negative gains a little easier to accept.

When we stopped for a lunch break, we looked over the map while we ate. Sandy was asleep in minutes and although I tried, my mind wandered and kept me awake.

I thought about how lucky I was to be able to take on this new adventure. It had taken some effort to reach this point in my life. Due to injury, I'd retired from training horses, teaching students to ride, and showing horses on the local hunter/jumper circuit. I was twenty-eight and single when I purchased the twenty acres that I called Hadley Hill Farm, and worked it for five years before the day my regular veterinarian sent out his new associate.

The new guy seemed nice and appeared to know what he was doing, but he had a beard and I don't care much for beards, so I didn't pay much attention to him. Between boarders and lesson horses, I cared for twenty-five to thirty horses, so I often had visits from the vets. As I got to know the new doctor, I started to like him in spite of his facial fur. When he shaved his beard, I couldn't help noticing that he was really good looking. Why would he cover that face up with hair?

It wasn't be long before we started dating, and were married three years later.

We'd been married for several years when Don decided to grow another beard and I discovered, from a closer vantage point, why I was unimpressed with his earlier attempt. The whiskers on one side of his face are well behaved, the hair growing downward along his strong jaw line. But on the other side, it looked like someone took an egg beater to it, with hair growing in all directions. Even though I loved him, or perhaps *because* I cared so much—I had to tell him, "Your beard has all the charm of a disemboweled mattress at a road-side dump." He held on to his beard for a few more weeks, just to prove he could, before I saw his handsome chin again.

Sandy was still sleeping, so I pulled out the *Nature Guide to Vermont's Long Trail*. Books are considered too heavy for most backpackers, but I like to read in the evenings after making my journal entry. The nature guide is a wealth of information about the plants and animals found along the trail, as well as the geology and ecology of the spaces we were moving through.

The nature guide taught me that the boulders we were seeing, that appeared to have been dropped by a sloppy giant, were called *glacial erratics*. I read that the orange salamanders we saw were called *efts*, and were juveniles of the red-spotted newt. Their bright coloring protected them, indicating that they were toxic, similar to the brightly-colored poisonous frogs seen in the amphibian house at the zoo. The relationship between bright coloring and poison is evidently not a coincidence in nature. I shared this information with Sandy as we started up the trail after lunch.

We passed several open areas and I wondered if it had been recently farmed or if they were the result of a natural event, like a fire, shearing wind, or disease among the trees. The result was that the forest floor was taken over by lush ferns. The ferns would eventually be replaced by sun-loving trees, then shade-tolerant trees, and ultimately the climax forest of maple and beech. Forest succession is an incredible thing. I tried to guess how long ago the disturbance occurred.

Other hikers shared that the weather forecast called for a clear, dry night, but that we should be ready for three days of rain after that. Everything was wet and dull, except our spirits. When we got to a marker and realized we were struggling to hike at one mile an hour, we would walk a little faster for a while, inspired to pick up our speed. I wondered if Sandy was sad to be stuck with such a slow hiker; she could have made better time without me. She usually hiked ahead and waited for me at trail junctions or tricky areas. I wondered how much ground she could have covered if she hadn't spent so much time waiting for me.

We made it to Congden Shelter by 3:30, having averaged one mile an hour, and it felt good to sit on a rock in the stream, allowing my crock-clad feet to feel the water rush over them as I pumped purified water into my CamelBak and water bottles. We heard more hikers come into camp, bringing our occupancy for the evening to ten. We'd met two of them at Seth Warner: Quick Toes, who was doing the LT and The Bulgarian was on the AT.

I had to commend The Bulgarian on his chosen brand of hiking boots; he wore Asolo boots, the same as me. He said the name so easily and it didn't sound like swearing—I tried several times, but it still sounded like ass-hole-o.

Sandy set up her tent with the rainfly flipped back halfway, so she could look out at the stars. I, on the other hand, did not trust the weather.

My nightly journal entry was almost complete when it began to rain and I heard Sandy unzipping her tent door. Luckily, it wasn't raining hard yet, and I heard her re-enter her tent as the drops went from tapping to pelting. Within my fabric home I was comfortable, content, and thinking about sleep. It was only 6:30.

I picked up my journal and reviewed the second weekend hike I'd taken, figuring that should put me to sleep. I didn't find anything worth reading aloud to Sandy, so I put my journal away and listened to one of my favorite sounds. When my sister Fay and I were kids, we liked to sit in the car, listening to raindrops falling on the metal roof. We usually fell asleep, one in the front seat, one in the back.

I nestled deeper into my sleeping bag, thinking about the many times we'd slept through storms in Dad's car.

CHAPTER SEVEN

JORDON RIVER

Look deep into nature,
and then you will understand everything better.
Albert Einstein

I was better prepared for my second distance hike on the Jordon River Trail in Michigan. We met on Friday to camp near the trailhead, and set out to cover twenty-seven miles in two days. I now knew: how to set up my tent, not to attach anything to the outside of my pack, always have tissue or soft green leaves available when answering nature's call, and my new hiking boots were properly worn-in. Over the past two weeks I'd trained on the steepest hills I could find to prep my legs for keeping up with Ewa's pace.

On the Jordon River Trail, I forgot to pack my pen, so I made no journal entries. I promptly made entries when I got home, but I lost valuable information due to that mistake. Note to self: *Always keep an extra pen or pencil in my pack.* I hadn't purchased a camera small enough to hike with, so I had no images to jog my memory, either.

Ewa was our leader, and Nancy and Joe also were in our group, so I knew about half of our group. My backpack was crammed tight, with nothing hanging from the outside. I still had to figure out how to carry my walking stick in a way that allowed me to get at it when I needed it and have it out of the way when I didn't. The CamelBak allowed me to drink as I walked, and I was happy to note that there was no plastic taste.

On my first hike, I'd learned that when going up steep hills I needed to slide my hand down my walking stick to help pull myself up. The metal part of the pole was often slippery from perspiration, but it was especially slick in the rain, so I'd wrapped my stick with enough duct tape to create a secondary handle, a few inches below the handgrip. As we began our first uphill of the day, I slid my hand down for a firm grasp on my duct tape handgrip.

I'd been breaking in my new boots for almost two months, but they turned on me in the first hour on the trail. I could feel my toenails gouging into the flesh of adjoining toes; four digits were going through punishment they'd not experienced before. During our lunch break, examining my bare feet, I was surprised to find no broken skin. They were red and angry, but there was no blood yet.

I sat near my fellow hikers but turned away, embarrassed to be carefully examining my feet while everyone was eating. I had to figure out how to make my boots work for another day and a half. Could I wedge something between my toes? I let my feet air as I ate my midday meal, wondering what to do—I had twenty miles left to walk. My mind wandered to shoe stories from my childhood.

With four siblings, time alone with my parents was rare, so I enjoyed any opportunity to feel like an only child. One time when my parents and I were at a shoe store, Dad told the salesman that I needed a good, solid shoe. The salesman brought out cute girly shoes and my mother shook her head. I spotted a pair of Keds—I knew from the commercials that wearing them would allow me to "run faster and jump higher," but when I pleaded for the coolest shoes in the store, Dad shook his head. "You'd wear through them in a week."

Mom pointed to a pair of black and white saddle oxfords. "This is what she wants." I'd already told them what I wanted, and black-and-white saddle shoes were *not* on that list. I didn't dare say that, but I thought it very loudly and kept looking for a better shoe. We eventually settled on gray oxfords, making everyone happy.

Those shoes could take a beating—for the first time, I outgrew a pair of shoes before they wore out. We returned to the store for same shoe, one size larger, and I went home to beat the hell out of another pair.

I was walking home from school one day when a stone made its way into my gray oxford, but I couldn't be bothered to stop and pour the pebble out. I was less than a block from home and it didn't hurt that much, so I just accepted the discomfort. When I got home, I sat on the porch steps, unlaced my shoe, and pulled forward from the heel. I don't know what surprised me more, the fact that my shoe would not move or the degree of pain related to the effort. I called out for Mom with a little-kid inflection that stopped just short of a wail. She must have heard the earnestness in my plea, because she came running to the door with my sisters, Fay and Renee, close behind.

"I can't get my shoe off."

"What do you mean, you can't get your shoe off?"

"It won't come off," I said, trying not to panic.

Mom sat down beside me, took my ankle in one hand and pulled down on the heel of my shoe with the other. I'm not sure if it was my squeal or the puzzling fact that the shoe didn't move that stopped her, but she promptly aborted the attempt. She turned my foot to look at the bottom of my shoe and without looking up instructed: "Fay, go into the junk drawer and bring me a screwdriver and a pair of pliers."

What was on the bottom of my shoe? I pulled my foot from her hand, turning it so I could see what she'd found, and there, just behind the ball of my foot, was the head of a nail. It hadn't been a pebble—I'd stepped on a nail and then walked on it for half a country block. When Fay came back with the tools, she squatted on the porch, positioning herself to see what was going on. Her response was immediate: "Wow, is that a nail? How long is it? It's all the way in there."

Fay's running commentary was not helpful as Mom pried the screwdriver between the sole of my shoe and the nailhead to lift it enough to grasp with the pliers. I ouched and squirmed, which did not make the task easier or less painful. When the nail was removed, my shoe dropped away, exposing a puddle of blood. Another "Wow" from Fay. Mom instructed me to lean on her and hop to the bathroom so she could clean the wound. It had been a roofing nail, so it wasn't that long, but it had held my shoe firmly to my foot, and the amount of blood in my shoe was impressive.

As evening approached, I lay on the sofa with my foot elevated, an ice pack wrapped around it. I could see into the kitchen where Fay and Renee lay in ambush as Dad came through the back door. "Dad, you won't believe it." Fay couldn't wait to make the big announcement. Renee stood next to her, quivering with excitement. "Ceil nailed her shoe to her foot. She walked all the way home and didn't know there was a nail in her foot. There wasn't much blood, but that nail was all the way in there!"

Fay was hopping up and down with enthusiasm; Renee barely got a word in. Fay told Dad that Mom had to pry the nail up with a screwdriver and pull it out with pliers. She closed her report with a statement that lives in family infamy: "She nailed her shoe to her foot and didn't even know it!"

I was packing my food away, preparing to put my feet back into boots that felt like torture chambers, when my walking stick rolled off the rock I'd been sitting on. A glint of sunlight reflected off the duct tape handgrip, inspiring me to try wrapping thin pieces of duct tape around my toes; I was dubious about whether it would help, but desperate for relief.

I used the scissors of my ParaTool multitool to cut precise, thin strips. I'd received conflicting advice about the ParaTool: "It's heavy."

"It has many uses."

"It takes up too much space."

"You'll never use it."

"No one should hike without one." I wasn't sure who was right, but I'd put one in my pack before my first hike, just in case.

The ParaTool is a cross between a pair of needle-nose pliers and a Swiss Army Knife: within the handles of the pliers are knife blades, scissors, screwdrivers, a bottle opener, etc. It came in handy to splice the duct tape, so it was in my pack to stay.

When we set off after lunch, my toes thanked me. On our first serious uphill, I congratulated myself for the duct tape solution. Hurrah for me, damn it!—I hope I didn't say that out loud . . . That incident instilled in me a greater appreciation for duct tape.

I also learned something new about my Jetboil on that hike, when one of my fellow hikers saw me lighting my stove with a lighter and asked, "Is the starter broken?"

"Starter? What starter? There's a starter?"

He showed me how, after turning on the gas, to press the button next to the gas knob instead of applying a flame —to my amazement, a flame burst forth!

"Duh! I guess I should have read the instructions."

I was happier with my pace on the Jordon River Trail. I didn't find my group waiting for me at the top of every hill, and I wasn't as tired at each day's end. I knew I still needed to do more to prepare for the Long Trail, but my performance had improved in the two weeks since Red Bridge.

Early in the day, one of the new hikers commented, "I didn't know this was going to be a race." He obviously hadn't been warned about Ewa's hiking pace. I felt better about not being able to keep up on my first hike when he and another hiker, both fit and experienced-looking, put themselves in the lead to slow the pace. By my watch, our morning pace had been just under three miles an hour. Although I'd been slower than most, I was hiking easier and could comfortably keep up with the pace set by our new group members.

During our lunch break on Sunday, Joe took off his boots to address hot spots on his feet that had the potential to become blisters. Unlike me, he wasn't shy about sharing his foot problems over lunch. We talked about how duct tape could be used, but Joe didn't have any. I used my ParaTool to cut a couple pieces from my walking stick's handgrip. Joe applied the tape to the rubbed area to reduce friction, saving him from blisters.

At our afternoon break, Joe declared, "My feet are fine, not a hint of soreness." Duct tape to the rescue!

When I got home, I added a pen and a pencil to my pack and wrapped several extra layers of duct tape around the pencil, above where it would rest in my hand. This extra tape would allow me to make repairs on gear or feet without compromising my walking stick's second handle.

At a trail junction, Ewa allowed us to choose between a steep path and an easier but slightly longer approach to our destination. Without a consensus, she allowed us to split into two groups, and I chose the more difficult trail. One among us, who'd done a lot of mountain hiking, advised me: "Take it slower. Set a steady pace that you can maintain and slowly walk up the hill."

I'd been pushing myself to keep up—or catch up—with the others, but would often have to stop to catch my breath. By following that advice, I was able to walk up Dead Man's Hill with ease. Historic markers told me that it was called Dead Man's Hill because of a logging accident that happened years before, when logs had careened down the hill and killed the team of horses pulling them, as well as one of the loggers.

I'd purchased my hiking boots from a young clerk (who did not hike) at a small sporting goods store in Vermont. The price had *screamed* quality—they were not cheap, and I'd spent weeks breaking them in. But the results had been disappointing, and in fact quite painful. Clearly, another trip to REI was in order. When I told the clerk at REI (who was a hiker) about my foot issues, she measured and said, "Your feet are different sizes."

I looked down at my feet. "My right leg has been broken twice . . . I guess that foot does look different."

"Having different-sized feet is not that unusual. We'll need to fit your smaller foot and stretch the other boot. You cannot pack a boot that is too large, even slightly, and have it work on uneven terrain."

She brought out several pairs of boots, and it was the Asolo—the most expensive pair—that fit best. When my right boot fit perfect, she felt around the left boot with her hand and knew exactly where it was too snug. She took the boot into the back and sent me off to finish my shopping. When I returned to try them on, both boots fit perfectly, like I'd already broken them in.

Now it was time to buy my own backpack. I'd borrowed Janine's for training and my practice hikes, but it was time to get my own. I tried on different packs without noting their brand, and it turned out to be the Osprey Arial, the same brand as Janine's, that felt the best. Getting the right fit is important; the distance from shoulder to hip is key. When I told the clerk that I was planning to hike the Long Trail, he thought I might need a larger pack, but Janine had warned me that a large pack might be able to carry more, but I was going to have to be able to lift it. She'd stuck with a smaller pack on long hikes, arranging more food drops to compensate for her smaller load, so I bought the smaller pack with confidence.

With my new gear and our Long Trail expedition fast approaching, I was determined to train harder. In two weeks, I was planning to hike thirty-two miles in three days; not much by backpacker standards, but it would be my longest hike yet.

Two days into the Long Trail, the thought of worrying about thirty-two miles made me chuckle, but I stifled my laughter. I didn't feel like reading to the tents around us. Even so, Sandy heard me. "What are you laughing at now?"

"Oh, nothing."

CHAPTER EIGHT

BENT BIKE

I was never happier, never more my best self,
than when I was in the woods.
Paul Doiron , "Massacre Pond" [4]

The Melville Nauheim Shelter was 5.9 miles from the Congden Shelter, but Sandy and I thought that traveling less than six miles would be too short a day. Getting to Little Pond, where we were told we could camp, would give us our first ten-mile day, and we thought we were ready.

Early in the day, the trail had been flat and I'd tucked my walking stick into my pack belt to walk with my arms at my sides, but my hands were soon swollen. I had to curl my fingers into the sternum strap of my backpack to give them a break, easing the swelling by bringing them up above my heart. My fingers looked like angry cigar butts until I started moving them around.

The walking stick which had been a problem on my Michigan hikes was almost constantly in use on the LT. The stretches of flat ground were usually so brief that I didn't have time to think about tucking my stick away. I needed it to pull myself up slope after slope, and used it even more when easing down inclines.

The steps down to Route 9 were more difficult than anything I had hiked. The descent seemed endless and there were few tree trunks or branches to grab onto for assistance. The steps, as they are optimistically called, were extremely irregular. They were saturated from the overnight rain and slippery. I fell twice and had a four-inch cut above my right wrist, just deep enough to bleed. I cleaned and bandaged it when I got to the road.

Patty-O met us on the descent to Route 9 and walked us to his truck, which was full of hiker goodies. After my second fall, he commented that I might be wearing the wrong boots. Wrong boots? These are great boots. I love these boots. Do Not talk that way about my boots.

I felt a need to defend my footwear, so I shared with a stranger the fact that I had a neurologic condition. I told him about symptoms that had showed up years before, making me feel for months as though I'd just recovered from the flu: dizziness, lightheadedness, balance issues, light sensitivity, intermittent hearing loss, ringing in the ears . . . One doctor thought I had brain damage due to the large number of head injuries I'd incurred. Another thought I had a brain stem virus. Dr. Ball did more tests and concluded that I had the combo platter: brain damage and a virus.

His prognosis was the same, regardless: sometimes it gets better, sometimes it gets worse, but most of the time it stays the same. His treatment for both conditions was the same: get used to it and do things to improve your balance. So I took up tai chi and kickboxing, and pulled a bike out of the cobwebs of my parents' garage; I filled the tires, oiled the chain, and took a short ride down the road.

When I returned, I told Fay, "This thing must have been hit by a car or something. The wheels are not aligned."

Fay got on the bike and went for a spin. When she came back, she held the handlebars out to me. "It's not the bike."

Patty-O wasn't thinking about boots when he asked if I had a trail name. I'd tried a couple, Yogi and Oven Bird, but I wasn't happy with either one. Patty-O decided that my trail name should be Bent Bike. I wasn't thrilled, but decided to try it out for a while.

I'm glad I hadn't shared another story about my symptoms—the day I wanted to show Fay a great horned owl's nest near our home in Michigan, with two young owlets in it. We were on a hill opposite the nest, far enough away not to be a bother, yet close enough to see the fluffy young. After Fay watched them for a bit, I took the binoculars from her to look for myself. I panned to the tree trunk that I knew was their base and then raised my head to find the nest, but it wasn't there. After the third try, Fay said, "Do that again."

"Why?"

"Just do it again."

I panned to the trunk, raised my binoculars, but still could not find the nest. I looked at Fay, who was smiling, and asked, "What?"

"Do you remember Lady Bug, that cat you had that was hit by a car?"

I remembered Lady B's condition well. For the first few days after the accident, she'd walked in circles with her head tilted to the left. The vet recommended keeping her in a quiet place and allowing her to heal on her own. She gradually improved to the point where she seemed normal, except when she looked up. When she raised her head, it would tremble. Once her head was facing up, it would stop quaking, but during the raising process it wobbled quite severely.

Fay shrugged. "That's what you look like—a hit-by-car cat."

"I have no sensation of tremor."

"I don't know how you could not feel that. Your head was shaking, big time."

If I'd shared that story with Patty-O, my trail name might have been Bobble-Head or Hit-by-Car-Cat or even Brain Damage. All things considered, Bent Bike wasn't bad.

We were dreading the uphill from Route 9 that promised to be as steep as the downhill had been, so we declined the warm pizza Patty-O offered. We drank icy-cold sodas and set off up the trail while Patty-O headed back up the steps to carry tidings of great joy regarding pizza, soda, and beer to those yet to endure the steps. Trail Angels are purveyors of random acts of kindness known as Trail Magic. Patty-O was our first Trail Angel.

After the ascent from Route 9, the trail was relatively level and covered with leaf duff and evergreen needles. A gray mist was hanging in the tree tops, creating a feeling so quiet and shaded, I could imagine every fairy tale that had ever been written, as having taken place there. Hansel and Gretel could have left bread crumbs along that very path. A gust of wind grabbed the trees, reminding me of the Haunted Forest from the Wizard of Oz. I imagined winged monkeys peeking through the thick canopy. One gnarled sugar maple looked like a warrior Ent from *The Lord of the Rings*. The trail morphed from one fantasy forest to another. It was refreshing to walk at a decent pace on level ground, and I folded my walking stick, tucking it into my pack belt and stretching my legs over the easy terrain.

The best part of getting into camp that day was the phone message from

Don waiting on my cell. I'd called him from the Seth Warner Shelter to tell him how slow we were going and that we were OK but disappointed in our progress. He'd been on the golf course, where calls are frowned upon, and his message was an apology for not talking longer or being more supportive. "If you only get to two shelters in the nine days, I will still be proud of you. I admire what I you're doing and I love you."

I don't cry easily, but that almost did it. There are times when Don and I disagree, times when I need to get away from him or argue, but when it comes to the important things, he's a keeper. Not many husbands would understand this adventure, let alone support and encourage it. But he's proud of me. How cool is that?

We got to the Melville Nauheim Shelter at 2 p.m., had lunch and decided it would take too much time to get to the next shelter that day. Who were we kidding? Goddard Shelter was 8.5 miles away and at our pace, we'd be lucky if we got there by 10 p.m. We weren't ready to cowboy at Little Pond. (*Cowboy* is the term used when hikers camp outside of a designated campsite.)

We rolled out our sleeping bags in the shelter and quickly fell asleep. When we woke, we filled our water bottles, set up our tents, and returned to the shelter for dinner and chat-time with the other hikers. They'd all hiked the thirteen miles from Seth Warner that day. We'd barely done six, but we were tired.

Serious hikers sleep in the shelters to save the time and effort of setting up and taking down their tents. They can carry a fourteen-ounce tent for those occasions when one is required. Blue Jay, back at Seth Warner, advised taking it easy "until your legs tell you they're ready for more."

Our legs were still not ready for much. We were one-third of the way through our goal for the week and according to our hiking friends, there was more rain in the forecast. The next day would be our longest—almost nine miles to the next shelter.

There was a table and bunks in the Melville Nauheim Shelter, so that's where I sat to make my journal entry. When I retired to my tent, it was too early to sleep, so I read my journal entry from my third Michigan training hike.

CHAPTER NINE

NO WATERLOO

Wilderness is not a luxury
but a necessity of the human spirit,
and as vital to our lives as water and good bread.
Edward Abbey , "Desert Solitaire" [5]

Pinkney/Waterloo, my third training hike, would be my longest hike yet. In three days, we would hike over thirty-two miles, from the Pinkney Recreation Area to Waterloo State Recreation Area. I got an early start on Friday morning and found myself mentally reviewing the contents of my pack as I drove. Preparation had felt different this time; the sun was shining as I placed my pack, boots, baseball cap, and walking stick in the car like I knew what I was doing. I was electrified by anticipation, but also felt the familiar childhood comfort of setting off to see what I might find.

I've loved to walk since my first tottering steps. Once I was tall enough to operate the doorknob, I did most of my walking outdoors. My first solo walks began with trips around the block. My siblings and parents stayed at home, but when my friends joined me, we'd point out important sites along the way, like the tree Billy fell out of, the spot where Barb caught the biggest fish ever, and the place Jeff and I crashed our sleds.

Walking alone, I could stop and sit under my favorite tree for no reason at all, or walk as fast and hard as I could, also for no good reason, and there was no one to ask me why. I could pretend to be walking beside a covered wagon, crossing hot dessert sands, or imagine I was in a dense forest, pushing through deep snow.

Emily Dickenson wrote: "There is no Frigate like a Book," and as I walked, my mind revisited my favorite stories, inserting my body into whatever adventure the writer had shared. Often, I would revise the conclusion to suit my whim and there were times when I found myself surprised by my imaginary path. Even as a child, I wondered how I could concoct a story that shocked me. How could my own brain sneak up on me like that?

My imagination could take me to places that the gravel roads in our neighborhood never could. A country block may be longer than a city block, but I was still less than a block from home, walking anywhere on this planet—or beyond.

Saturday mornings were magical. I'd rise early and wash the bathroom floor— the chore that won me my weekly allowance. With that out of the way, I'd wait for the charmed hour; Mom wouldn't let us leave our yard until 10 a.m. on weekends. She didn't want us bothering other people who might want to sleep in, so I sat on the porch waiting for freedom. "Mom, what time is it?"

I asked that question so often, I got a watch for my birthday. I was thrilled—none of my friends had watches and it looked so grown-up on my wrist. I didn't realize that the watch Mom gave me was for her. I would now sit silently on the porch, aching for the hands to move faster, and then catapult into my day without asking what time it was. I thought my watch was cool; Mom thought it was bliss.

If I was in a bad mood or angry because of some injustice cast upon me, I learned to walk as therapy for my angst. I'd let the anger out at a fast, hard pace, feeling my heart pumping, my lungs stretching, and at some point my anger would disappear, floating off like vapor, like a dream fading to wispy strands. With my anger resolved, I could walk home to the sister who'd made me angry or brother who was being mean, leaving my rage in the woods along the way. Gramma called it, "Walking Off the Stink." I didn't know where the anger went, but I knew how to get rid of it.

Anger was easy to be rid of, but disappointment required a long, slow walk. I think it was the time as much as the walk that would turn the corner on disappointments. Sitting on a log listening to peeper frogs would ease the pain of seeing one of my brothers receiving freedoms that I was denied because of my age. They don't realize how mature I am, I'd think.

A slow walk under trees with leaves beginning to fall could ease anxiety brought on by a tough classroom problem or that boy who made fun of me for not being able to spell the word *else* in the spelling bee. I knew how to spell that word, but my mind had gone blank. Roger teased me all the way home from school, so I stomped in the door, dropped my lunch box, called out to Vena and took her with me for a long, slow wander in the woods.

The birds didn't care about spelling, or Roger, or even me. They just went about their business as we walked beneath them. Their tranquil calls created a veil of serenity, and I forgot about the embarrassment and I forgot about Roger. I would listen to the birds, catch a frog and look into its eyes before returning it to the water. I'd walk among the trees and wander home in a better state of mind.

> *I found nature's indifference*
> *to my cares and concerns oddly consoling.*
>
> Paul Doiron , "Massacre Pond"[6]

On the Pinkney/Waterloo Trail, I was hiking with Ewa. She and Nancy had dropped a car off at our destination and returned to our starting point to begin hiking at 9 a.m. On the Manistee River Trail, I'd learned to tuck everything inside my pack; on the Jordon River Trail, my boots had been a problem. The Pinkney/Waterloo Trail was long and difficult, but my pack felt soft against my spine and my new boots hugged my feet like slippers. I lifted my face to the sun and felt like I was playing in the woods on a Saturday with Fay.At dinner, I noticed that Nancy carried Cup-a-Soup packets, and was glad to know that other people were also not hungry after hiking all day. The soup looked like a great idea, and I added it to my mental shopping list.

I'd broken some of my single-serving meals into two Ziploc baggies and written cooking instructions on the bags with a Sharpie, so I'd remember to add half the water and how long to cook it for. I placed those bags inside the foil cooking pouch the food had come in. It worked; half of a single-serving was perfect at the end of a hiking day. I'd stocked up on chicken teriyaki, mac and cheese, beef stroganoff, and lasagna. I saved the lasagna for the last day of our hike, because it was too messy to split in half and difficult to clean from the pan and spork, but I never considered going without it—it was soooo good.

While talking around the campfire, I was surprised to find a tick walking along my forearm. I crushed it between my fingernail and the top of my thumbnail. This was the first tick I'd seen while distance hiking, perhaps because the longer hikes tended to be at higher elevations, and it made me more alert to their presence.

I've heard non-hikers mention ticks as though they were ever-present man-eaters, but few hikers give them much thought. They're usually easy to spot, and if you don't find them before they bite you, the engorged tick is hard to miss.

Gazing into the fire, we became silent, drifting into private thoughts, and the quiet sent me floating to the research I'd done before my first backpacking trip.

Beyond the hours spent preparing myself physically, I'd read books written by hikers. Bill Bryson's *A Walk in the Woods* made me feel better about my age as a new backpacker. He was younger than me, and didn't finish the AT's twenty-one hundred miles, but he did hike eight hundred and seventy of them. I gleaned information from his book about what I might expect as an older hiker new to the sport.

I read *Not Without Peril* by Nicholas Howe, thinking it might sober me, making me more careful about the potential dangers of hiking New England's mountains. Howe chronicled disasters resulting in deaths on New Hampshire's Mount Washington. I didn't share that book with Don. Mount Washington is higher than anything we would hike in Vermont, and there could be snow on its peak any month of the year. It was nice to know that most of the disasters occurred because people ignored weather conditions and advice from guides or experienced hikers. Moral to that story: Don't be stupid.

One disaster story was about a family who decided to head for Mount Washington's summit shack at two o'clock on an October afternoon. The family, traveling without lamps of any kind, was stopped by darkness. The father chose a site in a cleft of rocks to shelter himself and his children, and they hunkered down for a dark, cold night. When he awoke in the morning, he could see the summit shack from their rocky nest. But that did not help his daughter; she had succumbed to the cold. It happened many years ago and the protagonists are gone from this Earth, but I couldn't help wondering: What was he thinking?

When *Wild* came out, I read Cheryl Strayed's account of hiking the Pacific Crest Trail, another distance of over two thousand miles. I was stunned that she began her hike without previously putting on her boots or picking up her pack. She seemed otherwise intelligent, so why would she do that? I had to admire her fortitude, but it seemed like a dumb way to start. I would be far more prepared than that. One of my friends thought that reading those books might dampen my enthusiasm, but instead, they inspired me.

The next morning, I was still in my tent at 8:45, listening to the rain. I duct taped my toes out of habit, though it didn't seem necessary with my new boots, which I loved more each day. They were heavy by hiker-standards, but so comfortable.

We broke camp in the rain and I had my gear stowed and ready to go before anyone else; it felt good to wait for them for a change. My right leg ached with my first steps of the morning, which was no surprise since that leg has had six fractures and is held together with eleven screws and seven inches of titanium plate. Early-morning pain is common for me, but it hadn't occurred on the trail under the weight of a full pack. I was worried about how it would respond to my normal treatment: walking it off. It felt like a metal hose clamp had tightened around my tibia, gouging into the bone's surface. I walked past the deep bone ache in the first half hour, and as the throbbing dissipated, found myself smiling, with rain dripping from my hat's brim. I was feeling good—very good.

That evening around the campfire, I shared a story about a class I'd taken through the Green Mountain Club, called SOLO Wilderness First Aid. It was a weekend seminar with classroom information followed by hands-on sessions, where students took turns playing the injured and the rescuer. It was a wealth of information I hoped never to need, but it inspired me to make changes to the items I kept in my backpack, for day hikes as well as distance.

During one of our exercises, I was told to pretend to be having a diabetic episode and my rescuer was supposed to surmise from my less-than-lucid responses what the problem was. My rescuer was from Chicago and looked like he'd walked off the set of The Godfather. He was no wimp, but when I failed to respond appropriately to his questions, his breathing became quick and shallow. When the exercise was over, I asked if he was all right. He said, "I suddenly realized that someone might really need my help and I may not know what to do."

"I know what you mean. I hope I never have to deal with some of the problems we're learning about."

Important lessons learned:

- How to splint a fractured appendage using trekking poles and a sleeping mat.

- If you come upon a diabetic who is not lucid, Do Not use their insulin injection pen. Hikers are usually low on sugar, not high. Giving someone who has high sugar something sweet will not kill them, but giving that shot to someone low on sugar could.

- If available, use the contents of the wounded hiker's pack for treatment, rather than your own.

- Add a syringe that I could use to flush a wound to my pack.

- Make sure my daypack contains the necessities for spending the night in the woods.

Driving back to our cars, I was surprised how long it took to travel the distance we'd just walked. When we passed a site where the trail crossed the road, someone said, "We're only halfway back to our cars. We hiked further than I thought."

The Long Trail was feeling closer.

That first day home after the Pinkney/Waterloo Trail, I went through my post-hike rituals, cleaning up cooking gear, airing out my tent and sleeping bag, and going over what remained of my food. This time, however, I was prepping my gear for the Long Trail. The real thing was coming and I had to be sure I had what I needed—we'd be hiking for at least a week, hopefully ten days.

Our spare bedroom was my staging area and my pack stood on the floor agape, awaiting its heaviest load yet. Strewn across the bed were my clothing, sleeping bag and mat, cooking gear, and an assortment of food packets. Sandy and I had decided to leave a food drop at what we hoped would be our halfway point, so I had a pile of food for my pack and another pile next to a cardboard box.

In the first few days on the LT, I realized how much harder it would have been if I hadn't done the practice hikes in Michigan. I couldn't imagine my first day on the LT with my water bottles, walking stick, and boots tormenting me.

CHAPTER TEN

FOG WALKING

I understood at a very early age that in nature,
I felt everything I should feel in church but never did.
Walking in the woods, I felt in touch with
the universe and with the spirit of the universe.
Alice Walker [7]

S andy and I broke camp under a cloudless sky and had been on the trail for about an hour when a light rain began. Within minutes, the light rain gained weight and turned into a downpour, then a deluge. In spite of the weather, I felt good. There were moments when I felt like I could keep going forever. I was the Energizer Bunny wearing a backpack.

We hiked through a haunted forest engulfed by a dense fog, the eerie calm making the joyful birdsongs sound ominous. A light wind jostled the trees against one another, sounding like a huge crowd chanting, just out of sight. That invisible throng had us surrounded and followed us as we walked deeper into the forest. We pushed through a miasma that opened and closed around us, and we both jumped at the sudden flutter of partridge wings. We looked at one another and laughed. Were we both being stalked by fog creatures, or was it just me? Walking through that fog reminded me of an early morning ritual that my grandmother had shared with me, and I played the old footage in my head as I moved through the haze.

Our family was staying with Gramma at her cottage on White Lake, and I was always awake before everyone else. One morning, Gramma walked out of the kitchen and saw me looking at my picture book, pretending to read. She wore her usual calf-length dress with small floral print in muted colors, and her head was wrapped in a dull green Rosie the Riveter bandanna. The hair that poked out from under the cloth was graying, but I didn't know how long it was—I never saw it down. On rare bandanna-free occasions, her hair was swept up and pinned against her head. She wore sensible laced shoes with chunky heels.

She hesitated when she saw me awake, smiled and motioned for me to follow her quietly. I wasn't sure what she intended, but I was glad when she handed me my jacket and headed for the door. The windows were barely lit by the coming day, and fog pressed against the glass. I thought that if we opened a window, even slightly, the fog would ooze over the window sill, drop to the floor, and slowly fill the room. I hurried out the open door so the fog wouldn't slink in past us.

We walked toward the lake through a haze as dense as the one the partridge had just jumped out of. I stayed closer to Gramma than usual, knowing I'd lose sight of her if she got one step ahead. Her hand was visible against the dark cloth of her dress and I could have reached up for it, but I didn't want her to know I was afraid. In general, the only time she held my hand was to guide me across a street. I knew that hand was callused and warm, and I used its swinging motion as my guide.

The fog was disorienting. At first, I was confident that we were walking toward the lake, but then I thought we may have taken a turn toward Mother Orr's house, next door. It seemed like we'd been walking long enough to have gotten to the lake, or to Mother Orr's, but we kept going. I trotted to keep up, confused by how far we'd traveled without seeing anything I recognized. The boat dock appeared out of the darkness, but even then I wasn't sure if it was our dock until we stepped onto the wooden surface and I recognized our rowboat. I hoped we were going out onto the lake, but we walked past the boat. I wondered if we were going swimming in the not-quite morning fog, but I didn't like swimming off the end of the dock because I couldn't really swim and the water was deep—someone had to hold me up. I was glad to see that Gramma didn't have a swimsuit or towel, but I wondered what she had in the tin can she carried. Were we going fishing? But she didn't have a fishing pole . . .

Gramma wasn't talking, so I didn't ask. She did that when we walked in the woods. She'd walk silently until she saw something interesting and then hand-signal me to stop and look. When she was silent, I walked silently, waiting for her to point out some new marvel.

She stopped at the end of the dock and gazed out at the lake, where I could barely make out shadows gliding toward us on the glassy gray surface. The first one I saw clearly was a swan—then another, then two ducks, then more. There were ducks, swans, and geese moving toward us as if we were magnets pulling them from the fog. Gramma opened the can and threw food pellets out onto the water. Mouths grabbing at each morsel made the sound of tiny splashes. She gave me a little handful. "Throw it out as far as you can."

I watched the food pellets leave my hand and land in the water near a mama duck with little duck-babies. Gramma and I threw until the can was empty. The birds knew when breakfast was over, and drifted back into the mist. We watched until the last shadowy figure disappeared before walking back to the cottage where everyone was still asleep, and I sat back down with my book.

I didn't tell my brothers about the swans and ducks and geese. Whenever Gramma saw me awake early in the morning, she and I would go out and throw food pellets on the lake. It wasn't always foggy, but the foggy mornings felt special, like the day was waiting a little longer to begin. When I asked Gramma why she didn't feed the birds during the daytime, she said, "Other children don't understand the way you do, that ducklings can drown. If the mamas came during the day with their babies, other children might chase them and try to catch them."

That made the secret even more important. We were helping the birds and keeping them from being bothered by children that didn't know about ducks and swans, the way I did—never mind that I didn't know it until a few minutes ago. On those mornings, I felt a softness in Gramma that her usual gruff exterior kept well-hidden. She was not the cuddly sort, and did not hug or talk cute, but she shared with me her interest in nature and I often feel her presence as an adult, when I walk in the woods.

Later in the day, Sandy and I passed a couple of old stone foundations. The stones were now covered with thick soft moss, but years ago someone had collected them and carefully set each one in place. How long ago had they been pulled from the damp earth, and what had these buildings been used for? Was this a homestead or a community, a town or a single family living in the wilderness? Was it destroyed by fire or storm, or did it die slowly, as things sometimes do? Were there trees on these mountains or had the International Paper Company been through, cutting whatever they could? Some of the roads we hiked past were IPC roads, reminding us of a time when Vermont's landscape was denuded by large-scale lumbering.

I was reminded of two communities near our home in Michigan. I'd done some research and discovered that Oakwood had been wiped out by the "Great Cyclone of 1896," an F5 tornado. According to the record, the entire town was destroyed and never rebuilt. In an old newspaper article, the reporter noted: "almost all the trees were gone and the few that remained were totally debarked, down to the smallest twigs." Forty-seven people died and over one hundred were injured. I wondered what percentage that was of the community's population. Now there is only a crossroads with a four-way stop and a convenience store, built long after the cyclone, of brick and glass.

I thought Independence had suffered the same fate, because there had clearly been a town where now there was none. There are old homes and a few businesses remaining, but they are few and far between. Independence was founded in 1836 and prospered when the railroad came through in 1856. The farming village began to fail when the main road, Dixie Highway, was paved in 1924. Many of the residents drove to Pontiac and Flint to work in the auto industry instead of the fields. Over time the homes fell into disrepair and the hotel was torn down. There are a few shops and homes left but not what anyone would call a town. I thought of those two stories as I looked at the moss-covered stone foundations on the LT and wondered what fate had befallen that site. I imagined the trees around me debarked down to the tiniest branch, and my mind walked through a forest of pale ghost trees.

We were meeting a lot of hikers as we walked and camped, and there was a feeling of camaraderie. The age variation was great, from people in their teens and twenties to those in their sixties, seventies, and eighties; but most were either college-aged or retirees, with few in between. It was encouraging to find that I was not the only hiker trying to get this adventure in before my aging legs failed.

We were making good time in spite of the rain. When we got to the Glastenbury Wilderness sign, we were way ahead of schedule. Our legs were finally talking to us instead of shouting. Blue Jay had said it would happen. Shortly after that, we walked through a balsam forest so fragrant that we floated on balsam perfume and trail-legs.

We refilled our water bottles at Goddard Shelter with a hiker in that middle-age group that we didn't see much of on the trail. He said that his feet were killing him, and pulled off his croc to show me a foot that resembled hamburger. He had blisters upon blisters and some of them were bleeding. I gave him the Moleskins foot pads I carried on every hike. I kept a couple, just in case, but gave him most of my supply. I hadn't used any of them, and my feet had been blister free, so far.

That night we were so energized by our successful day, we planned to do another long segment the following day. It was less than five miles to Kid Gore Shelter, so we decided to hike 8.9 miles to Story Spring Shelter.

I did not feel well overnight. I had a digestive upset that may have been from a change in routine, or from freeze-dried meals. This had happened before, but it usually disappeared in a few hours—this bout lasted longer and made me ill. Usually my discomfort was eased by a few more bio-breaks in the woods, but that night I was vomiting. My stomachache was not bad, but I felt chilled even in my sleeping bag, wearing my fleece jacket.

I lay in the darkness, waiting for sleep to ease my woes and wondering how I would hike feeling the way I did, carrying the weight of my pack. I pondered the distance to the nearest road and strained to hear highway sounds, but heard only the night forest. All of that happened between 10 p.m. and 1 a.m. I finally dozed off and awoke again at 3 a.m., feeling a little better, with no privy urges or nausea as I drifted back to sleep. By morning, I felt fine—a little short on sleep, but happy to be feeling better.

The hike to Goddard flowed under our boots, and we arrived in camp feeling almost as geeked as we had the day before. We set our packs down at the shelter and I headed for the privy.

The privy was downhill, and I walked carefully because if I leaned one way or another without the weight of the pack, I might topple over. I could usually catch myself without much effort and laugh about adjusting my posture to the relative weightlessness. The path was awkward, with rocks and deep gouges from rain washes, and I began to lose my balance, walking faster to catch myself. I jogged and careened a bit to the right, a bit to the left, before landing in a heap. Sandy was watching from the shelter deck and called out through her laughter, "Are you all right?"

"Thanks for asking. The bruises will heal."

Sandy laughed louder. "I wish I had a film of that. It would be a money-maker in any home video contest."

"I could live without that, thanks."

It was raining, so we decided to have a shelter experience. Once we made that decision, the rain stopped, but we were already set up inside. Goddard Shelter had no tables or bunks. The floor served as the sleeping area, but it had a covered porch along its open front. There were no tables or benches outside, either, so I sat on the porch steps to make my journal entry.

We shared the shelter with three male hikers, another hiker chose to tent outside, and one more who showed up long after dark and quietly set up on the porch. I placed myself along the right side wall, with Sandy sleeping on my left. The mice were active all night along the wall, and Sandy's snoring was a delight compared to the hikers on the other side of the shelter, who snored like lumberjacks—so I didn't get much sleep.

Looking out over the balsam trees, I was impressed by their perfect silhouette, like the background of an animation cel: a wall of trees consistent in conical shape until the very top, where they narrowed like rockets prepared to take off from the tree. I wished I could remember how to take pictures without the flash, but Dad's voice whispered, "You will remember this for the rest of your life."

The hiker who showed up after we were asleep was up and gone before 5:30. I wondered how many miles they put down in a day and how many of them were done by headlamp.

The rest of us were up and getting ready to start our day by six. There was no sleeping-in at a shelter. Trying to sleep at all was a challenge with quadraphonic snoring, an occasional gas emanation, and tiny rodents scurrying about. At least in a tent, you'd have a little distance and wouldn't be woken by the early-risers. I decided that I preferred the comfort and privacy of my tent.

We stopped for lunch at the Kid Gore Shelter, and it felt good to get to a shelter before stopping for the night. We ate lunch at a picnic table, discussing the value of peanut butter relative to its weight. I didn't realize how heavy peanut butter was. It added valuable protein and flavor to our meals, but it was the heaviest food I had in my pack. It can also be hard to eat out of a Ziploc baggie, which got us laughing, making it all the more difficult. I pointed at Sandy. "Is my face as peanut-butter smeared as yours?"

"You've got peanut butter on your chin, both cheeks, and your forehead. How did you get it on your forehead?" Laughter shook us again, and the process became messier.

The remaining five miles got us to Story Spring Shelter at 3:30. We heard thunder in the distance and quickly set up our tents, got water from the spring, and decided to take a nap before dinner. The rain started as I crawled into my tent and hadn't stopped by 7:45, when I woke up. The wind snapped at the rainfly, and the rain hammered a steady drone. The sky brightened briefly, but I could hear the thunder of another storm approaching.

"Sandy, I'm happy to dine in my tent. How about you?"

"I'm with you." The rain was spitting again.

Water soon flowed beneath my tent, creating a water-bed effect. Sandy called out through the rain, "I sure am glad my tent weighs more than fourteen ounces."

"A Saran Wrap ground cloth wouldn't be much protection against this," I agreed.

I could feel the water flowing beneath my tent, but I was dry.

I listened to the relentless rain until I needed to urinate. I weighed the pros and cons of making a privy run; the privy was not close. I estimated how wet I would get making a trip to the forest instead, and made a decision. Desperate times call for desperate measures. My uphill vestibule was my primary entrance, and I could inch my backside into my downhill vestibule and allow my water to flow away with the rain. It was awkward and chilly, but it worked and I crawled back into my sleeping bag dry and relieved.

Day six would be our longest, with 10.5 miles to Stratton Pond. We got out of camp at 7 a.m. and arrived at Stratton Pond at 5:15 p.m. According to the guidebook, we should have gotten there at one thirty or two. The sky had been crystal clear all day. Everywhere we turned was beautiful, so we'd stopped often to take pictures, not caring about the time.

At Black Brook, dark stones lay everywhere like giant jacks thrown on a sidewalk. The black stone of the brook's bed gave it its name. A huge spider web, stretched between two hemlock branches, caught the sunlight. Shimmering beads of water glistened on the silvery filaments with the flowing blackness beneath, creating the illusion of a jeweled silver necklace against a black velvet case.

CHAPTER ELEVEN

ODZIHOZO

Today is your day!
Your mountain is waiting, so . . . get on your way!
Dr. Seuss , "Oh the Places You'll Go!" [8]

I woke twice in the darkness, learned from my watch that there were hours before sunrise, and drifted back to sleep. When I could see the first hint of light filtering through my tent, I lay there with eyes closed, floating on the edge of slumber.

In that semi-wakeful state, I heard the first birdcall of the day: a single clear chirp, then a pause followed by another single chirp, then a slightly shorter pause followed by seven close clear chirps in a row. Then the forest fell silent. A few minutes later, I heard the same series: chirp, pause, chirp, pause, seven chirps, silence. This went on for over an hour. I had no idea what bird I was listening to and wished I was more knowledgeable. It would be nice to hike with an ornithologist who could say with confidence, "Oh, that's the Ruby-Slippered wood thrush or the Butterfingered booby. I hear them often, don't you?"

Finally, I heard a different call: a softer, almost gurgling song. I imagined a bird sitting atop her eggs telling the tiny birds within that the time was coming for them to push out of their shells and into the world. The sweet melody felt like gentle urging. "Don't worry," it was saying. "When the time comes, you'll be ready." I felt myself pushing up through the soft membrane of slumber, but I didn't feel the need to push out of my shell just yet.

I'd heard similar birdsongs from my bed in the winter, but they were muffled by a windowpane. In summer, they came into my room through the screen but remained distant, beyond the windowsill. On that morning, I felt like I was curled up in my own nest among hundreds of Mother Earth's nests. I was awakened as nature intended; not by an alarm or a timetable, but by the pleasant sounds that open each day. I woke up right where I was supposed to be.

We'd encountered many hikers by this time, but for the first time, one bothered me. Sandy was usually ahead of me, often out of sight, but I could see her when I met this SOBO hiker. At a glance, you could tell he'd just come onto the trail. He looked like he would smell like soap. Hikers *do not* smell like soap. He carried a full pack and other than being way too clean, seemed normal. I thought he might be back on the trail after going off to restock and clean up. I was going to ask him, but his first question threw me.

"Are you hiking alone?"

I answered the question I had expected to hear. "I'm doing the LT."

"Are you hiking alone?" he asked again.

I looked ahead, at Sandy's backpack. "No, I'm with my friend up there. I don't know where the guys are. They're usually ahead of us, but they've been goofing around back there."

He didn't say another word. I stood aside and felt a wave of relief as he walked by. He did smell like soap.

At our next break, I told Sandy. "That way-too-clean hiker asked me twice if I was hiking alone."

"He asked me the same question and it gave me the willies."

"I told him we were hiking together and the guys were messing around somewhere behind us."

Sandy looked south on the trail. "Let him think we have big, burly guys with us. I'm glad we're NOBO and won't see him again."

As we entered the Green Mountain National Forest, we arrived at our first real mountain. We were at once eager and anxious to climb Stratton Mountain. The hike so far had been difficult enough without four-thousand-foot mountains.

But getting to the top of Stratton was easier than I'd anticipated. There were a lot of switchbacks and not much rock scramble. I'd hiked my first real mountain, and yet there was no view—we were encased in a cloud. Sandy couldn't resist going up the fire tower anyway. I stayed on the ground, taking a break before we began our descent, and I could barely see Sandy. "How's the view up there?"

She leaned over the rail. "I can almost see you."

At Stratton's summit, there was a bronze plaque on a huge stone with information about the 3,936-foot elevation, its significance to the Abenaki people, specs on the fire tower, and the Nature Conservancy's purchase of the site from the International Paper Company. This is the paragraph that struck me:

> Stratton claims a unique role in hiking path history. It is here, in 1909, that James Taylor conceived of the idea of a "Long Trail" extending from Massachusetts to Canada. Then, in 1921, after construction of Taylor's Long Trail had begun, Benton MacKaye – forester, author, philosopher – further expanded that concept into a footpath linking all the scenic ridges of the entire range – and the Appalachian Trail was born.

I sat on a bench where these two trails had been born.

The plaque mentioned that Stratton Mountain had significance to the Abenaki people, but it didn't say what that significance was. I knew little about Vermont's Native Americans but I'd read that Abenaki means "people of the dawn," and that they believe stories have lives of their own. I was curious what they called this mountain, and what the story behind that name would have been.

Upon my return to the world of roads and people not carrying their lives on their backs, I couldn't wait to get to the Woodstock library to find information about the Abenaki people and their stories. I'd wandered into the Norman Williams Public Library on one of my first visits to Woodstock. Its architecture had drawn me and I was not disappointed when I walked through the triple-arched entry. The white vaulted ceiling contrasted perfectly with the ornate wooden support beams that reflected the chandeliered lighting. It was so beautiful, I nearly fell over a chair.

I feel at home in libraries; our mother had taken us often to Clarkston's tiny clapboard library. Fay and I were constantly checking out and returning books. I went into the Woodstock library just to look at the building, but sat down feeling at home among the books. That library was grand compared to the tiny square building I'd grown up with, but I felt it envelope me as if it were my own private space.

I discovered that Woodstock's library had been built in 1883 by Edward Williams, as a tribute to his parents, Norman and Mary, "to ensure that their love of reading and books continues for generations."

I wondered why, if the building was dedicated to both of them, it was the Norman Williams Library and not the Norman and Mary Williams Library. I thought Mary deserved a little credit. Still, it was nice that Edward created an exquisite memorial to his parents, even if his mother's name was left out.

Years later, when the library was remodeled, I cringed at what might be going on inside and stayed away long after the work was complete. They'd installed a long wheelchair access ramp on one side of the arched entry and edged it with a marble wall that looked OK, but I was afraid to see what they'd done to the interior. I heard they'd added a second floor and I was saddened to think of losing the view of the vaulted ceiling and beautifully shaped wooden beams.

When I worked up the courage to step through the doors, I was stunned. They had added a second story, but it was a donut around the inside of the building, leaving intact the central view, past a new wooden railing that matched the wood of the vaulted ceiling. It was beautiful. They'd created more space without adverse effect on the architecture. I should have come back sooner.

After hiking Stratton, I was looking for information on the Abenaki people. I'd done some research online, but I like the feel of a house of books. I informed the librarian of my quest and she guided me to the appropriate area. After I gathered a pile, my librarian brought folders of articles, booklets, and more books that might interest me. I didn't have to move, she was finding everything I could possibly want, and was happy to do so. I found so much more than I had online, because of my oh-so-helpful librarian. I had to remind myself to go out and feed the parking meter. I can spend almost as much time in a library as in the woods.

Here's what I learned about the significance of Stratton Mountain to the Abenaki people (if I err or fail to convey proper significance to any part of the tale, I hope the Abenaki people will forgive me): the name they applied to Stratton Mountain is Manicknung, meaning "place where the mountains pile up."

As for Stratton's significance to the Abenaki, there is a god, or nearly-god, who resides there. He is called Odzihozo, which means "he makes himself from nothing." He is an assistant to Tabaldah, The Owner. The Owner would be equivalent in Christianity to The Creator or God. After Odzihozo made himself from dust leftover from Tabaldah's creation of man, Odzihozo was placed in charge of this land by Tabaldah. Odzihozo's job was to watch over the people and report back to Tabaldah if problems developed.

According to story, Odzihozo went into a village but found no one there. He heard sounds coming from the forest and discovered the people lying on the ground under maple branches that dripped maple sap into their mouths. The sound he had heard was the people making contented noises as the sugar fell onto their tongues.

When Odzihozo reported this to Tabaldah, that the people were doing nothing else and the village had been abandoned, Tabaldah instructed Odzihozo: "Go to the river, gather water, and place it in the trees to dilute the sugar."

When Odzihozo did this, the people went back to their village and carried on with their lives. And that is why maple sap must be boiled down to get to the sugar, a.k.a., maple syrup.

That story helped me understand Odzihozo's place and why he may reside on the first of the Green Mountains, to keep an eye on things going on below.

As we began our descent of Stratton Mountain, the sun burst out of the clouds. We walked through a stand of yellow birch with masses of hobblebush viburnum and sedge beneath their golden branches, dripping with rainwater.

The golden tree trunks surrounded us and I wondered what the Abenaki people thought about yellow birch trees. The Abenaki were storytellers who used stories to entertain and teach. Are there stories living within the yellow birches that I cannot hear?

We crossed several roads and in our guidebook I read the same advice in italics for each crossing: *Use caution when crossing the road; traffic moves at high speeds.* We'd noticed how fast the cars appeared to be going when we crossed Route 9. Our hearts and minds had slowed to the pace of our legs and the speed of the cars seemed excessive. Could our outlook have changed that much in a few days?

At the Stratton-Arlington Road crossing, there was a notice encased in plastic, stapled near the logbook that read: "Attention: A section of trail between Bourn Pond and Stratton Pond has been affected by a large wind event and is now partially under water due to beaver activity. Hiking in this area may be challenging."

Much of what we'd already hiked felt challenging, but had not been described as such in the guidebook. I could hardly wait to find out what *challenging* would feel like . . . Even though we were tired when we got to Stratton Pond, we tried to hike to the tenting area, in spite of the notices. The enormity of the beaver construction was impressive; we turned back to camp at the shelter.

I sat gazing across the pond to the far shore that was shrouded in fog, and wondered if the Abenaki had a story here. I tried to conjure a story, but my imagination didn't know Native lore and I couldn't guess what was out there in both physical and story-form. Was the story floating on the glassy surface or living in the depths that I would never see?

CHAPTER TWELVE

LOON CALL

There's no such thing as bad weather, only inappropriate clothing.
Sir Ranulph Fiennes

We hiked into the Stratton Pond Shelter discussing a personal hygiene question. "We should stop using scented wipes for our trail showers," I said. "I thought being scented would be a plus, but the addition of that scent to my natural bouquet makes me smell like rancid cookie dough."

Sandy was walking backward, looking at me. "How would you know what rancid cookie dough smells like?"

"When I was a kid I swiped some cookie dough from Mom's kitchen and hid it in my room for future consumption. I forgot about it until it smelled like this." I sniffed down the front of my shirt.

There's usually a caretaker at the Stratton Shelter, and because it's one of the more popular day hike destinations, there's a fee to camp. I'd been told that once a thru-hiker has paid a camp fee, their receipt would take care of any future fees. The caretaker was not around as we set up our tents, restocked our water, and crawled inside. We heard thunder getting closer with each clap.

Sandy and I had decided to go off-trail at Route 30. I'd made a call to Wib and Audrey, and they were leaving my car at the trailhead parking area, rather than picking us up, because we weren't sure if we would be there in one day or two. It would depend on the trail and weather conditions—both unpredictable.

I lay in my tent listening to the rain when the call of a loon took me to a loon encounter from long ago.

When we stayed at Gramma's cottage, I slept on the screened porch. One night, I was frightened by an eerie sound from the lake. The next evening, Gramma walked with me down to the dock where the glassy surface of the lake was being painted by the setting sun. I'd never been out on the lake at night. I took my usual seat in the back of the boat; she sat in the center facing me and began to row toward the far end of the lake. The sunset was golden, but the blackness of the water was ominous, so I tried not to look down—something might float up from the depths. During the day, I could see the weeds undulating beneath the surface. I couldn't see it in the inky water, but I knew it was there, moving back and forth.

The painted sky was fading when I heard the eerie call. It was so close—the hair on my arms stood up and I looked at Gramma, hoping she would turn the boat and row us to safety. But she smiled and pointed at an oddly-shaped duck floating just yards away from us. She held her index finger to her lips, telling me to be quiet. I stared at this strange being. It floated like a duck, but its bill was pointed, its body low in the water, and it made a sound that shouldn't come from a duck.

With white-knuckled hands wrapped around the edge of my seat, I wished for Gramma to get us out of there, away from that thing, but I did not speak. Gramma turned the boat toward the strange duck that wasn't a duck and leaned toward me. "It's a loon, watch it and nod your head if it dives."

She rowed toward the loon. I knew its name now, but I didn't want to get any closer. Oh, Gramma, please, please, please take us home. She didn't hear my thoughts and continued to row.

Suddenly it was gone; there were surface ripples glistening in what remained of the light, but it was gone. I looked up but saw no bird in flight. I nodded, nodded, nodded. It's in the water. Is it coming after us? Will it jump in the boat and peck us with its sharp beak? Will it poke holes in the bottom of the boat? I don't want to be in that dark water, with darker weeds. I can't swim. Gramma, remember I can't swim.

Gramma reached for my hand and pulled me forward to sit beside her, whispering, "Let's see where this crazy loon comes up. You look that way, I'll look this way. Squeeze my hand when you see it but don't say a word."

We sat holding hands and watching for a crazy loon. I was pleased by this closeness and forgot for a moment about odd creatures in the darkness, with her warm hand engulfing mine. Gramma spotted the loon and when she squeezed my hand I jumped and the boat wobbled. Don't fall in, don't fall in. I clamped hard to Gramma, gripping the plank seat with my other hand. She put her arm around me, she didn't do that often, and as the boat settled she whispered, "They're fish ducks. They can dive way down in the water and catch fish. That's why their bills are so sharp, for catching fish. They make strange sounds, but they're just silly fish ducks. That's why some people say, 'He's crazy as a loon,' when someone isn't right in the head."

She put me back in my seat, turned the boat, and began to row toward the silly fish duck. It didn't dive this time, but spread its wings, lifting its body, flapping as its feet splashed on the lake's surface. Gramma laughed and said, "That silly loon didn't know whether to fly or dive, so it went for a walk."

We whispered back and forth about how far they could swim under water and how funny they looked, and when I heard the loon call again, I giggled and we turned toward home.

When I slept on the porch after that, I listened for the loons and when I heard one I thought about fish ducks low in the water with the setting sun behind them, and holding Gramma's hand.

⚹

Loon memories guided me to sleep.

Route 30 was eleven miles from Stratton Pond, so we were relatively sure we'd hike out on day seven, but we knew better than to make a prediction.

We broke camp at 7:30 a.m., just before the rain started again. It rained often and hard, and the temperature dropped as the day progressed. Sandy's thermometer read fifty-six degrees. The wind at the summits was so strong, our rain gear whipped and snapped in our wake. We kept our heads down and walked.

The guidebook said that the day's hike would not be demanding. The grades were not as steep and there would be smooth path under foot. With less rock to deal with, we made good time until we met our most difficult water crossing.

We unhooked our pack straps and Sandy carried her pack across the churning water, then came back to get mine. I argued that I could handle it, but without much conviction. We both made it, but it was slow going. The other crossings that day were also difficult. I didn't hand Sandy my pack on those, but we unhooked our pack belts and sternum straps two more times, in case we fell in.

We managed to cover 11.5 miles in nine hours. I wonder how we would have done in normal weather, but I don't know if there is normal weather on the LT.

Before we got in the car, we changed into the dry clothing we'd left in the backseat. I let a couple cars pass, waiting to pull out of the parking area. I was surprised by their speed. I waited for another car, thinking of Fay's comment when she was behind a too-cautious driver: "This guy is waiting for the road to be clear for a hundred miles in both directions. Move it, buddy."

I *moved it* and drove at what seemed like a good pace. I usually drove at or above the speed limit, but cars were now piling up behind me. I looked down at the speedometer. I was going thirty-nine in a 55 mph zone. I pulled over to let the other cars pass. My perception of velocity had been altered by our week in the woods.

I pulled out again and moved up to speed, glancing up at the mountain ridge we would be hiking in a month. It was enclosed in cloud cover. I said, "We were probably walking in that cloud."

Sandy added, "I think it will be waiting for us when we come back in September."

We were hungry for real food, but didn't want to go inside a restaurant looking and smelling the way we did, so we watched for a takeout place. We didn't find one until we got to the Kentucky Fried Chicken in Rutland. I placed our order at the drive-thru window and wondered if our fragrance might be noticeable through the window. We decided to eat when we got back to our house, about twenty minutes away. But when we rounded the first corner, Sandy pointed to a drugstore parking lot. "This looks like a lovely place to have lunch."

I pulled in and we scarfed down our food like a pair of starving animals.

Once we got to the house, and after our showers, the weather cleared and the cold rain turned to warm sunshine that allowed us to air out our gear. When I came out onto the porch to see if Sandy wanted to go around the corner to the Long Trail Brewery for dinner, she was slumped in a chair, sound asleep. When she woke, we walked to the brewery and had what would become our traditional post-hike meal at a brewery named after the trail.

Sandy and I learned a lot on our hike; we got tired, got stronger, and got through it. We saw beautiful sights that only those who hike are privileged to enjoy. We were left with a feeling of accomplishment coupled with a pleasant fatigue. I couldn't wait to do it again.

CHAPTER THIRTEEN

SEPTEMBER SUN

Each fresh peak ascended teaches something.
Sir Martin Conway

"It's September and I can see my breath." I held the door open for the dogs. Don laughed. "Yeah, but it's not raining."

"Yet," said Sandy, sorting through her gear.

The next morning, Sandy and I set off into a fifty-three-degree downpour. Don and his brother Chris doubted our sanity, but we smiled for a picture at the trailhead, wearing full rain gear. We laughed while walking up Bromley Mountain into a blustering cold rain. "This weather has been waiting for us since July," Sandy called over her shoulder.

It rained all day, but we were ready for it. In two months we hadn't lost much of our hiking fitness and we did almost eleven miles on day one. The walk up Bromley was easy by LT standards, and the trail itself was unusually open. My mind wandered to a John Ford western, with the image of a wagon train trailing to a distant prairie horizon. We could see our path winding up the open slope ahead of us and fading into a mist that made the trail seem vast beyond imagination. We stopped at Bromley Shelter for a break, a snack, and to get out of the driving wind and rain.

The weather on Bromley was fierce, the temperature still in the fifties, and as I reached the peak I found myself gasping in a wind so stiff that I had to turn my head to breathe. On Styles Peak, the wind was worse. "The rain feels like ice pellets," I commented. The temperature was dropping.

"I think it *is* ice pellets." Sandy's head was turned in my direction.

We entered a stand of trees where we could walk with our heads up, but the break was brief. By the time we got to Peru Peak, the wind and rain felt normal.

The trail was wet and we knew better than to attempt to avoid the deep puddles. We marched along as if we'd been hoping for cold rain and wind. At our first bridge of the day, over Bromley Brook, the water rushed in a foamy rage around huge black boulders. The color contrast made the water look faster and deeper. "I'm glad we don't have to ford this on foot."

Sandy stomped on the wooden planks, looking into the sky. "Thank you, bridge builders."

We hiked three mountains on our first day in cold rain and high wind. We saw moose tracks in the muck and noted that the efts were beginning to show the spots for which the red–spotted newt is named.

Sandy's flight had come in late. We'd gotten to bed at 1:30 a.m., and I was awake and eager to get started by 6:30. With less than five hours' sleep and a hike of ten miles over three peaks under our belts, I thought I would sleep soundly on our first night out, in spite of the wooden tent platforms. The wooden floor was hard, and I missed being able to nest on the forest floor. I had to use rocks to secure the tent in lieu of tent stakes.

Sandy was wearing gators over her zippie pants. She had new boots and between them and the gators, her feet had stayed dry. I'd seen hikers wearing shorts with gators, but hadn't tried them myself. They looked like they'd be useful not only for keeping feet dry, but also for keeping dust and dirt out of socks and boots. I thought I might try my cross-country ski gators; they were lightweight and waterproof, and I added them to my mental checklist for our next hike.

We arrived at Peru Peak Shelter having hiked almost eleven miles in eight hours. According to the guidebook, it should have taken five and a half, but we didn't care. We had hiked over ten miles on day one in awful weather. Over dinner we chattered like children on Christmas Eve.

Hearing from other hikers that the weather was supposed to improve fed our enthusiasm as we pored over maps and set goals for the next few days. If we had twenty-four hours without rain, it would be the first we'd experienced on the Long Trail.

Sandy and I talked about training hikes and I shared an incident that had happened on my Nordhouse hike. After our July hike, eight weeks before I would be on the Long Trail again, I relaxed for two weeks before returning to my training schedule. I walked local roads and hiked for a weekend at Nordhouse Dunes with Ewa's group. The Nordhouse trail was easier than the LT and a fellow hiker commented, looking at me on a steep uphill, "Look how easy she does this." I was surprised by the compliment and happy to be feeling so good. I was now one of the fastest hikers in the group.

I never get far from the trail when I take a bio-break in the woods. I usually set my pack on the trail where I can see it and do not walk beyond its view. At Nordhouse there were many campers and I felt the need to walk further, for privacy. The forest floor was undistinguished and on my return I walked with confidence into the wrong campsite. When strangers looked up at me, I continued toward the lake as if that had been my plan. Lake Michigan was my only source for orienting myself. When I got to the shore, I looked back and spotted our camp.

During my next bio-break, I took a long stick and dragged a scar in the soft soil that I followed back to my tent after my business was taken care of.

I was more enthusiastic than I should have been on day two back on the LT, after not sleeping well the night before. I'd had a hard time falling asleep on the unforgiving wooden deck. It was after 1 a.m. when I finally nodded off, and we started the day early, walking into bright sunshine reflecting through dripping trees.

Mount Baker was the first exposed vista on the LT that we approached without rain, fog, or dense cloud cover. We passed a sign indicating a bad weather route and didn't give it a thought. In my backcountry first aid class, I'd learned how important foul weather alternatives could be. Being on exposed rock in a thunder storm is not a good idea. I also learned to watch for approaching weather, since most lightning incidents occur as a storm approaches.

We walked up Baker's rocky surface and noted a pair of garter snakes sunning themselves on the moss-covered stone. The blazes, usually found on tree trunks, were painted on the rock instead, and we decided that this would be a perfect place to take a break and enjoy our first expansive view.

We gazed into the distant horizon, but my mind came back to our perch and the snakes that had been sunning themselves on the warm stone. These snakes are often referred to as garden snakes or common garter snakes, but I resented the use of the word *common* in regard to the first snakes my grandmother taught me how to catch.

Gramma taught me to use a forked stick to gently pin them just behind the head. "Now don't press too hard. You want to catch them, not hurt them."

Gramma would pick them up to let me look at them, appreciating how pretty they were and how soft their scaly-looking skin was. Then she would let me hold them and feel them gently twine around my wrist before I carefully set them on the ground to slither away. After watching her, I was able to catch them myself.

Gramma and I found many garter snakes, but we also caught water snakes and milk snakes. We could catch the water snakes by hand as they swam along the surface of the lake, next to Gramma's rowboat. After we looked at them briefly, we would release them and they would glide away from my hand, leaving a thin serpentine wake.

The splotched skin of the milk snake was different and Gramma said, "They act tough, but they're no more dangerous than a garter snake."

The first milk snake I saw coiled its body and arched its neck. I jumped back, but Gramma easily picked it up to show me how pretty it was. "They're called milk snakes because farmers used to think they would steal milk from their cows, but that's just not so. They come into barns and around houses to find rodents. They help the farmer by catching chipmunks and mice that might get into their grain stores."

I held the milk snake carefully, looking at its strange coloring. In comparison to the garter snake, its mottled coloring was exotic. But it still seemed dangerous to me; it had coiled its body and hissed. No garter snake had ever lifted its head.

I caught a snake all by myself one day. I had not seen another snake like it, and carried it into Gramma's kitchen to show her. She was sitting on the right side of the table, Mom was on the left, and I held up my prize so Gramma could tell me what it was.

She calmly took it from me, the way she had allowed me to take snakes from her hands. "Let me see this little guy," she said.

She held it and explained that our other snakes had round heads and this one had a triangular head. She pointed out the little dip between its eyes and then said, "This is a pit viper, a copperhead. All pit vipers are poisonous."

Mom leaned back, taking in a breath that might have frightened me, but Gramma's reaction was a question. "Where did you find this snake?"

"Down by the lake."

"I am going to ask again. Where did you find this snake?"

In a small voice, I said, "Down by the lake."

Gramma leaned toward me. "I am going to ask one more time and I want you to tell me exactly where you found this snake."

She was getting angry. She didn't do that often and I didn't like it. In a slightly smaller voice, I said, "In the stone wall."

Gramma leaned closer. "In the stone wall across the street, where you're not allowed to go?"

In my tiniest voice, I said, "Uh-huh."

She stood. "Show me where you found it."

We walked to the street, where she directed me to stop and look both ways before we crossed the narrow road. She placed my snake on the ground near the wall and stepped back. My copperhead disappeared in an instant. Gramma placed her hands behind my shoulders and guided me back to the street, looking both ways before we crossed to the cottage. As we walked she told me that going across the street alone was very bad, but telling a lie about it was worse, and since I had lied twice, I was in big trouble.

I was sent to Gramma's bedroom to await my punishment. The dim room with the glow-in-the-dark crucifix on the wall did little to ease my anxiety. When I looked at any crucifix with Jesus hanging from it, I was sad and I felt sorry for him. I didn't understand why anyone would want to hang something so miserable on their wall. Wouldn't it be better to have a pretty picture of Jesus with a halo?

Mom and Aunt Dorothy once took me to see a particularly striking crucifix. The life-sized figure towered over us. I could see the tension in his calves and thighs and it made me hurt. Mom and Aunt Dorothy were gazing up in awe. "Isn't it beautiful?"

I looked up again, directly into his eyes. They looked like fear and pain. I turned away.

I had seen a dog hit by a car, and before Dad could pull me back, I'd looked into his eyes. They looked like the eyes of Jesus hanging on that crucifix. I understood it was a credit to the artist to create so realistic a sculpture, but I

85

wondered what people would think if the owner of that dog took a picture of it, near death, and framed it to hang on the wall. Would they say it was beautiful, or would they think he was weird?

I turned my head away from Gramma's image of glowing agony and on the opposite wall was another glow-in-the-dark image. Why would Gramma have a glowing dead person on one wall and Donald Duck on the other? But there he was, walking in front of a radiant picket fence. She'd hung that picture for her grandchildren, but I didn't know that then. I just thought that Gramma had strange taste in decorations.

I lay there in the gloom, awaiting my sentence, knowing that it was going to be awful. However, I have no recollection of what the punishment was. The dread I felt while I waited crept into any thought I had of telling a lie in the future.

My reverie of childhood snake catching was broken by the call of a hawk, and I watched it tilt and soar at eye level. I don't know where Sandy's mind wandered while I stumbled down memory lane, but we both watched the red-tailed hawk drop out of sight below our rocky throne and reappear several times before we took one more look at the view and got back on the trail.

Dropping down from Baker's summit, we reached a step that even Sandy, with her long legs, could not reach. She took off her pack and was able to stretch down, then retrieve her pack. I took off my pack and set it near the edge of the step where I sat and dangled my feet two feet above the nearest foothold. Sandy laughed as I rolled onto my stomach and slithered backward to find a rock to step on. We were soon back under our packs and on our way, but we would perform that exercise more often as we traveled north.

Our plan was to get to Big Branch that day, but we arrived earlier than expected and we weren't ready to stop, so we kept going. We regretted that decision halfway to Lula Tye Shelter, but it was too late by then. Walking through an open area that was alive with golden rod and blooming asters lightened our fatigue, but just slightly.

Back in the forest, we came upon a rock the shape and size of a coffin. Its resemblance to a sarcophagus was unmistakable, but in the mottled sunlight, with orange jewel weed at its base and crimson viburnum berries draping its sides, it didn't feel foreboding. What if it were a fallen hiker, or Abenaki warrior of ages past? I picked a small bouquet of jewel weed and set it on the flat stone surface, just in case.

We were weary when we got to the shelter. Sandy said her feet were hurting and I was feeling drained. We dropped our packs and walked to Little Rock Pond to restock our water and talk to the caretaker who lived in a tent near the pond. The Little Rock Pond Shelter had a custodian because this lovely spot affords easy access for day or weekend hikers from the road we'd crossed a mile back. The caretaker had a kayak, which he allowed Sandy to take for a spin as the sun was setting. Her sore feet and fatigue disappeared. With my balance issues, I wanted to avoid the embarrassment of needing help getting in and out of the kayak, so I watched Sandy for a few minutes before walking back to our campsite.

CHAPTER FOURTEEN

GHOSTS

Memory is like riding a trail at night with a lighted torch.
The torch casts its light only so far, and beyond that is darkness.
Ancient Lakota saying

That night, we planned to make the next day's hike an easy one, just a few miles to Greenwall Shelter. It would be short, but we could spend some time playing tourist, taking in the sights that were supposed to be impressive: white rocks (whatever that means) and cascades worth stopping for, according to the guidebook.

A short day would give my right leg a needed rest. It ached as we'd hiked our last mile to Little Rock. Old fractures were speaking to me, their tone moving from a whisper to a shriek, but they became silent after my break beside the sunset-painted pond. Watching Sandy's kayak glide across the water had soothed me, body and mind.

Sandy and I were the only people at Lula Tye. Within my dark tent, the quiet of the forest was disturbed by an animal moving outside, inches from my ear. I couldn't see what was rustling through the leaves so close to my fabric home, but Sandy had her rainfly flipped back and she could see what I could not.

"Sandy do you see something near my tent?"

She shone her headlamp in my direction. "It's a rabbit."

"It sounds like a rhinoceros."

The moon was bright and the shadows of individual leaves were crisp against my tent flap. A slight breeze created the visual effect of a foliar kabuki dance. I was lying there, mesmerized by the show, when a loon's call floated from Little Rock Pond. Oh cool, sound to go with this fabulous visual!

Beyond Sandy's tent, two barred owls called to one another. A screech owl, some distance off, enhanced the audio, creating a triangle of woodland sounds. I envisioned the forest full of night birds.

I was waiting for sleep when I heard a sound that sat me straight up. No, it wasn't a bear, or a rhinoceros, but an owl that I'd never heard before. It made a single, deep resonant hoot. Could it be a great gray owl? They're rare and don't call as often as some owls, but I think they hoot in little groups, not a single call. I sat in the darkness, straining to hear it again. I was about to give up when I heard it, a single call—deep and close. That was a big owl. It wasn't a great horned owl; I've heard them before. It may not have been a great gray, but I'm going to remember it as such until someone informs me to the contrary.

I didn't hear it again, so I lay back in my sleeping bag thinking that the night couldn't have been any better. But I was wrong. Two barred owls moved in and began chatting, one in the beech tree near Sandy's tent and one in the maple next to mine.

Nestled against the forest floor, I drifted toward sleep listening to a barred owl serenade. My sleepy thoughts turned to my dad's prediction: "You will remember this for the rest of your life." And I will.

After breakfast, we set off into the sunshine past a set of cascades and into the forest. A moss-covered stone foundation emerged as if it had been waiting for us. The rocky wall awakened me from my hiking trance and several others appeared on both sides of the trail, continuing deep into the forest around us. They were accented by bits of rusted iron woodstoves, metal wheels, and tools discovered by other hikers and stacked in artistic arrays along the trail and on top of the stone walls.

This had been a town. I would have liked to look around to determine how large it had been and guess the number of inhabitants. It made me think of how remote the area must have been for the settlers who'd left the artifacts. I knew, if we looked closer, we would find more remains of their community.

"Sandy, I wonder where the cemetery was. I should come back to look around. I love exploring ghost towns. My favorite vacation memory with my parents was hunting for ghost towns in Michigan's Upper Peninsula. We learned so much, without realizing we were being taught."

We kept walking as I talked. "Last summer, Don and I took a hiking tour of Fort Independence, the garrison on the Vermont shore opposite Fort Ticonderoga. Our guide led us into a dense forest, to a site that had recently been discovered. He pointed out stones—some large, some small. They were the head and foot stones of a military cemetery."

I remembered standing in the Fort Independence woods, imagining it clear of trees with units of soldiers in sharp rows, saluting their fallen brothers. That image evaporated into a forest with crumbling stone markers, symmetrically spaced. We had the good luck to be with a guide who was not afraid to drag us through brambles to a site he found interesting. From the path a few feet away, there was no indication of the sacred place hidden by the forest.

I wondered if similar markers might be found in that village on the Long Trail. The night before, I had read in my LT nature guide about the ghost town we were walking through. It had been the hamlet of Aldrichville, and we were on what had once been the main road to Wallingford. This was a road?

The Aldrich brothers had founded the town in 1879 and it thrived until 1898. When the best lumber had been removed, the sawmill was deconstructed and the settlement abandoned.

How strange to build a town only to walk away from it after twenty years. I wondered where they went, and why. Were some of them glad to leave and get back to where they'd lived before, or were they off to start another town to be abandoned when the trees were gone?

After nineteen years, there must have been children living there who maybe felt awful about leaving the only home they'd ever known. When my family moved from Waterford to Clarkston, I was nine years old and I thought they'd ruined my life. I would never see my friends and I would never have friends like Jeff and Billy and Barbara again. It was winter when we moved, in the middle of the school term. I walked around my new neighborhood thinking that there was no canal to skate on in the winter and hunt for frogs or mud puppies in the summer. My favorite trees and hiking places were gone. It was a gloomy gray place and I was certain it would never feel like home.

I sat beneath the arching branches of the shrubs on our property line, thinking I would sit there until I froze to death. Then they'd be sorry. I heard them calling as darkness neared and I wrapped my arms around my knees, determined that by morning I would be frozen to the ground. Then they would realize that if they hadn't brought me to this terrible place this never would have happened.

My determination was strong and I could out-wait them, but Vena pushed her black muzzle through the drooping branches, licked my face, and it was all over. How could I leave Vena? She would miss me and it wasn't her fault my parents had ruined everything. She and I crawled out from under the hedge and I survived to make new friends and find new places to explore.

Were there children who felt that strongly about leaving Aldrichville? Did their dogs make them feel better? I walked away from the aging foundations, past an area of hemlock, their branches arching toward the ground, where I imagined a young pair beneath the drooping limbs. They sat shoulder to shoulder, arms wrapped around knees, defiant in their resolve not to be separated. I saw a young boy and girl of nine or ten; their families were going in opposite directions. They'd been friends all their lives and Aldrichville was the only home they'd ever known.

The Aldrich brothers were moving on to build another logging town and Sarah would go there with her family; James would be going back to Boston where his mother could live in a "civilized world" and he would attend a "proper school." Did I imagine this or was I seeing their ghosts in the shadows?

White Rocks looked like an antediluvian giant had cast white stones like seeds for a wild garden. Hikers had stacked them into creative displays of balance and art, and cairns lined both sides of the trail. Some were balanced on rocks the size of cars and others were composed of miniature stones. The rocks were white or light gray, no brown or black among them. Perhaps Odzihozo had painted them for Tabaldah. I wish I knew the Abenaki story hiding among the white stones of the cairns. My camera was busy saving images, as if they wouldn't last in my mind.

With our cameras stowed, we returned to the woods on an even path of pine needles that took us to a second collection of white rocks. This mass of white stones was equal to the first, but with fewer boulders. The smaller cairns created a greater feeling of solemnity. We had talked back and forth at the first rock display, but at the second, the click of cameras was our only sound.

Perhaps the site was revered by ancient peoples and we were sensing their primordial wonder, passed to us by spirits forever standing guard. The path beneath our boots was soft with needles that muted our steps. The White Rock spirits wanted our feet to whisper their presence.

We got to Greenwall at about 1 p.m., looked around the empty shelter, set our camp, restored our water supply, and went for a walk to the cascades. It was downhill all the way, which meant uphill all the way back, creating another what-were-we-thinking moment. It was easier without our packs, but we discovered that we would see the cascades as we hiked the trail the next day, and kicked ourselves for wasting the time and energy. There were people at the shelter when we returned.

Everyone at Greenwall was making better time than Sandy and I.

The dispute over the LT being more difficult than any hike in North America and who had the better boots ended when Moose Jaw said, "My wife is a saint letting me come out here for months, leaving her to take care of everything at home."

Jelly Bean added, "Is she understanding or glad to be rid of you? Since I retired, my wife keeps looking for things to get me out of the house. She may change the locks or move away while I'm hiking." The way he said it let us know he was kidding, and the boyish-innocent grin on his face confirmed that.

There were seven people in camp, and as I made my journal entry it sounded like more were arriving. When I retired to my tent, I could hear people talking at the shelter and at tent sites nearby, but as the night settled I heard only the raspy tone of wood frogs. It was not the serenade I'd experienced at Lula Tye, but that would be a tough one to match. I imagined the frogs' brown bodies glistening in the dappled moonlight as they sang their nightsong.

CHAPTER FIFTEEN

TRAIL–LEGS

*Those who contemplate the beauty of the earth find reserves of
strength that will endure as long as life lasts.*
Rachel Carson , "Silent Spring" [9]

I experienced the best distance-hiking day of my life, slipping into a hiking rhythm I'd never felt before. I had the sensation that I could walk forever. I was breathing hard, but felt an even, steady pace flowing from my boots. We gained more than a thousand feet in an hour, and I was hiking at two miles an hour on a mountain ascent under a full pack. It was magical. I floated into the Minerva Hinchey Shelter on a cloud. We rested there, laughed, and regaled ourselves with how impressed we were with our hiking.

While Sandy napped, I looked around at the plants growing near the shelter. My legs felt good, but there were plants along the trail that threatened to slow me down. I wanted to identify them now, while we were stopped, and I wished my friend Janet was with me. As a gardener/instructor/speaker she is a wealth of information, and whenever I work in a garden or walk in the woods with her I learn something new.

I recalled a day when Janet, her husband Steve, Don, and I walked up the carriage paths to the Mount Tom overlook in Woodstock. It was cold and rainy, the kind of weather that does not stop hikers or gardeners, and we pointed out interesting plants to one another as we walked. Janet and Steve are both horticulturalists and Don worked for a tree service in his high school and college years. Don pointed out an old sugar maple and Janet said, "No, it's a silver maple."

They stood discussing this tree and the reasons for their identification choices. Steve is a photographer, and he and I were preoccupied taking pictures of a viburnum in particularly stunning fruit. When Steve was asked to adjudicate the maple dispute, he walked to where Don stood and said, "You're right." Then he walked over to Janet and said the same thing. They were looking at different trees.

If I hiked with Janet, my problem would be keeping her on the trail, because she might become enthralled with an interesting plant community and wander off, spending more time than I wanted to spare. I wished she'd been present when I saw a plant that looked like blue cohosh, but then again it wasn't. Get moving Ryker, I thought, don't let this botanical puzzle slow you down.

I was walking around the woods at Minerva Hinchey with my LT nature guide, trying to find the plant I'd seen earlier. When Sandy woke up, I stashed my guidebook, hoping to see the plant again along the trail and this time taking its picture to ID later. It was time to get back on the trail.

Hiking down to Route 103 was as surreal as the morning had been. Parts of it were difficult, but the ground flowed beneath me. Perhaps this was influenced by the fact that Route 103 meant a half-mile walk to a *Vermonster burger* with fries, coleslaw, and a cold soda. Distance hikers are alert to any opportunity for real food close to trail/road junctions. Notable food-stops are passed on by word of mouth or in the logbooks at the shelters. It was heavenly to dine on real food, sitting on real chairs, at a real table, but it was still more than I could eat. We ate on the open deck, not inside the restaurant; we were aware of how we smelled.

Walking back, Route 103 paralleled a railroad track, so we got off the road to walk between the rails. Sandy asked me to take a picture of her and with arms extended, she announced, "I am a NOBO HOBO."

We were surrounded by a field of asters, alive with pollinators, that transitioned to a mass of goldenrod with the occasional purple aster as accent. It was a walk in the park.

I was worried that eating a real meal would make the hike to Clarendon miserable. I knew from others that it was a steep uphill with no switchbacks. The trek began with a walk through more wildflower fields, heading north over a farmer's fence via stiles, and then we began our ascent. The walk is always more difficult after lunch, but in a few minutes I found an easy walking pace that emerged from my legs like they didn't belong to me.

I burped a few times and fouled the air behind me, which is what real food can do to you after days of dried meals. The climb flowed in a way that made the sweat and difficult steps feel like a lovely woodland walk. The rocky gorge that marked our ascent was a cathedral of towering rock walls topped by skyward evergreens. We gazed in awe. I worried that stopping to take pictures and gape at the beauty would slow us down, but we couldn't help ourselves.

We covered the rocky mile to Clarendon in less than an hour, and I was excited about putting down a nine-mile day that felt easy compared to our best day in July.

That night provided few serenades, with a couple of barred owls early on and coyotes in the distance later. I was surprised that I didn't hear more coyotes along the trail. The coyote calls stopped and while I waited for them to begin again, I heard the song of a distant train. Although it was not of nature, I found the sound calming.

"Today I experienced trail-legs. I felt them hover over soil and stone to find the right notch or slope. They felt no pain or fear but marched with a will driven by the hiker's spirit."

It sounds schmaltzy, but that was what I wrote in my journal, and I stood at Sandy's tent reading it to her. "IT FELT SO DAMN GOOD! I felt like I could walk up a cliff."

"So this is what trail-legs feel like." Sandy was feeling it too.

I felt stronger, and that strength was pumping from my legs, through my entire body, with my mind floating above it all. I know it sounds goofy but, DAMN!

That night, we looked over our maps, knowing that we were planning what could be our toughest day. We were heading for Cooper Lodge and the peak of Killington, the second-highest mountain in Vermont. It would be a ten-mile day, starting with a short steep climb, then a ridge followed by a drop that looked tough. After that, we would begin our mountain ascent. It's hard to tell from the map how difficult the hike will be. Elevation changes can be made easier by switchbacks, tougher by rocky gulches, and nearly impossible by irregular stone steps. Our final climb up Killington would be a twenty-five-hundred-foot elevation change. I was less apprehensive since my trail-legs had kicked in, but I was not delusional. I had no idea how difficult Killington might be.

CHAPTER SIXTEEN

THE VOICE

*Thousands of tired, nerve-shaken, over-civilized people
are beginning to find out that going to the mountains is going home;
that wildness is a necessity . . .*
John Muir , "On National Parks" [10]

Killington Mountain would require a degree of effort that Sandy and I had not faced before. We felt stronger and more capable than ever before, but the day's distance and elevation change (ten miles and two thousand five hundred feet) weighed on us. We crossed Lottery Road early in the day, walked past farm fields, and climbed over a gate with a white blaze on the gatepost and a sign that read, *Keep Gate Closed.*

Past the Clement Shelter Road, the trail was getting steep when we saw something white in the distance on our path. The closer we got, the less sense it made. There was a white cooler alone in the woods, and when I lifted the lid it was full of ice and Mountain Dew—my favorite. Next to the cooler sat a chair with a plastic container on the seat that revealed our invitation to tea. The Mad Hatter advised us to take a moment to enjoy a cold, refreshing drink and put our empties in the container provided. Next to the note was a register similar to those found in the shelters. The number of grateful tea party attendees indicated that the Mad Hatter did this often.

There were fallen trees to sit on, but Sandy and I didn't take off our packs. We didn't want to get too comfortable. We were anxious about what lay ahead and eager to keep going. The cool bite of carbonation refreshed us, but we couldn't relax.

We added miles to our day by missing the sign at a road crossing, and had to backtrack. We didn't go far off course, but we'd wasted energy we would need. Killington's enormity played on us and Sandy backed off to let me lead. I think it was her mind more than her body slowing her. I was anxious but felt when Sandy faded that I could carry on, and I hiked well most of the day.

We continued our ascent and soon came upon an expanse of level ground and a shelter without a signpost. It was a three-sided stone structure with a fireplace, dirt floor, and a solid-looking roof. It might be fun to camp there sometime, but we were on a mission. I looked in my guidebook and Sandy examined our map, but found no indication of that shelter, which had clearly been there for many years. It would have been nice to find out when it was built and by whom. It was no longer in use, but it was so inviting, we dropped our packs to walk around, taking note of the distinctive stone work and wishing we had more time to explore, but the difficulty that lay before us wouldn't let us rest for long.

We could feel the summit coming when Sandy got her second wind and I began to fade. I couldn't wait to get to camp. My legs were feeling every inch of the elevation change. I thought we were nearing the Cooper Lodge for an hour and a half before we actually did. When I ran out of water in my CamelBak, my degree of concern was inappropriate to the situation; I had water in my bottles. I was in no danger and although the grade was steep, it was not difficult. Sandy, sensing my frustration, asked, "Do you want to stop and take a break?"

I stomped to a halt, planted both feet, slammed my stick to the ground and yelled, "No! I just want to get there!"

Cooper Lodge was still eluding us when I heard something unfamiliar in the distance. At first I thought it was a bird, then I suspected a coyote, but coyotes rarely call during the day. I couldn't make it out. It was a continuous call—could it be an animal in trouble? It was soon clear that we were hearing a human voice, a singing voice.

Its clarity and beauty were enhanced as it neared and I thought to myself: This woman has an incredible voice.

The lovely voice drew nearer and Sandy said, "Do you hear that?"

"Yes, isn't it amazing?"

"I'm glad you're hearing it, too. I thought I might have died and an angel was calling me home."

I thought of the angel that had topped the first Christmas trees in my life. She was fragile, never touched by children's hands. Her hair and body were made of spun glass and she reflected light like a prism. When the tree lights were off, the filaments in her hair and gown reflected a soft glow from the hall night-light. Our angel glowed even when she slept. If she'd had a voice, it would have sounded like the song now wafting through the trees.

Killington's angel walked into view; her hair was not spun glass but a warm, slightly frizzy brown. She walked with calm confidence. She had not yet seen us. Her blouse was tan, her slacks a dull green, but her voice glowed. We stood on the path watching her approach. When she spotted us, her song stopped and her voice called out, "Isn't it a lovely day?"

She was day-hiking and having a wonderful time descending Killington in the afternoon light. We spoke briefly and she noted our heavy packs. Her daypack was small; it would barely hold a water bottle and an apple. She assured us that we were almost there.

As she walked away singing, we realized our tension had disappeared. I no longer cared about my empty CamelBak, and the summit would come in its own sweet time. We walked into the Cooper Lodge camp feeling lighter than we should have after the longest uphill of our hiking-lives. I wondered if our singing angel had any idea of her impact on tired hikers, like us.

Cooper Lodge was our campsite for the night. Our packs came off, our shoulders relaxed, and we began to examine our home. We set up our tents on platforms, used the privy, refilled our water containers, and stopped inside to look around. It was a classic lodge: a stone building with four walls, windows without glass, and a door. Inside were six bunks and a large table flanked by benches. A typical Long Trail shelter is a three-sided building that may or may not have rustic wooden bunks and a table inside. Some shelters had covered porches, but none had a door. Cooper was our first lodge.

There was a single hiker, Scotty, setting up within; he was hiking in a blue and red plaid kilt. Most hikers wore lightweight quick-drying fabrics, but some had different tastes. I'd seen one woman hiking in a skirt, and a man wearing blue jeans. The skirt made more sense to me than denim. If jeans got wet, they would be difficult to dry. But the kilt ranked as the most unusual hiking garb either of us had seen. I wondered what sort of fabric it was made of, how heavy it was, and how long it took to dry. Kilts are traditionally made of wool, but that one must have been from some other fabric, considering how heavy wet wool would be. I should've asked, but it was getting late and we wanted to get to the Killington summit before sunset.

"Scotty, we're heading for the summit. Do you want to join us?" I was feeling generous, expansive—my legs weren't tired and neither was I.

Scotty sat on the edge of a bunk rubbing his calf. "No, I'm done for today."

We were back at our tents, putting our cameras in our pockets, when Sandy said, "He must be spent. I can't imagine passing on a summit in good weather when you're this close."

We hiked without our packs for the two-tenths of a mile to the summit, gaining thirteen hundred feet in elevation. Clambering along rock scramble without our packs was a treat. I was disappointed by the antennae and guy-wires we found at the peak, but they were isolated to one area; in the other direction we had a spectacular 180-degree view from the first open mountaintop of my life.

In my years of day-hiking in Michigan and Vermont, I'd never been on an exposed summit above the tree line. I looked out from that grand perch and flopped to the ground like a wet ragdoll. The area I lay on was a quarter-acre of solid flat stone, but I felt like I was falling off the mountain; not like I was going to fall, but like I was in the process of falling. I was clinging to the mountaintop, my fingers clutching at rock, my boot heels, shoulders, and butt cheeks trying to find a grip.

Sandy stood casually surveying the world before her. When she looked my way she paused. "Are you OK?"

"Great." I was sitting up, no longer clinging to the rock, but feeling a little nauseous.

"You look pale." Sandy was walking around like the world wasn't sideways.

Once the nausea passed, I was awed by my bird's-eye view of the world. It was so impressive, I knew Don had to see it. Killington would witness our first mountaintop kiss. Being at the pinnacle of that rocky mass was more impressive than I had imagined, and I'd imagined it being pretty damned special.

Leaning back on my elbows, watching the setting sun streak the clouds pink, the mountaintop was my throne. It elevated me to a view I didn't know I needed to see.

Sandy was writing her name with the small stones that littered the summit. "I wish we'd brought up our headlamps. I would love to watch this sunset."

"That would be cool." Why did I say that? I looked at the rocky trail back to our tents, with miles of trees around it. The potential danger of getting lost in the dark was greater than any sunset view might be.

The sun was sinking as we wriggled backward down the steep scramble. We were back at our tents when the shadows of night grew long and faint. I noticed a few scrapes on my hands and Sandy had wounds on her knees. They looked fresh, but we couldn't recall how we might have gotten them.

Sleep came slowly on the wooden deck. I heard the forest sounds around me, but it was the memory of a woodland angel that lulled me.

On our last hiking day, we were up early and heading toward Route 4 by 7 a.m. We wanted to get to the trailhead early and we had no idea what the 6.3 miles to Route 4 would be like. The map images looked more daunting than the guidebook description indicated.

The trail to Route 4 turned out to be relatively easy. My legs were tired, but my spirit was soaring when we landed at the trailhead parking lot by noon. I called Don to pick us up and we stopped at the Corners Store on our way home for sandwiches. Eat first, shower later.

After we'd showered and changed, and Don left for the golf course, Sandy and I set out our equipment to air and I started the laundry. She was sitting on the porch reading and throwing the frisbee for our dogs, Frankie and Ringer. When I came out to ask about going to the Long Trail Brewery for dinner, the dogs were circling her chair and Sandy was asleep. I sat down to enjoy the sunny afternoon, knowing I'd nod off in a few minutes. Dinner and the dogs could wait.

Over dinner at the Brewery, we set up my laptop and looked at the pictures we'd taken on our hike. When we got to the Killington shots, Sandy said what I was thinking, "We should have taken a picture of our angel."

I nodded. "She will have to live in our memories."

CHAPTER SEVENTEEN

COME AWAY WITH ME

Walking takes longer, for example,
than any other known form of locomotion except crawling.
Thus it stretches time and prolongs life.
Life is already too short to waste on speed.
Edward Abbey, "The Journey Home" [11]

Sandy's flight came in at 7:30 p.m., and we were at our house by 9:30 with sandwiches from the Corners Store. We discussed our hike and shared ideas about lightening our packs, arranged our gear across sofas and chairs to be ready to pack in the morning, and didn't get to bed until almost 1 a.m. Even so, I woke at 4:30 and couldn't get back to sleep. Excitement would not let me rest.

I was sad that Don couldn't be there to drive us to the trailhead. My hiking adventure was enhanced by his support and encouragement. While talking to a friend about distance hiking, she said, "Your husband lets you do this?"

It didn't dawn on either of us to seek or give permission. Don didn't stand in my way, he promoted and cheered me on. I'd even heard that he sometimes bragged about me.

Although supportive, Don had no interest in carrying everything he needed "like a turtle," and walking for days without access to bed or shower. He was glad that I enjoyed it and equally pleased not to be doing it himself. He benefited from my finding new areas for day hikes, which he did enjoy, like White Rocks and the Killington summit.

We've walked through waist-high ferns and grassy meadows, taken refuge from rain in hemlock stands, watched for wildlife and their tracks and nests, listened to rain on our metal roof, and kissed on a mountaintop.

We opened our wedding dance with our song: Stevie Wonder's "I Just Called to Say I Love You," but the first time we heard Nora Jones's "Come Away with Me," it became our Vermont song. She describes rain on a tin roof, walking in knee-high grass, and kissing on a mountaintop like she knew us. I can't hear that song without seeing a mental collage of our days exploring Vermont.

Nora was ringing in my ears now, but it was too early to get up. I should have been sleeping, but my body would not go there. My mind slipped from Nora to youthful hiking.

As a kid, I preferred to walk alone, but my sister Fay, four years my junior, often joined me as she got older. We didn't call them hikes, we didn't carry backpacks, and we rarely had what anyone would call a plan, but we could walk all day. Sometimes other children joined us, but often, especially for our longer walks, it was Fay and me and our imaginations. When we got into fields and wooded areas, away from prying eyes, we could ride our imaginary horses. I always rode Fury, who was jet-black with a white diamond on his forehead, his coat glistening as if he'd just been groomed— although I never imagined the grooming part. Fay rode Trigger, a golden palomino with a white blaze, white legs, and flaxen mane and tail. When we were younger, we rode these horses down sidewalks and in ours and our neighbor's yards. We were getting too old for that, though there were times when we just couldn't resist an imaginary ride on fabulous horses that we would never own.

Eventually, we did own real horses, but our imaginary steeds are a cherished memory. Perhaps we'll ride them again in our aging minds, when we're too old to walk.

As adults, discussing the horrors of dementia, Fay and I decided that if one of us became senile, the other would defend her by telling people, "Oh, she's not nuts, she's just drunk again."

Renee, two years younger than Fay, never joined us on our adventures walking or riding invisible horses. Fay and I returned once from an all-day trek and dropped onto the picnic table benches to recount our day's activities, when Fay pointed out that Renee had been washing doll clothes again. On a string clothesline hung tiny dresses, pants, blouses, and tinier undergarments held with equally tiny clothespins, all in a line next to the full-sized human clothing that Mom had hung out to dry. Fay mused, "On a beautiful day like this Renee spent her time washing doll clothes that never get dirty. What a waste."

These thoughts rattled in my head until it was clear I needed to get up and get moving. Sandy and I had a leisurely breakfast with our maps out on the table between us. All talk was of the trail and our pack choices. Audrey picked us up at 9:30 to put us on the trail by 10 a.m.

The Maine Junction, just north of Route 4, is the point at which the Appalachian Trail branches east toward Maine and the LT continues north to Canada. Standing in front of the sign, we could see the first AT sign several yards to the east, and to the north, our first LT sign, containing information about Canada, 165.9 miles ahead. Could we begin to think of getting to Canada?

It had been sunny at 6:30 a.m., clouding up by the time we hit the trail at 10, and raining lightly as we took our first break at the Tucker Johnson Shelter, 1.5 miles into our day. The rain stopped as we left the shelter, but began again as we neared the Rolston Rest Shelter. That was as far as we would go that day, just over five miles. Getting to the next shelter would have meant a thirteen-mile first day.

The LT was quieter north of the Maine Junction. The shelter logbook noted many solo stays and no one had been there the night before. We stayed in the shelter that night, not my favorite choice, but it looked like we might have the space to ourselves.

We'd hiked that morning in humid heat, but the late-day rain brought a cool breeze and I was comfortable in my fleece jacket as we performed our camp rituals. My shirt was wet with sweat, so the dry fleece felt especially good. My wet shirt was unlikely to dry without a fire, so I hung it on a nail in the shelter. Later I would stuff it into my sleeping bag. If it wasn't dry by morning, it would at least be warm.

Another hiker showed up as night drew near and told us that he built a fire every night because he didn't carry a stove and would heat his food over the fire. That explained his trail name, Firefly. His fire allowed us to dry out our boots and sweaty shirts before we turned in for the night.

In conversation around the fire, we learned that Firefly was thru-hiking the LT and had been on the trail for two weeks. He'd taken the bus into Rutland the day before to restock his food supply. He did not have boxes of food mailed from home, but stopped at towns along the way to shop for his trail needs. When I asked, "What happens if the stores don't have what you want?"

"Then I decide to want something else."

"An interesting philosophy." I hadn't heard that before, but it made good sense. Over dinner, Sandy and I planned the next day's hike to the David Logan Shelter, just eight miles away. The map showed PUDs (pointless ups and downs), but no big elevation changes. We talked about our trail-legs being days away and that the next eight miles could turn out to be more difficult than the map and guidebook indicated. We had learned to read between the lines.

On day two, our morning ritual felt as though we'd been walking for weeks. Eating breakfast at the table in the shelter, I shared with Sandy a tale of my Nichols Lake training hike, two weeks before, where I'd suffered the first blisters of my hiking career.

The trail had been a flat, easy walk in the woods and I was stunned to find blisters on my feet at the end of the first day. The bottom of each big toe had a blister covering the entire toe, and on the ball of each foot I had blisters bigger than silver dollars. I shared my shock with the others around the campfire and Ewa said that walking an easy trail was like walking on a road. Taking the same step over and over again was different from moving up and down hills. Repetitious steps could be worse than walking in the woods, because your foot moved within the boot on uneven terrain, but it didn't on the flats. Her suggestion for traveling on level ground was to remove your boots at every break and as you walk, move your foot around inside your boot.

The LT was never flat enough to worry about that issue, but the walk to David Logan seemed longer than eight miles. There were a lot of PUDs, more elevation change than we expected, and it rained lightly off and on. I was still in my poncho, Sandy in her rain jacket, but we were both in shorts and gators. I could zip on my pant legs at the end of the day while Sandy put on lightweight sweat pants in camp.

I had my first fall of the trip that day, slipping in heavy slop and landing hard on my right hip. Later, as I was working my way across a slippery boulder, I fell again, landing hard on the stone, again on my right side. After two falls, I slowed down. I was worried about my right leg with its six fractures, seven inches of metal rod, and eleven screws.

The first fall had been a tough one, but the second had been literally tooth-jarring. I heard my hip hit the rock as my teeth slammed together. I had no loose teeth and saw no evidence of bruising, but my right leg was oddly shaped already, so I couldn't be certain whether it was swollen or not.

As we hiked, I was reminded of a conversation at our Christmas party. There'd been a few hiking friends present that evening, along with family and friends. My cousin Dick and his wife Jennifer attended, and Jennifer was surprised by how far we could travel in a day. She said she couldn't imagine walking that far, especially in the woods, and was curious about what we carried and where we camped. She seemed to be interested, but couldn't understand why we would do that to ourselves.

That might be why it was Jennifer's presence that I imagined during the most strenuous moments that day. The first time I pictured her, she was standing next to a steep rock while I was descending backward, groping for a foothold. I imagined her laughing as I fumbled blindly for a place to rest my boot. Most of the time, I simply imagined her smiling as I struggled at this spot or stumbled at that one. It was reassuring to think of someone I knew watching as I trundled up and down, and then down and up, only to do it again and again. It was another day to be glad that I wasn't hiking with a mind reader.

We saw more evidence of wildlife after the AT branched east away from us, and that day we saw the biggest moose track I'd ever seen. I photographed the track with my boot beside it to show how big it was. The mud came in handy for spotting wildlife tracks. We saw evidence of bear and bobcat sharing our trail.

The David Logan Shelter's deck was too high for me to step up onto, so I sat on the edge and turned to pull my legs inside or climbed on logs or rocks, holding onto the side wall to pull myself onto the deck. The object is to keep the sleeping deck above any water that may flow beneath, but sometimes it made getting in and out of a shelter tricky for those with short legs.

In my journal, I recorded the PUDs, the falls, and the slop, but my final entry for the day read: *"The day was good, other than that. We had a few good views over Chittenden reservoir and it felt great to be hiking again."*

Proof that *everything is relative*.

I worried about my leg as I retired to my tent. Before I hunkered down into my sleeping bag, I massaged the injured areas and looked the leg over for swelling or heat before dropping off to sleep.

When I woke in the morning, the sky was bright and the birds were in full voice. I was shocked at having slept so late. When I pulled my legs out of my sleeping bag, I was appalled. My right leg was swollen and purple, almost black, with odd yellow streaks in the muscle tissue. I was surprised that it wasn't painful, because the skin was pulled tight and oozed serum in several places. I panicked that the lack of pain might mean paralysis. Settle down Ryker, you just moved it.

I was about to call out to Sandy when I jerked myself awake in full darkness and looked at my watch, it was almost midnight. The dream was so real that I turned on my headlamp to check on my leg. Relieved to see a relatively normal form, I fell back asleep.

We broke camp during a brief break in the rain. I examined my leg as soon as I woke, but all was well and it didn't hurt much.

It began to rain again as we started to walk. The wind picked up but there was none of the thunder or lightening that often came with such a downpour. When we reached a sign that put us at the halfway mark for our day, I was disappointed to find that we were an hour behind our hoped-for pace. We encountered steep, slippery steps with viscous mud everywhere and after two falls the day before, I was being extra careful. My leg had been throbbing as we ate breakfast and cleared camp, but I decided to take no pain killers and see if I could walk the pain away. The ache eased as I began to walk and after the first hour, I forgot all about my dream. But the slightest slip reminded me that I didn't want to chance another fall.

At 1 p.m., we reached a marker indicating that we were 2.1 miles from the Sunrise Shelter. The trail had become easier and we were making better time. I was feeling good, pushing it a bit, and we were at the shelter by 1:30. Was the sign wrong or had we hiked at four miles an hour? I'd never done four miles an hour with a full pack—ever. I looked at the map to be sure of our distance and still couldn't believe it. Don't get giddy Ryker; you're usually slower than the average snail.

It felt so good, we thought about changing our plan and pressing on to the next shelter, six miles ahead, but decided instead to take advantage of a clearing sky to set out our gear to dry.

A few hours later, we stowed our dry gear just before the rain began again. It rained so hard, a tiny creek formed and flowed beneath the shelter. It was so deep, Sandy was able to set the coil of her water filter into the shallow stream beneath the deck. We sat at the edge of the shelter floor under the roof overhang, pumping water without going out in the rain. Sandy smiled as she pumped. "Indoor plumbing."

Based on its name, I expected Sunrise Shelter to have a view to the east and we'd hoped we might see New Hampshire's White Mountains, but Sunrise was nestled into the forest.

There was no fire to gaze into that night, but the sound of rain on the roof and water babbling beneath our sleeping deck reminded me of the rainy hikes Don and I had shared. My last thought of the night was of Don and me laughing in the rain, watching our dogs playing in a puddle.

CHAPTER EIGHTEEN

MOUNT CUPCAKE

Come forth into the light of things,
Let Nature be your teacher.
William Wordsworth, "The Tables Turned"

It was an interesting night. Minnie Mouse and Ultralight, who had camped at David Logan and stayed there during the day to dry out their gear, showed up at Sunrise at about 6 p.m., and three young men hiked in just before dark.

Nightcap talked about why he slept in his knit cap. "I had a raccoon bite me on the head at a shelter. That's why I wear this hat every night."

His friend Twitch swished his long blond hair back and forth. "No hat hair for me. I'll take my chances."

Lug Nut, the third member of their group, rolled his eyes. "Raccoons and hat hair, I hear this story every damned night."

We covered other topics, but it was remnants of that story that woke the entire shelter in the middle of the night.

Snoring noise is normal, but Ultralight talked in his sleep. It was all gibberish until he called out, "There's something in here. There's something on my face." Sitting up, arms flailing, he said, "Get out of here. Get out. Get the hell off me!"

He'd been asleep during his outburst—you could tell by his dazed expression when his eyes came into focus with everyone looking at him. We were all awake and shining headlamps around, looking to see what might be in there with us.

I said, "I was awake, and I didn't see or hear an animal."

We kept looking around while Ultralight apologized for making so much noise over a stupid dream. When nothing was found, we tried to get back to sleep. Ultralight was snoring within minutes.

Nightcap said, "Is that son of a bitch asleep?"

Twitch said, "If he is, somebody needs to kick him."

Lug Nut added, "Kick him hard."

The next morning, no one mentioned the midnight outburst. Everyone was busy planning their day.

As Nightcap stowed his hat, he said, "Well, I didn't need you last night."

Twitch swished his hair and opened his mouth, but Lug Nut cut him off. "Don't even say it. One more word out of you two," he said, jabbing a finger at one and then the other, "and I'll drop that fucking hat in the river and tie your hair in knots while you sleep."

Nightcap and Twitch hit the trail before Lug Nut was ready. I watched Lug Nut disappear into the forest, trying not to look like he was hurrying to catch up. "I think the three musketeers may be breaking up."

Ultralight shook his head. "Nah, they'll be fine."

We left the Sunrise Shelter at a leisurely 8:45 a.m. Our first mountain ascent of the day was Mount Horrid and we agreed that it was appropriately named. The stone was slick from an all-night rain. Don and I had friends who'd day-hiked the area on a bright sunny day and declared that Mount Horrid would be more appropriately called Mount Cupcake—not so in my experience. Both Sandy and I ended up crawling part of the ascent, because the stone was steep and slippery. Seeing Sandy struggle made me feel less inept.

We moved easily along Mount Gillespie, where we flushed two partridge families, both moms going into their wounded ploy to draw us away from her brood. Shortly after that, Sandy came eye to eye with a bull moose who stared back at her from twenty feet away. She took cover behind a tree and fumbled for her camera while the moose thundered off through the woods. She called out, "Celia there's a bull moose heading your way."

I stood near a tree trunk and enjoyed seeing him in flight, five yards from me. This had been our closest wildlife encounter of any size; snakes, newts and birds did not count.

On Gillespie Peak, we found a swamp near the summit that looked like a kettle carved into the stone surface. Kettle is the term for a depression, formed during the retreating ice age, that has filled with rain water, rather than being fed from an underground source, to create a lake, pond, or swamp. This one was clearly home to many moose. I saw more moose poop there than I'd seen in my life. It was everywhere. We also found what appeared to be a moose rib. I wondered where the rest of the carcass was. We looked around for more bones, but all we found was more poop.

The first time I'd seen moose droppings was on my first visit to Vermont. I noticed it was made up of pellets similar to deer droppings, but larger. They were about the size and shape of the foil-wrapped chocolate eggs I'd found in my Easter basket as a child. I thought of my brothers and how they could have put this natural wonder to use. I'm certain, given the opportunity, they would've saved pastel foil wrappers and used them to disguise the lovely little eggs at my feet to put into some poor target's Easter basket.

We walked into the Sucker Brook Shelter at 2:30 and saw a note among the logbook entries indicating that we could use the ski patrol shed on Worth Mountain as a shelter. We looked at the map and decided to cowboy on Worth Mountain. The weather was great, but it might not stay that way.

Moving up Worth Mountain was easier than the elevation indicated. The only shed we could find was full of junk, so we set up our tents on one of the ski area's mowed access paths. We cooked and ate dinner sitting on the chairlift platform, looking east to the White Mountains. It was perfection. We'd summited three mountains that day: Mount Horrid (and it was no cupcake), Gillespie Peak, and Worth Mountain.

We pored over our maps and planned for the next day—eight miles to Skyline Lodge. We hoped to get to Cooley Glen the day after that and hike out to our ride home at Lincoln Gap early on Friday.

The white-throated sparrow on a tree branch just above us serenaded us throughout dinner. Watching his head tilted back with beak slightly open, silhouetted against a late-day sun, added a fabulous visual to his lovely song.

Chapter Nineteen

GRILLED CHEESE

Forget not that the earth delights to feel your bare feet and
the winds long to play with your hair.
Khalil Gibran, "The Prophet" [12]

We set off for Skyline Lodge at 7 a.m., but struggled to find the trail. The blazes were few and the mowed ski-area paths confused us. Our actual departure from Worth was therefore after 8.

The climb out of Middlebury Gap was difficult, with much of the trail described as challenging, and no views to reward our efforts, but getting to Skyline was a treat. It was a lodge with four walls, a covered porch, glass windows, and a door. Inside were two levels of bunks, enough for fourteen people, and a table with benches. We passed five college-aged trail-workers on our way in, who were staying at the Skyline Lodge while working on new punch-ins along the wet trail sections.

We stopped for a few moments to talk with them, and they explained that they were not allowed to use chain saws or other noisy tools in wilderness areas. They were hand-sawing and hewing logs to create the steps we used to move across marshy ground. Their conversation when they returned to camp was a delight. They talked about where they went to school, what their majors were, what they hoped to do with their futures, what area of trail they would work on the next day and what needed to be done there, and (most importantly) who'd be cooking and what they'd be making. Their youthful banter was a joy, partially making up for the fact that they did not offer to share even a tiny piece of their great-smelling grilled cheese sandwiches with tomato soup. They fired up a hibachi grill on the porch, and when I saw the number of sandwiches being made, the huge bowl of salad, and the vat of soup, I thought there might be a chance for a half-sandwich or some other nibble of non-freeze-dried food, but that was not to be. They ate two or three sandwiches each and did not leave enough scraps to satisfy a chipmunk on a diet.

The view from the lodge down to Skyline Pond was spectacular. The pond was covered with yellow water lilies, the opposite shore edged with evergreen trees, and the White Mountains stood ghost-like in the distance. The beauty kept us from giving a thought to going on to the Emily Proctor Shelter. We took pictures from the porch and the edge of the pond. The images are lovely, but I still smell melting cheese when I see them.

As usual, over dinner we planned the next day's walk, which would get us to Cooley Glen in eight miles, over some areas described as challenging and past several areas with great views, if the weather held.

Three hikers came in after we'd all been in our bunks for over an hour. These late arrivals tried to be quiet while heating up food before they turned in. They used the green and red lights on their headlamps, so it wouldn't be too bright. They barely spoke and when they did it was in whispers, but everyone in the building was awake. I take that back: teenagers full of food may not have noticed the disruption, but Sandy and I were awake for quite a while. Another great reason to stay in my tent.

We left Skyline in a light rain that continued off and on for much of the day; so much for the great views. At one point, we had to remove our packs to crawl on hands and knees through ankle-deep mud under a fallen tree. I recorded an image of Sandy skirting a deep basin of water on the trail, where the water swirled like nature's broken toilet bowl.

When we arrived at Cooley Glen, the temperature was forty-eight degrees and the winds were high. I'd been wet with perspiration, which is usually the case, but didn't think to change into my fleece jacket. I didn't realize how cold it was until I was chilled—then I was suddenly and seriously cold. I put on my fleece and crawled into my sleeping bag on the shelter floor, thinking I would get warm in a few minutes. An hour later, I lay there shaking and began to think about what I knew about hypothermia. I'd read about a family found floating in their life jackets around their overturned canoe. They were within easy swimming distance of the shore, but they'd allowed themselves to drift about in the icy water until they succumbed to the cold, and they were all found dead. I'd been told that one of the first areas of the body affected by cold is the hypothalamus, which is largely responsible for cognition, helping us make daily decisions. My understanding is that a person suffering hypothermia can walk in circles around their own house and not recognize it.

In a book of Vermont ghost stories, I read about two women, described as experienced hikers, who were on an October outing when one of them fell into a stream. She decided to go back to their campsite and change while her friend continued. My first thought when I read those words was: Don't separate, she's too cold to be left alone for a minute. She may not be able to find the tent even if she sees it.

The story tells how the woman was never seen again, and suggests that she must have suffered some ghostly attack and/or she is haunting the forest in which she was lost. But to me, it wasn't a ghost story but was a tale of two people lacking common sense. Falling into a stream in October is cause for concern and hypothermia is a real possibility. Experienced hikers should have known that they both needed to walk back to camp and the dry hiker should have watched over the wet one until she was warm, dry, and thinking clearly.

In *Not Without Peril*[13], a book about a number of people who'd lost their lives on New Hampshire's Mount Washington, I read about a young man separated from his surveying team in a sudden fog. He was seen by several people over the next three days, and asked them each if they knew how he could find his family's farm, giving his family name as a hint to the farm he was looking for.

He was working on Mount Washington for the summer as a visiting student. The family farm he was asking about was in Wisconsin, and the people he spoke to were unaware that a member of a survey team had gone missing. The conclusion was that he'd been suffering from hypothermia as he wandered around for days looking for his home. Then, he disappeared.

These stories circled in my head as I lay in my sleeping bag shaking. I instructed Sandy not to leave me alone until I was warm and toasty.

I was beginning to feel less cold when we decided to have dinner. Warm cider helped a lot, and after dinner I felt much better. I should have warmed some cider earlier, but I thought I would get warm without much effort; then again, maybe I wasn't thinking clearly.

We decided to sleep in the shelter instead of our tents. I snuggled into my sleeping bag with dry pants, my fleece jacket, and my head pulled down into my sleeping bag.

We shared the shelter with a thru-hiker who was putting down sixteen-mile days. This woman was hiking the LT end-to-end for the second time. As she treated the angry blisters on her feet, she shared with us some insights into how she did the hike. She carried no tent, which saved time and weight in her pack, and her partner met her at road crossings to resupply her food.

Overnight, the lows dropped into the high thirties. I was OK in my twenty-five-degree sleeping bag, but I'd forgotten my longies (long johns, for those not from the Midwest) and had deliberately left out my knit cap because I never used it, but I would have used both that night. Why did I take them out of my pack when they weigh almost nothing? They would be returned to my spare-clothing bag and stay there—forever.

I was heavy on planning, but in previous post-hike reviews, the list I'd made while on the trail was forgotten in my journal until I was back on the trail: too late. The list I made that night, I tore out of my journal and stashed in my food bag where I'd find it while preparing for my next hike. I planned to bring more tissue, longies, a knit cap, and a long-sleeved T-shirt on our next stretch. I put the knit cap on my list twice.

On our last day, we planned to hike 4.7 miles to Lincoln Gap Road and our car. I'd hiked the area on day hikes, so I knew the views and what the decent into Lincoln Gap would be like. It was a treat to know what to expect.

The sun was shining and the temperature was in the sixties when we left Cooley Glen. We took a break at Sunset Ledge, 1.2 miles above Lincoln Gap. I sat in the sunshine remembering the day I'd sat in that same spot on my first-ever hike of Lincoln Gap, when I'd first entertained thoughts of hiking this trail that I knew nothing about. This was where my Long Trail vision had been born.

CHAPTER TWENTY

HUMBLE PIE

"This is the first day of eight in a hike from Lincoln Gap to Stowe and Route 108."

That was the first journal entry of a new section-hike, and it sounded so confident. Our plan was to hike three major peaks in eight days: Mount Abraham, Camel's Hump, and Mount Mansfield.

I'd been concerned about a head cold that sailed through Don's office and clinic staff, but had dodged it prior to leaving Michigan and was feeling good as the hike date approached. That is, until the night before Sandy was due to arrive. I thought my mind might be working overtime, so eager not to be sick that it was making me think I was getting sick. I spoke clearly to my brain that night: Don't think about it, it's not happening, go to sleep.

I was also concerned about the degree of difficulty we would face, so I'd trained harder. I arrived in Vermont four days early to lay down training hikes with my pack, in real mountains. It had been difficult, but as of that morning I was feeling good. By evening, though, I had a nagging cough.

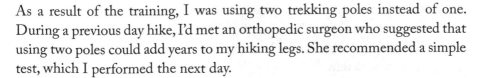

As a result of the training, I was using two trekking poles instead of one. During a previous day hike, I'd met an orthopedic surgeon who suggested that using two poles could add years to my hiking legs. She recommended a simple test, which I performed the next day.

I chose a short loop for my test hike, with steep rocky areas that reflected the sort of trails I would encounter on the LT. I hiked it with my single trekking pole and made the trip in two and half hours with ease. Two days later, I hiked the same loop with two trekking poles. I felt like I was hiking at about the same speed and found that using two poles made the steep areas, both up and down, easier. I didn't find the double poles awkward, and when they were not necessary, I could carry both loosely in one hand. The miles rolled with ease. I didn't look at my watch until I got back to the car, when I discovered that I'd hiked the same track, with less effort, in one hour and fifty minutes, cutting my time by forty minutes; double trekking poles were here to stay.

The plan for our first day was to hike north out of Lincoln Gap, heading for Battell Shelter, just two miles away. Wib and Audrey were dropping us off again and we'd decided to start late. To get to the shelter beyond Battell would have meant a nine-mile first day.

We began our hike under a clear sky and I felt good even though we'd only traveled two miles—or maybe I felt good *because* I'd only gone two miles. I felt a little congested as we set camp, but that often happens in the cool damp of a hike. The bug that I was worried about had sent employees who usually worked through illness home to bed for a day or two. I did not have time for that. Trying not to think about my symptoms was making me think about my symptoms. I tried to distract myself with my journal entry, but I ended up writing about the very thoughts I was attempting to ignore.

We were on the trail out of Battell at 7 a.m., but didn't get through the nine miles to Theron Dean Shelter until almost 4 p.m.—twice as long as it said in the guidebook, even with two trekking poles. Sandy and I had taken off our packs for some of the severe areas. Some of the rock steps were armpit-high with no footholds, and we had to set our packs up or down the shelf and then clamber to them and put them on again, only to repeat the process within the next half mile. The trekking poles made no difference on that terrain. However, I discovered another plus to hiking with two poles: having both my hands elevated, rather than one dangling, meant that my hands did not swell. The swelling hadn't been a huge problem with one pole, but with two it disappeared completely.

We didn't receive the reward of a view on Mount Abraham or Mount Ellen. It didn't rain, but felt like it could at any moment. As we neared our shelter destination, the weather cleared and the sunshine boosted my mood.

I'd known that this part of the hike would be difficult, but it was harder than expected, and coughing and blowing my nose did not help. I felt light-headed a few times, which made me doubtful about the wisdom of proceeding. I couldn't deny it; I had a cold. It had been a difficult day and there were more to come. If the trail got harder, as I thought it would, I might reach a point where I'd have to stop. I found myself torn by the fact that we had both been planning and working toward this hike for months. Sandy had taken time away from work, and I would feel awful stopping because of a few sniffles.

Some of the more severe ups and downs of the trail were so harsh that even Sandy could barely pull it off. And if she struggled to make the reach with her long legs, my only choice was to crawl along the rock or scoot on my butt, reaching for rocky footholds. I became more concerned each time we met another stiff up or down. And we met our first ladders on this trail. I'd been anxious about the prospect of climbing ladders while wearing my backpack.

"This is easier than I thought it would be," I said, stepping away from a heavy wooden ladder that provided side-bars that allowed me to hold on until I was standing. "I was afraid I was going to have to crawl on and off the ladders."

"I wonder how old it is." Sandy was walking away. "Who maintains this stuff?"

"It looks solid to me." I was surprised by her concern.

"I trust rock and tree roots more—especially rock."

I looked down at the rock around the ladder and wondered how we would have managed without it. Sandy was looking back at me. "It's just wood and nails that rot and rust."

"Thanks for putting that in my head."

At the next ladder, my mind wandered to my cousin BJ. I didn't know why until I was halfway down the ladder and my memory flashed to an abandoned barn. BJ and I had climbed down a ladder from the hay loft, where we'd thought we might find some lost treasure but all we encountered were cobwebs and moldy hay.

I don't remember why BJ and I were alone that day, we usually traveled as a pack with my sister Fay and BJ's siblings, Kathy, Freddie, and Howard. The

117

barn BJ and I were in was near the railroad tracks in a distant field behind their house.

I walked through my day worried about a cold knocking me out of my hike, but I kept thinking about BJ when I got to a tough spot or saw a great view, but especially when I went up or down a ladder. As adults, we cousins seldom see one another. We live about an hour and a half apart, and each time we get together for a Christmas party, wedding, or funeral, I'd wish we got together more often. But we don't. It was helpful, having those memories from my youth interrupting my worry about cold symptoms.

I lay in my tent that night trying not to think about my cold or how difficult the trail might be in the coming days. We had eight miles to cover the next day—eight hours of hiking.

On one uphill that morning, I'd felt like The Little Engine That Could, and visualized a tiny green locomotive. My walking mantra became: I think I can, I think I can. Later in the day, I switched to: I know I can, I know I can.

As I drifted toward sleep, the mantra morphed: I hope I can . . . cough, blow nose, and go to sleep.

As morning broke the next day, my cold had not diminished and I was a little light-headed, coughing, and headachy in addition to my constant runny nose. Without a thermometer I couldn't be sure, but I thought I might be running a fever. I talked to Sandy about my symptoms and we decided to hike to Route 17 and decide what the best course of action would be from there.

I was moving along the trail with relative ease when I stretched for a long step to what looked like solid ground. My left foot slid forward and down, my right knee bent back severely, and I slid down a muddy slope with my left leg extended and my right leg twisted oddly beside me, knocking my head against a tree stump as I came to a halt. I was worried about my right leg: that foot was bent back, up next to my hip. My mind flashed to previous fractures of the same limb and I wondered why my head didn't hurt from striking the tree. Was that a good sign or bad? Sandy had heard the start of my fall and watched me slide to a halt.

"My right foot's in the wrong place." I pushed my foot down and addressed my leg. "Don't turn on me now . . . And I banged my head on this tree." I reached out and found it rotted to the consistency of a wet sponge. I pulled out a handful of pulpy wood. "That's why it didn't hurt."

I was moving my leg around and it seemed OK. Sandy walked toward me. "I'm more worried about your left arm."

"Left arm? My arm isn't hurt." I looked at my left arm, but it wasn't there. It was twisted oddly behind me—but it didn't hurt. I untwisted my arm and lay on the ground in a heap.

"We're going off at Route 17," Sandy announced.

"You think?"

I was spooked by the fall, but my leg and arm unwound to their rightful places with no visible injury. Should I keep going or should I stop?

"Sandy, I'm not hurt. I can keep going." We'd been walking for a while and I was feeling better than I thought I would.

"If you weren't coughing while you said that it would be more believable. I think we should come off today and make our decision based on how you feel tomorrow."

I was relieved and saddened by the decision: sad for myself and Sandy but relieved that the choice had been made.

Walking toward the Appalachian Gap (App Gap in hiker-speak), we were quiet for miles. "If I feel good tomorrow we could hike Camel's Hump. Frankie and I snowshoed that trail and it's fabulous. With a daypack my cold would weigh less."

"I don't know, you might be really sore tomorrow."

"If I'm not sore—if my cold isn't worse—if the weather is good."

"That's a lot of ifs." Sandy didn't want to be disappointed again.

"If the ifs converge, we day hike Camel's Hump tomorrow." I tried not to cough and needed to blow my nose again. Sandy was laughing and shaking her head.

When we arrived at the App Gap, we had no phone reception and needed to call for a ride home. We talked to a couple of day-hikers who were heading north, and they took Audrey's phone number and climbed a rock that allowed them to get a call out where neither of our phones could find a connection. That stranger made the call for me, telling Audrey that we were coming off the trail at Route 17 and needed a ride home. Before I could ask them to tell her that there was no emergency and no one was hurt, the connection failed.

We knew our ride was coming, but I was concerned that Audrey might think something was wrong. We started walking down the road that Wib and Audrey would arrive on and I kept checking the bars on my phone. My leg and arm were surprisingly pain-free, but my cough was getting worse and the runny nose was constant—and I was running out of tissues. We finally found a faint cell signal and got a call out, reassuring Audrey that there was no hurry, we were both OK.

Audrey said she had been a little worried, but Wib had assured her that if there was an injury: "They wouldn't be waiting for us to come and help. They would've called an ambulance." I could hear in her tone that she was glad to know we were fine. They didn't seem to mind coming to pick us up, and I told her that we'd hiked partway down from the trail crossing and would be waiting in a parking area at a restaurant on the south side of the road.

We sat on our packs at the edge of the driveway to be sure we were visible. Resting, we talked about what we'd be doing for the next few days. Planning made me feel a little better, but Sandy had to be disappointed. How could I make it up to her? I hoped to feel well enough to hike Camel's Hump the next day. According to Sandy's phone, the weather forecast was for perfect hiking conditions. I resolved to hike whether I felt better or not.

Our conversation waned as we waited for our ride. My mind drifted to a book I'd read years before. In *Running to the Mountain*, Jon Katz found himself sitting on a guardrail near his home; the road was blocked by police, because of a fire. He wasn't in danger and he didn't think his house was in peril, but he had to wait. As he sat there with his dogs, he had time to think about where he'd been, the changes that had been thrust upon him, and the changes he was choosing for himself. He felt humbled by what he'd lost and by how unprepared he felt for the new life he'd chosen.

Waiting there with Sandy, I was feeling humble. I'd been so organized—planning, training, acquiring the right gear, and yet here I sat questioning whether I was waiting for a ride home because of a virus or fear—both were present. As we moved our packs to follow the shade, I wondered which of the two was the strongest, and which had driven my decision.

It is not the mountain we conquer, but ourselves.

Sir Edmund Hillary, "View from the Summit" [14]

CHAPTER TWENTY-ONE

AIR SHOW

I have walked myself into my best thoughts.
Søren Kierkegaard, from a letter to his niece, Henriette Lund, in 1847 [15]

I was putting bread in the toaster when Sandy walked into the room. "How's your shoulder?"

"Not bad."

"I saw you rubbing it a minute ago."

"OK, it hurts more than I thought it would, but I'm ready to hike."

"I heard you coughing last night." Sandy wasn't giving up.

"If we don't do something today, I'll go nuts. I can cough anywhere and my temp is back to normal." Trying to be more convincing, I added, "Remember our ifs: One, my cold is not worse; Two, the weather is great; Three, I'm not very sore. If I can't make it to the summit, you can go on without me. I'll walk back to the car and you'll get to see Camel's Hump."

"OK, we're heading for Camel's Hump." Sandy's hands were up.

Our plan was to hike the Forest City Trail to the Long Trail, then hike to the summit and return to the parking area on the Burrows Trail. It was an eight-mile loop that I'd hiked on snowshoes in January.

My head wasn't as congested, my cough was almost gone, the sniffles were less, and I was beginning to wonder if my cold symptoms had been a figment of my imagination. The reality may be that I am just too old and fearful. That was what Wib said as we drove home from Lincoln Gap: "Celia, maybe you're just getting too damned old for this shit."

121

There was a part of me that thought he might be right.

My right leg tightened and my left shoulder throbbed as we began to walk, but I was sure they'd loosen up with movement. Within a few strides, my leg did begin to loosen. The shoulder pain came and went in the first few hours, and then it got tired of following me around and disappeared. The sunshine and my relatively weightless pack made the day feel light, which may explain my not feeling the cold symptoms as much.

The trail was difficult, with some steep ups and downs, but the views were worth the effort and I got sun for the first time on the Long Trail. We rarely hiked in areas open enough to be called sunny, even on cloudless days, and on most of the open summits we'd hiked in rain or dense cloud cover—there'd been little need for the tiny bottle of sunscreen I carried.

Camel's Hump's summit was even more impressive than Killington's. There were no towers to block a 360-degree view from the pinnacle. I felt a little shaky when I stood alone at the summit marker, but not like I had on Killington. We walked carefully around the rocky crest to avoid treading on the delicate plant community that was marked off with string to remind us where we should not step. These fragile plants could take extremes in weather, but were easily destroyed by foot traffic. There was a Green Mountain Club steward instructing those who did not read the signs, telling them that this extraordinary plant community is found only on the higher summits of New England and nowhere else in the world.

It was the Fourth of July weekend, so there were lots of day-hikers at the summit. They'd hiked up; there was no road that came close. Perhaps the effort required to get there made those who arrived more respectful than day-hikers I'd seen in more accessible parks, who left trash and ignored areas marked off-limits. Many were eating snacks or lunches before they hiked back to their cars, but there was not a bit of food or debris anywhere.

We sat under a cloudless sky enjoying the view in one direction, then turning and observing another. Everyone was talking quietly, eating, and looking off into the distance, when we inhaled a collective gasp. A glider aircraft had popped up out of nowhere, right next to our mountaintop. One young boy reflected what I was thinking: "Dad, did you see that? It was so close I could almost touch it. I could see that guy's face!"

Without a sound, the pilot had snuck up on us. Our chatter about the strange event had just settled when the glider jumped up next to us again and everyone applauded. I wondered if he could hear the applause. We sat and talked, looking out over the beauty, wondering if the air show would be repeated, but our pilot did not return for a third performance.

I get a sense of physical relief on a mountain peak, perhaps it's a concept of distance, oddly enhanced. I pondered how many people were walking under the trees on the hillsides below us. What animals were walking, flying, perching, or hiding there? Looking down upon roadways and homes, I thought about the people in those homes. Were they standing in their living rooms unaware that I was looking down at their houses? Was someone looking out the window at this mountaintop, wondering who might be up here?

From that prominent point, I witnessed complexity: from man to animal, snails, earth worms, and microorganisms. When I was above the rocks that had scraped my knees on the way, up I could see the minutia of life; the fragile web was obvious. When one delicate string broke, all of the strings were threatened.

I was looking at the big picture while thinking about its tiniest aspects, and it made more sense from here. If more people could see the world from that angle, perhaps they would be more conscientious with our planet. From my perch on high, the need to protect our planet seemed apparent. How fragile and connected we all are. How small, in the grand scheme of things. Imposing our will over nature could tip the scales of ecology beyond repair. In fact, it probably already had. The view made me feel solemn, reverent.

I coughed a little more on my way down the Burrows Trail than I had coming up and my right leg was tight, but my nose wasn't running as much and my shoulder wasn't sore at all. Perhaps I should have kept going after the App Gap. But then again, we would have been hiking in the green tunnel on that beautiful day and would have missed the air show.

CHAPTER TWENTY-TWO

THE RUSSIAN

The body advances,
while the mind flutters around it like a bird.
Jules Renard

The next day's plan was to hike the section between the App Gap and the Hedgehog Brook trailhead. I dropped Sandy off at the App Gap and drove to Hedgehog Brook to leave the car for Sandy to pick up with the spare keys. Sandy would hike north and end at Hedgehog Brook, and I would hike south from there to App Gap. We'd meet along the trail and have lunch together.

That part of the trail was not as challenging as Camel's Hump and I welcomed the new experience, even with a head cold. The weather was fabulous. The trail started and ended with difficult stretches but the middle was as easy as the LT gets. Still, it took me seven and a half hours to walk the nine miles that took Sandy six. But my sniffles were gone and my cough was improving.

We ate lunch at the Birch Glen Shelter, and as we were getting ready to leave, a young Russian hiker passed through, appearing exceptionally tired. I spoke to him for a few minutes and he seemed OK, but he walked like a person nearing exhaustion. I didn't see him again until after I'd passed the cutoff to the Cooley Glen Shelter. I was sitting on a log, eating a protein bar, when I saw him walking toward me.

"I took a rest at Cooley Glen." His English was very good.

"Sometimes we need to stop and rest a bit." I thought he might need more than a bit of a rest, and asked him some questions I'd learned in first aid that would let me know if he was in trouble.

"My name is Celia." I put my hand out. We shook hands and he told me his name and trail name, but I've forgotten them. I'm usually good with names, but I must have been so focused on his condition that his name just didn't register.

He knew his name, what day it was, where he was, and where he was going. We talked about his homeland and when I asked why he'd left Russia, he said, "You have obviously never been there."

I felt better about his mental state, but he still walked like a person struggling with fatigue. But maybe he just walked like that; he might have had a disability. He still walked faster than me.

When I arrived at Route 17, Sandy was waiting in the car and I asked if she'd seen our Russian hiker. She said, "He crossed the road and continued south on the LT. He looks like a guy on his last leg."

"I talked to him for a while and he seemed all right, mentally. Maybe he just walks funny?"

The section of trail we'd scheduled for the next day, Bamforth Ridge, was about the same distance as the App Gap to Hedgehog Brook, but much of it would be difficult. I questioned how long it would take to finish; my guess was nine to ten hours, perhaps more. We decided to postpone for a day, and go to the Fourth of July parades and celebrations nearby. We could do Bamforth Ridge the day after. Sandy wanted to drop me off this time, because she hiked faster and that would make our timing more even.

But the Bamforth Ridge hike did not happen. Though my cold symptoms were gone, the weather turned on us. We looked at the map, looked out the window, looked back at the map, and decided to pass on Bamforth Ridge. But we couldn't sit still for long, and found ourselves stomping around our property in spite of the weather.

When I took Sandy to the airport, we'd accomplished little of our planned hike and it was my fault. Sandy seemed OK, but I was feeling like I'd squandered her vacation time. I was disappointed in myself, but I would get over it by the following year, when we'd try it again.

The following spring, at the Green Mountain Club's headquarters, I was talking with the person behind the counter while I picked up a detailed map of Mount Mansfield. I told him how far I'd hiked on the LT, and that my hiking partner would not be able to join me that year. He said, "You've already done the most difficult parts. You should keep going alone if you really want to finish."

I don't know how we got on the topic, but I mentioned the tired Russian hiker I'd encountered the year before. He stopped counting out change. "Where did you see him?"

"He was southbound at App Gap."

"A Russian hiker went missing. They found his car south of the Gap. He'd left his car, taken a ride to the Canadian border, and was hiking back when he disappeared."

My neck was cold and the back of my knees ached. As Don and I drove home, I kept thinking about what I could have done, what I should have done. I could have had him wait for me at Route 17, where Sandy and I could have taken him to dinner to make sure he was all right. What else could I have done? There must have been something.

When we got back to the house, I took my laptop to the library to get online. I looked up *Russian hiker missing in Vermont* and found a website for this missing person. His parents had come to Vermont looking for him, but he'd never been found. The pictures they showed might have been the person I saw, but I couldn't be sure. On that website, I entered the information I had about the person I'd spoken to, and where I'd encountered him, but it wasn't much, and I couldn't remember the name he'd given me. Why didn't I write it down?

The next day, I received a phone call from the lost Russian's sister, who told me that her brother had gone missing the year before I was on the trail. We concluded that I'd seen a different person, but his sister continued to ask questions about what he looked like, where he was going, and what he was wearing. I felt bad for having bothered the family with misinformation, but she thanked me and told me to e-mail if I thought of anything else. I was imagining how I would feel if one of my brothers disappeared into the wilderness of a foreign country and a stranger thought they might have seen him. But they hadn't.

When I told Don about the phone conversation and that the missing Russian had disappeared a year earlier he said, "Maybe you saw his ghost."

CHAPTER TWENTY-THREE

SOLO

From one extreme to another: I went from thinking I might not finish my hike to attempting to complete the LT alone. I spoke to Sandy in early January; she had a lot going on in her life and wasn't going to be able to spare the time to train or hike. I understood being busy, but I couldn't help but wonder if she was hesitant to plan a trip that might get screwed up again—by me. Our hike the previous year had been disappointing for both of us, and I guess I was still carrying some guilt over the way it had ended.

After Sandy's call, I mulled over my hiking goal and knew I wanted to finish the Long Trail. Don was encouraging and my new physical training program was working in my favor. I'd been working on strengthening my legs, but my trainer instructed me to work my entire body. Carrying my pack and hiking in mountains required strong shoulders and core strength that I hadn't thought about. More cardio improved my lung capacity and I lost some weight, which was better for my knees. After some soul searching, I decided I just might have to finish the LT alone. I'd met plenty of solo hikers. Why not?

In mid-June, Don dropped me off at the Hedgehog Brook Trailhead at 9:30 a.m. I was heading north this time. Hedgehog was no picnic, but Burnt Rock Mountain was brutal, and it didn't improve much until after the Ethan Allen summit. Four times, I had to take off my pack—three times for steep downhills, and once for an uphill. The vertical reaches were almost armpit-high, with no step to help me. I removed my pack and set it up or down the steep part, and then clambered over the obstacle to get to my pack. I slipped and fell three times, but they were easy drops.

I didn't get to Montclair Glen until almost 6:30. It took me nine hours to travel 6.2 miles. That was an all-time slow pace for me. After all the training, weight loss, and preparation, I was still incredibly slow. I was fighting disappointment as I rested on the rock outcropping in front of the shelter.

I'd seen a few day-hikers along Hedgehog and up on Burnt Rock, but hadn't seen a distance hiker all day. I was beginning to wonder if the trail had been closed due to Hurricane Irene damage. It was strange not to see thru-hikers.

The view from Burnt Rock was spectacular. I ate lunch looking off from the mountain I'd just struggled up. I was hot and sweaty, and surprised by how comfortable I was dining alone on my stony perch, at ease in my solitude. When I finished my lunch, I sat quietly with eyes closed, listening to the birds singing and leaves rustling in the light breeze. I felt the air brushing against my skin and thought about the mass of stone I was sitting on, how it had pushed itself up from the depths of the Earth thousands of years before. It was incredible.

Leaving the Burnt Rock summit, I was rejuvenated by my mountain reverie. The sun shone on my shoulders and I stopped to tip my head back and bask in nature's glory. As I began to move my feet, I spread my arms and announced to the universe, "I love this."

When I arrived at the shelter, there were four thru-hikers who'd been in front of me when I came off Hedgehog. It was heartening to hear twenty- and thirty-year-old hikers who'd been on the trail for weeks, describing that day's hike as brutal. Pepsi, on his third end-to-end, commented, "We just hiked the most difficult part of the LT."

I suppose for a sixty-two-year-old to hike the most difficult portion of the LT on their first day out was not wise, but it did make me feel better about my pace. I refilled my CamelBak and water bottles and set them down next to my backpack while I prepped for dinner.

I decided to stay in the shelter that night, because the tenting area was another mile down the Dean Trail and the tent platforms at the shelter were already taken. When I got out my stove and food bag, I discovered that my CamelBak had been leaking. At first, I thought maybe I hadn't tightened the cap, but when I took it outside and examined it, I found a pinprick hole in the plastic next to the cap. If I kept it upright, it would be OK, but how long had it been like that? How often was my pack tipped to the side and how much water had traveled where?

The puncture must have occurred early in the day. I discovered that all of my extra clothing was wet, not just damp—wet. Part of my tent was wet (no big deal), and the edge of my sleeping bag as well. Now what? Hike with no dry clothes and a damp sleeping bag? The tent would dry. I was tired and hungry and decided to have dinner, chat with my fellow hikers, and address the issue in the morning.

I liked hiking alone. I'd worried I might feel lonely or vulnerable, but I enjoyed moving at my own pace and not worrying about keeping up with or holding back another hiker. I now understood the lone hikers I'd seen; they could schedule hikes when it suited them and walk at whatever pace they chose. In spite of the water issue rattling around in the back of my mind—like that rattle in the car dashboard that you only hear on a bumpy road, I was feeling better than I'd thought I might.

I lay awake well into the night, trying to stay away from the wet portion of my sleeping bag. But my toe kept creeping toward it the way your tongue can't leave a chipped tooth alone. I spent much of the night weighing the pros and cons of staying on or coming off the trail. Without Sandy there counting on me, I now had the option to quit when the going got tough.

Eating breakfast on the rocky terrace in front of the shelter, I mulled over what to do about my wet clothing and gear. The clothes I'd hung to dry overnight were a bit less wet. If I'd listened to the advice of the seasoned hikers who'd warned me, I would've had most of my gear sealed in a plastic bag within my pack. I would've been able to continue on, taking care to keep my bladder and its tiny hole upright at all times. I thought about continuing anyway, but in addition to bladder-sitting for the remainder of the trip, I would have no dry clothing. And although my sleeping bag was only wet in one corner, I didn't know how I would dry it. A bit of duct tape (the hiker's friend) might do the trick for the CamelBak, and the good weather looked like it would continue for several days. How could I pass up the chance to hike in good weather?

After discussion with fellow hikers, I decided to call Don and have him pick me up. I couldn't get a call out on my cell, but someone loaned me her phone that worked if I stood in just the right spot. Don and I would meet me at the Burrows/Forest City trailhead. I wasn't sure how long Don would take to arrive, so when I got to the parking area, I sat in the shade near the parking lot, leaning on my backpack and reflecting on the disappointment of another stupid blunder. Day-hikers moving on and off the trail nodded or chatted as they passed.

When Don arrived, he had the dogs with him and we decided to hike the Burrows Trail to the Camel's Hump summit. From previous experience, I knew that even our older dog, Frankie, would be able to handle that walk. He was beginning to have problems with tougher trails, but I thought this one would be gentle enough and we could help him if he needed it.

Don hadn't hiked Camel's Hump before and I would've hated for him to drive so far just to turn around and drive back. Besides, I'd been planning to hike. I wouldn't feel as bad about going off-trail if I could first share a summit as spectacular as Camel's Hump with Don.

The Burrows Trail was harder than I remembered. I'd hiked it in January, wearing snowshoes, and the rocky ground had been muted by the deep snow undulating beneath me. Frankie and I had walked it together, but his legs were stronger then.

Don declared, "If this is what the Long Trail is like, I'm glad I'm not doing it."

Hiking Camel's Hump kept the day from being a total loss for me. Don got to see a beautiful summit on a lovely day, and he had a better understanding of the difficulty of the Long Trail. Which made me feel better about thinking it was difficult.

When we arrived at the pinnacle, Don was impressed by the view and I was happy to share a special spot with him. We ate lunch from the stores in my pack and had a spectacular, sun-washed, 360-degree view. Don kept saying things to help me feel better; he knew I was frustrated with having to stop after only one day on the trail. He didn't complain about the distance he had to drive, or how long it had taken to get to the trailhead. Frankie and Ringer lay at our feet on the warm stone, enjoying their day. The four of us stopped to stand above the metal marker indicating the mountain's highest point. Don and I kissed on the most impressive mountaintop we'd experienced together, and then we all headed down the Burrows Trail.

In the car, I leaned back and closed my eyes so Don would think I was asleep. What I really wanted to do was think about whether I should get things dried out and set off again the next day. I didn't want to say it out loud and I wasn't sure if I wanted to ask Don to make the long drive two days in a row. I pondered what the weather might do and how tough Bamforth

Ridge was going to be.

The day after the Burnt Mountain debacle, the weather turned, so I decided to put off the next leg of my hike. I started working out harder, trying to improve my fitness and endurance levels.

Chapter Twenty-Four

WHITE LADY'S SLIPPER

Nature's peace will flow into you as sunshine flows into trees.
John Muir, "The Mountains of California" [16]

It was fifty-three degrees and raining like it meant it, but Sandy and I had started a September hike like that and the rest of the trip had been beautiful. Don and I heard on the radio as we drove toward the Monroe trailhead, that there were flood warnings in southern New Hampshire, but that was well south and east of my destination. I hoped the forecast would be better in north central Vermont.

The rain welcomed me to the trail, but the streams were like rivers and I stepped off a stone along the trail—not in a stream, mind you, and sank into water that was over my knee. That boot was wet and it wouldn't be long before the other was equally so. I thought I'd already been on the wettest trails possible, but that day was the worst.

I ascended the Monroe Trail; it was easier than the Forest City and Burrows trails had been, but the driving rain and deep slop complicated everything. I labored at the start, knowing I would catch my second wind and feel better as the day progressed. At one point, the rain stopped—but not for long. Although the trail and my feet were wet, I envisioned the day ending with me happily ensconced at the Bamforth Ridge Shelter. There were no views from the trail, due to the rain, but my legs felt good.

I took the Alpine Trail, knowing that it might be difficult, because it would shorten my hike by four-tenths of a mile. The Alpine was as tough as I'd thought it might be. There were some rugged, rocky PUDs. I didn't see another person along the Monroe or Alpine Trails, but figured I'd see some hardy soul when I got to the LT.

On a ledge along the Alpine, I couldn't walk the slick inclines, so I crept forward on my hands and knees. I reached a point where I'd not seen a yellow blaze for some time, so I hiked back to the previous marker, only to hike forward again, watching for possible twists or turns on the trail, but finding myself in the same spot. I was standing precisely where I'd been when I decided to retrace my steps, when I saw a blaze that I must have missed the first time. It was not on a tree, but on an overhead rock formation that I would be walking under. It was old and weathered, but it was right there looking at me as I stood in the tracks I'd been in almost an hour before. Damn.

A few feet past that marker, I had to squeeze between massive rock formations that were leaning toward one another, but I couldn't fit between them with my pack on. Ducking down or crawling under wouldn't work, either. I had to remove my pack and crawl through the opening backward, dragging my pack behind me.

When I reached the LT, the blazes were more plentiful and I was feeling good, but my feet were wet and I was beginning to talk myself into hiking to Duxbury Road instead of stopping at the Bamforth Shelter. Would I be able to get a call out to Don? I wondered if he could get to me before dark. I wasn't sure if I could even make it to Duxbury Road before dark. "You can do this. Your legs feel good, you are fitter and stronger and you can do this thing, Damn It!"

I was talking to myself again, out loud.

I reached a windy ledge that may have provided a view in better weather, when I felt my pack's rain cover tapping my right shoulder. Somewhere, perhaps when I'd dragged my pack between those big rocks, my pack cover had come loose. I reached my hands back to feel the bottom of my pack and I knew that it had been loose for some time, because the bottom of my pack was saturated. Had I learned from my previous experience and placed a waterproof liner in my pack? NOOO!

I didn't have to look in my pack to know that everything was soaked. The wet pack at Montclair Glen was nothing compared to this. I'd seen a plastic pack liner while shopping at Eastern Mountain Sports, but shuffled past it without a second glance and purchased a cool T-shirt instead. I could see it in my mental rearview mirror and had yet another reason to kick myself, but I kept the conversation brief, announcing to the universe, "You idiot!"

I'd had enough. I wasn't going to waste energy beating myself up. I called Don at the next high point with a cell signal, and kept going to Duxbury Road.

I didn't stop that day to take pictures as often as usual, but I got some shots of rain-enraged cascades and trails deep in water. When I show the photos to friends, they don't have the impact I'd hoped for, but they remind me how wet and cold the day was.

Walking with my head bent against the rain, I spotted a lone plant and it felt like a ray of sunshine. A white lady's slipper lay before me, rare and beautiful and in full bloom. Even in my sopping state, I had to pause to enjoy its beauty. I felt better after taking a break and I cherish that photograph above many others.

I struggled to find handholds and footholds while backing down the steepest inclines on Bamforth Ridge. Facing forward on that descent would have been like walking down a ladder the wrong way. I'm not sure how far I was from the forest floor in feet and inches, but looking to my right I would guess about two stories. The flat wooded area below was beautiful. I thought that if I weren't saturated, I might choose that lovely woodland for a break.

I inched along with relative confidence until, when reaching for a handhold with my right hand, my left hand slid off the rock it was clinging to. I was standing there with nothing in either hand when I felt the weight of my pack pulling me backward toward that beautiful park-like setting below. I threw myself forward, my fingernails clawing, desperate to get any grip I could find. I hugged the mountain like a tourist hugs their first redwood tree. My right hand closed on a solid anchor of stone just as the other found a sturdy root. I was frozen in place, my face squashed against wet rock, every muscle petrified.

My heart raged and my breath gasped sharp and quick. When my breathing eased toward normal, I forced a nervous laugh out loud, to settle my frazzled nerves. I struggled to calm myself by counting the raindrops falling from the brim of my hat: One ... two-three ... four ... five-six-seven ... eight ...

When I felt like I could move again, I silently vowed to be certain of my next handgrip before I let go of the one before. I flashed on a conversation I'd had with one of our exchange students. Rikke (pronounced Regga) had sailed on a tall ship from Denmark to New York, as a cadet. When I asked how she climbed into the rope rigging high above the ship's deck without fearing for her life, she said, "Never let go of one grip before you are certain of the next."

My trembling hand reached for the next root. I'd always been aware of possible slips or falls, and like every hiker young and old, I'd experienced my share of each. But this was different. I was alone. I'd been hiking for eight hours without seeing another human or even a fresh footprint. A fall like the one I'd just avoided would be major in any circumstance, but alone, on a cold wet trail . . .

I negotiated the rest of Bamforth Ridge without incident. My nerves calmed with the exercise of hiking, and my boots were happy to find the forest floor. The smooth path embraced me.

At the trailhead parking area, I found a spruce whose dense branches offered cover, and sat down on my sopping pack with my sopping pants, shook raindrops from my sopping head, and waited for my ride. When Don arrived, I asked him to take my picture—I'd never been so wet while fully clothed and I wanted photographic evidence. My gym bag was in the car with a change of clothes and I replaced my wet garments with dry jeans and a T-shirt under the shelter of the car's rear tailgate. As I piled my spent clothing on top of my backpack, Don asked, "What happened to your hand?"

"Oh, I slipped."

Just thinking about it made me slightly nauseous and I wasn't ready to talk about it yet. My right hand was still bleeding and a fingernail on my left hand was torn to the quick and oozing blood. I wrapped them both in napkins and leaned back into the passenger seat to listen to Don telling me about what he'd heard on the news regarding flood warnings everywhere. He'd been relieved when I called and was glad to come pick me up.

I talked about the rain and the pack cover coming off. I mentioned the lady's slipper, but when I thought about my near fall, the insides of my elbows ached in recollection of the tension of clinging to the sheer wall. I didn't tell Don for a couple of days about my most frightening hiking experience, and even then I played it down.

Seated in the car that day, I tipped my head back, almost asleep. In my cold wet disappointment I knew that I would find a way to finish, but I didn't know when or how. I'd heard that the definition of insanity was continuing to doing the same thing over and over, expecting a different outcome. I therefore decided that I was nuts because I was sitting there, wet and chilled to the bone yet knowing I would find a way to finish the Long Trail.

A white flower dripping with rain was my sign that I should keep going.

CHAPTER TWENTY-FIVE

LUCY'S LOOKOUT

The woods are lovely, dark and deep,
But I have promises to keep,
And miles to go before I sleep
Robert Frost

"I called Sandy in January for two reasons; I wanted to ask about hiking but I had a sad story to share. I had to tell her that Wib had passed away.

Don and I were in Vermont for Thanksgiving when Wib told us that he would be starting cancer treatment. I felt positive about his prospects because he looked just fine and was so optimistic. When I spoke to him in December he bragged about getting his treatment diploma. "I never got a diploma you know," he said. I was shocked when Audrey called in January to tell me about Wib passing.

Sandy responded to my message quickly with kind words and thoughts for Audrey and bad news about the summer hikes. She couldn't hike because she was moving back to Michigan. I decided to try to hike alone again. How could I expect a better result? I wasn't sure but I was going to try."

I considered finishing the LT in day hikes. I'd met people who were doing the AT and LT one day at a time, including a couple in the process of completing the entire Appalachian Trail in day hikes. They'd come all the way up to Vermont from Georgia over a series of years, driving two cars to leave one at either end of their hike. It was taking them a long time, but they seemed to be having a good time.

I met a hiker on Killington who was slack-packing the AT, with her husband following in a camper. He dropped her off at Route 103 in the morning and would meet her at Route 4 later that day. They would sleep in their camper at the Route 4 parking area, then she would head out from Route 4 the next day, to meet him that night at Route 12. That's why they called it slack-packing: she was hiking with a daypack— slacking. She was making good time, and although she was hiking alone, she had company every night and someone who knew where she was and when she should show up. Her pack was almost empty.

I mentioned these encounters to Don, hoping he would maybe want to try it, but he didn't seem interested in either approach. I admit, I was surprised but I couldn't be upset—he backed me in ways that many husbands would not.

I set off from Thundering Falls on a solo hike along the part of the Appalachian Trail that runs from the Maine Junction to the Vermont/New Hampshire border. That part of the trail is easier than much of the LT, and it would prepare me to set out later that summer on the LT.

I hiked into the hottest weather I'd experienced on any trail. I felt good, stopping at Stony Brook Shelter for an early break, then proceeding on the sunlit woodland path. My first height of ground was Quimby Mountain, which I consider an unfortunate name. As a child, *quimby* was a derogatory name applied when someone did something stupid. I don't know where the word came from, but I felt sorry for that mountain. I will probably learn that the Quimby family is a fabulous group of people that I would be proud to know. But as children, you were a *quimby* when you spilled your milk or stepped in dog poop.

The Quimby Mountain view was lovely, so I took a brief break. Don and I had day-hiked the area, so I knew where some of the prime rest spots were and had anticipated a Quimby-break.

I watched for the pond that marked the Continental Divide. The water flowing west was on its way to Lake Champlain, and to the east it was heading for the Connecticut River. I was struck by this auspicious location and wondered if the Abenaki people thought of it as a sacred place.

I saw few end-to-end hikers that far north in June, so the path was quiet. AT hikers usually start in March in Georgia and few make it to Vermont as early as mid-June. During a rest stop, I talked with a young couple from England who'd begun their hike in February. They said the heat had slowed them down, but they were happy to be ahead of schedule on their way to Mount Katahdin—the AT's northern terminus. They were both wearing short, light gators. I was still using winter gators and in the heat thought I might want to try something lighter.

Another end-to-ender passed me and we talked long enough for me to learn that he started in Georgia in early March and was making incredible time. His pack looked light, his shoes clean (he was wearing the little gators too), his gray hair was neatly cut, and he had no beard. Judging by his appearance, I was certain that someone was following his progress in a car and that he often slept in a motel or motor home.

I came upon an aluminum household ladder lashed to trees in front of a rock outcropping. Descending the ladder, I thought about my cousin BJ again. I flashed on the two of us dropping from the loft ladder to the dusty straw-cushioned floor of an abandoned barn that I hadn't seen in over fifty years.

When I crossed Chateaugay Road, I realized how close I was to Bob and Gina's house and that this had been where they'd first encountered the AT.

Bob and Gina had come from their home in Wisconsin to spend a week in our Vermont house several years ago, and because of that visit, purchased a piece of property in nearby Bridgewater Center. Bob was intrigued by my hike on the LT, and started hiking the year after I began my stumbling expedition. Bob owns an equine veterinary practice in Wisconsin, and when he and Gina are in town, the four of us get together to day-hike as a group and share a meal or two. Over dinner, Bob and I discuss where we are on the trail while Gina and Don talk about dropping us off and picking us up. As of that summer, we'd both made it to Jonesville. I had to admit, I wanted to finish before Bob, since I'd started first, but I reminded myself that I was a bigger person than that. I wanted him to finish the trail on his own schedule and I didn't care when that happened—as long as I got to finish first.

I stopped at a little stream and decided that it was hot enough to restock my water midday. The liquid dripping from my hat brim was not rain. I pulled off my hat and twisted it in front me, leaving a puddle of salty water in the dirt. How could I feel so good when I was sweating that much?

I began my usual water-pumping procedure, but the water moving through the filter into my bottle was only a tiny dribble. I opened and examined the filter system and everything looked right, so I tried again, but the dribble persisted. I opened up the pump area and as I did, a tiny metal washer disappeared into the leaf duff at my feet. I watched the silver reflecting in the sunlight as it fell to the forest floor in that slow-motion we experience when we watch something going terribly wrong. I searched carefully, but could not find the washer. I put the pump back together, hoping the washer had been in the way and the water would flow freely, but now it was not pumping at all.

I wasn't worried, because I carried iodine tablets. But when I pulled them out of my pack, I realized that I had the tablets in their foil packets, but I'd discarded the box and instructions that came with them. I thought I needed one tablet per bottle, but I wasn't sure. I thought it took a half hour to work correctly, but I wasn't sure about that either. Do these things have an expiration date? I had plenty of water for the day, but it would be a problem if I wanted to get to stay on the trail. I threw on my pack and continued.

I stopped at Lucy's Lookout for the night. It was only a couple more miles to Winturri Shelter, but I'd been to Lucy's on day hikes and wanted to spend the night in the cabin there, with its four walls, screened windows, fireplace, sleeping loft, and ladder to a roof-top observation deck.

On the map, it's simply called The Lookout, but I'd heard other hikers referring to it as Lucy's Lookout. Lucy may have been the owner or someone's wife or daughter. I wondered who she is . . . or was.

There were no fellow hikers at the lookout when I arrived, but I was sure some would come along. I sat on the porch for dinner and set up my sleeping area inside as darkness fell.

It was fully dark when I heard another hiker arriving. There is a sound that backpack water bladders make when they are low on water: a muted glugging as the remaining water sloshes back and forth in its plastic container. I heard that sound moving along the left side of the cabin where the trail came up from the AT. It moved past the open windows and I thought it would come around the corner of the building to the porch steps, and I would get to meet a new hiker. The sound did not make the turn, but continued past the building. I'd looked around the area on several occasions and never noticed a trail or tenting area nearby, but I must have missed one because my fellow hiker had gone by the cabin. Odd. I could check that out in the morning.

I was at that almost-asleep phase that lasts longer when you're alone in a strange place, when I heard the glugging sound again. This time it was at the right-hand corner of the cabin, near the porch steps. Maybe that sound was not coming from a hiker. What kind of animal might sound like that? Could a bear who'd just had a big drink of water be glugging around out there? How firm was that door latch?

My bear spray was in the boot near my head and I lay there in the darkness thinking I should get up and look outside. Another part of me wanted to pull myself down into my sleeping bag and hide under the covers like a child. But this was no boogey man and I was not a child.

With bear spray in one hand and headlamp (not turned on, yet) in the other, I crab-walked toward the corner near the porch steps. My eyes were adjusted to the darkness and I would be able to see out into the moonlight. I eased into a standing position in the corner, with windows to my left and right. What was I going to do if I saw something?

I tipped my head around to the right and looked out over the porch steps, gazing into the darkness long enough to allow whatever animal might be out there to move, but nothing happened. I pulled my head back and leaned around to the left, looking into the woods, but saw nothing.

The moon was not bright, but I could make out the shapes of trees, shrubs, and rocks and saw no evidence of animal or human. There had been no sound since I decided to look around, so I crab-walked back to my sleeping bag. Who was I hiding from? There was nothing out there. Why was I sneaking back to my sleeping bag? Still, I didn't stand up.

I listened for sounds from outside, but the quiet was profound. When I was comfortably in my sleeping bag, I heard the glugging again in the same corner. Now, that was more than creepy. Perhaps my presence was bothering a ghost.

"Lucy, if you're out there, I appreciate your lovely house. I will clean it up carefully before I leave. I'll just be sleeping now, if you don't mind."

The sound stopped, but I couldn't sleep. Each time I relaxed a little, I heard it again; sometimes near the steps, sometimes to my left, again to my right, but always outside. Was Lucy trying to get in?

Could a rodent be making a very odd chewing sound? It sounded like water, not chewing. I chuckled as I thought of a chipmunk using a spray of water, like a tile saw, to keep his teeth from overheating while gnawing on a tough acorn. I wanted it to be a rodent, so I decided the little guy must have a dental issue that created an odd sound. It made no sense, but neither did any other explanation. I wondered if he had a lisp when he communicated with his rodent friends. It was soothing to think about a cartoon chipmunk spitting out his words like Sylvester the cat.

After a long, restless night, the sun was finally rising and I hadn't heard the noise for a while. I shuffled out of my bag and prepared breakfast, being careful to conserve water. With my gear packed and ready on the porch, I made a bio-break in the woods. When I returned, I looked for evidence of what was making noises all night, but the surrounding area was either rock or tall grass and I saw nothing that couldn't have been matted down by previous hikers. I was glad to be heading back to the AT before the sun heated up the day.

When I shared my Lucy's Lookout story with Bob and Gina, they hesitated, looked at one another, and laughed. On a day hike to the lookout, they'd met thru-hikers returning to the AT after spending the night there. The hikers had been shaking their heads and saying that it was one weird place to spend the night. Bob and Gina hadn't gotten much more information, but I wondered what their unusual experience had been. It made me feel less paranoid, but I knew there were stories to be told. Who is Lucy?

CHAPTER TWENTY-SIX

ON THE EDGE

Thoughts come clearly while one walks.
Thomas Mann

The heat moved in quickly on day two and I would have been worried about water if I hadn't known that Route 12 was not far. There's a garden center and store called On The Edge Farm just down the road from the trail crossing. I hoped to either find instructions useful for the iodine tablets I had in my pack, or buy new ones with their own instructions. The store was well-known by end-to-enders as the place to stop and buy a pie. If all else failed, I could get a call out to Don and take a trip to replace or repair my water filter.

Hiking down to Route 12 was an easy walk, and it would have been fun to think I was making good time into my second day—but I had no water source, so the detour was necessary. As a last attempt to stay on the trail, when I got to the trailhead at Route 12, I sat on a rocky riverbank and tried again to get my water filter to work, but it would not pump a drop. I went through my pack, but still did not find the instructions for my iodine tablets. So I walked to On The Edge Farm.

At the farm, I walked past rows of potted plants backed by gardens in full bloom, left my pack on the porch, and entered the quaint shop full of baked goods and household items, but found no hiking gear. The woman who owned the shop welcomed me, but I knew immediately she was not a hiker. I needed to call Don.

My cell phone didn't work, so I asked if I could make a call. The shop owner, Dana, asked, "Is it local?"

I decided to call Audrey and have her relay a message to Don, who had an out-of-state cell phone number. When I mentioned Audrey, I discovered that Dana and her husband Bill were long-time friends of Audrey and Wib. I told her that our place was across the street from theirs and how much Don and I valued their friendship.

We talked about how Audrey was doing since Wib passed away in January. I told Dana that I'd come from Michigan for his funeral, but Don couldn't make it. Audrey had had friends and family around her, but I'd wanted to be there, too, to offer support in any way I could.

In his retirement, Wib had been in the habit of driving around the area to see what was going on. When Don and I had people doing repairs or making improvements on our house, Wib was there daily to see how things were progressing. When Hurricane Irene washed our driveway onto Route 100A, Wib watched over it, making sure that nobody stole our gravel; gravel was a prime commodity during the post-Irene days. It was nice to know he was keeping an eye on things for us, and when we were in town we enjoyed his visits. I was present for one of our improvement projects, when a worker heard Wib's four-wheeler coming up the driveway and announced, "The boss is coming. We better get busy."

I was glad to be there the day before the funeral, when Wib's family decided to put his casket in his truck and drive him around his usual circuit, one last time. The funeral director changed plans, allowing the casket to remain in Wib's truck, which was driven behind the hearse by Wib's brother Macky. The rest of us followed in procession. When we looped around the Corners Store, an employee came out with a cup of coffee for Wib. Macky accepted in his brother's name, then we drove up Route 100A. I was touched to see people who'd heard about Wib's last drive standing at the end of their driveways in the icy weather to wave goodbye. It was a stirring tribute, and I was especially glad to be present for Wib's last drive around.

I carpooled to the funeral service with our friends Mary and David. Knowing that parking near the church was limited, we arrived an hour early. I was stunned to find the church full, a half hour before the service, with standing room only long before the ceremony began. People were seated in the choir area and standing along every inch of wall space, with a crowd that backed out the door onto the church steps.

After the service, there was a meal served by friends at the Grange Hall. I'd thought the Grange building was large, but it was so full I could hardly move. Audrey was proud of the turnout as a demonstration of Wib's value to the community. I hardly had a chance to speak to her as we shuffled around nodding hellos and looking at the pictures displayed on tables and easels reflecting Wib's time on this earth. It was nice to see people acknowledging a man for being a nice guy.

As Dana and I talked, I told her how I still found myself looking for Wib when I went to the Corners Store. In unison we said, "I miss him."

I told Dana that I thought it might be a while before Don arrived, and she invited me to sit on the covered porch behind the store to enjoy whatever breeze existed in the afternoon heat. I purchased a cold drink and she let me take the newspaper to read while I waited. I felt better than I should have after getting so little sleep. After my drink and a few minutes of reading, I lay down on a wooden bench with my head on the newspaper, waking to see Don standing over me, smiling.

Another aborted mission, and I knew what Wib would've said because he'd already said it: "Celia, maybe you're just getting too damned old for this shit."

Maybe I was, but that wouldn't keep me from making another attempt next month. I planned to finish the LT, and when I did, I was going to go to Wib's gravesite and sit on his bench to tell him about it.

CHAPTER TWENTY-SEVEN

IF YOU'RE ASKING THE QUESTION, YOU'VE MADE UP YOUR MIND

If you are walking to seek, ye shall find.
Sommeil Liberosensa [17]

Don dropped me off at the base of Bamforth Ridge where he'd picked me up the year before. I was glad to be heading north, with my back to the ridge. I would not feel my trail-legs for days, but I did the first 1.7 miles to Duck Brook in less than an hour, doing almost two miles an hour on day one.

Leaving Duck Brook, things changed. I had trouble finding the trail and wasted distance and minutes wandering back and forth. After reading the guidebook and map, I still couldn't find the trial. I crossed the brook and was on the old logging road, watching for the trail that should have come up quickly on my left. When I got to a right-hand bend in the logging road, I knew I'd already missed my turn.

I hiked back to the brook and saw an area that led down into another brook. It looked like there was a small path, so I tried that direction, but the trail stopped abruptly. Other hikers had wandered that area before me.

I walked back to the brook and just as I reached the logging road, I noticed a miniature cairn of small gray rocks against a gray tree trunk beside a gray rock. All of that gray made the tiny cairn almost invisible. Next to that was a narrow separation between two tree trunks that may or may not have been a trail. As I stepped off the logging road, turning my body to fit between the trees, I saw a white blaze. Really? They couldn't put a blaze on one of the tree trunks on the logging road? What a waste of time and effort, and I'd been doing so well.

I tried not to let the delay bother me. I let the easy trail soothe me the way walking had in my youth. I felt my pace and spirits lifting as I moved through the mottled light. At Bolton Notch Road, the guidebook's directions were to cross the road and continue. When I reached the road, I spotted a little waterway directly across from me, and although the trail was small, I walked on as directed. A few yards in, the trail stopped at the edge of someone's backyard.

I hiked back to the road, watching along the way for a turn I may have missed. Like the false turn at Duck Brook, a lot of people had stumbled around that little swamp. Turning right on the road, I walked a short distance to another house and decided that, too, was the wrong direction. I returned to the trail and walked up the road in the opposite direction until I came to a house with signs telling me: NO PARKING and PRIVATE PROPERTY with no blazes or trail signs available. There was a gate beyond the unfriendly signs, with a large truck parked in front of it—it did not look inviting.

I went back to the trail, crossed the road into the little waterway, walked up the road to the first house, then went back to the uninviting signs. I walked past the unfriendly markers and around the obstructing truck to see if there was a sign on the gate. A NO PARKING sign was attached to the gate, but I saw no markers beyond it and nothing indicating that it was the trail. Yet the path looked right, so I ducked under the gate and walked a few yards and found a white blaze. I'd endured another long delay for nothing, but I knew that my walking legs would renew me.

I hiked on to the Buchanan Shelter with relative ease. The walk down to the shelter seemed longer than the three-tenths of a mile indicated on the map, but I was sure it was leading me to a water source deep within the quiet forest. I was beginning to wonder if I was on the wrong trail when I spotted the privy roof. The shelter was a few yards away. I sat on the steps, pulled off my pack, and looked around. There was no evidence of another hiker.

According to the logbook, no one had stayed there for three days. Being alone at a campsite was a little strange, but it didn't bother me much. On my second visit to the privy, I noticed a red Swiss Army Knife at the bottom of the steps. How could I have missed that on my first visit? It was shiny and bright—it couldn't have been there long, and the shelter hadn't been used in days. Could someone have stopped to use the privy and left without my noticing? But who would do that? Perhaps being alone bothered me more than I wanted to admit. I'd passed some people earlier in the day who'd said they had day-hiked to Buchanan for lunch. One of them may have dropped it. Relax Ryker. Eat some jelly beans and take it easy.

The next day's hike looked harder, but I could opt for a short day. I was hoping to get to Butler Lodge, but decided that Taylor Lodge might be a better choice. The guidebook's description made the trail sound tough, and the elevation indicators on the map looked daunting. But the weather was pleasant, with the forecast predicting more of the same. If all went well, I could get to Coddling Hollow Road in five or six days.

One of the people I'd passed earlier told me she'd hiked the LT end-to-end. She'd said, "It gets harder as you near Canada." She also said, "As tough as this trail is, I would not hike it alone."

Other people told me I'd already done the hardest parts of the trail. Who was right?

Two college-aged hikers that Don and I met while day-hiking Mount Mansfield had said they didn't think anyone should try the LT alone. The couple from England that I'd met near Lucy's Lookout had said the same thing, and they were both young and healthy-looking. But I'd met solo hikers, young and old, who thought nothing of it. A woman I'd met at our very first shelter was in her seventies and hiking the AT solo, end-to-end. When I told her I admired her for doing it alone, she said, "Look around. How many people are at this campsite? I am rarely alone."

The AT is a busy trail, but the LT north of Route 4 is relatively quiet.

I spoke with two SOBO hikers earlier in the day, one in his twenties, the other in his thirties. When I asked how difficult the ledges I'd read about, between the Puffer and Taylor Shelters, had been, Thirty-something said, "You don't want to know."

Twenty-something said, "Don't say that, you'll psych her out."

"She should be," Thirty-something replied.

I had to ask. "Then you wouldn't recommend doing it alone?"

"If I had known what it was going to be like, I wouldn't have done it *with him*." Thirty-something had strong feelings.

That didn't make me feel better. At all. I could rationalize, telling myself that Thirty-something was out of shape; and perhaps the woman I'd met earlier in the day didn't like hiking alone. But the college-aged kids on Mansfield didn't seem wimpy, and the British couple was into endurance conditioning. My mental argument was going in the wrong direction.

I set up my tent, refreshed my water supply, and dined at the table in the shelter, returning to my tent as darkness neared. It was nearly dark when I heard a male voice shout out: "I see a privy!"

A few minutes later, he announced, "I see the shelter." Then he saw my tent and I heard a loudish whisper, "Sorry, go back to sleep." There were at least two people coming in for the night and I thought I heard a dog. I would meet them in the morning. At breakfast, I met two young men in their twenties and their dog. Blue Boy, who owned the dog, had finished the AT and returned to hike the LT from Canada back to Route 4. Cracker Jack was hiking the LT SOBO, Canada to Massachusetts. He was the one who'd whispered apologies the night before. I learned that he was a kindergarten teacher; his whisper seemed fitting for someone teaching young people how to live politely in society.

We talked about hiking with a dog and I asked how they dealt with the ladders. Blue Boy said, "She can usually find a way up or down, but when that doesn't work, I pick her up by the handle on her backpack and carry her."

I'd met an AT thru-hiker who was traveling with a full-sized collie that carried its own backpack in the rain. I hadn't thought to ask how he handled the tricky spots with a dog that size.

I'd often thought it would be fun to distance hike with one of my dogs, but I couldn't carry either one of my border collies up a ladder. Perhaps once Flurry was old enough, I could take her on trails that I knew well. She wasn't a year old yet, so distance hikes would have to wait.

Frankie had hiked his last trail at fourteen. Prior to that, he and I had often day-hiked together. He was with me the first time I'd reached the Camel's Hump summit on snowshoes. As we walked up, I could clearly see the summit from the Burrows Trail, but when we arrived at the pinnacle, the cloud cover left no view further than a few yards of rocky surface.

There'd been a young couple at the summit trying to enjoy their break in a cold wind. They welcomed us to sit with them and laughed when I addressed my canine hiking partner: "Well, Frank, I think it's time to head back to the car. Are you ready, buddy?" I suppose talking to a dog like a short person seems odd to some people.

I can't walk the Burrows Trail without thinking about the times Frankie hiked it with me. I miss that funny little dog. Watching my dogs grow old gives me perspective on my own aging process. Frankie walked with me as long as he could and Ringer, too, is approaching the end of his trail days. Ringer hasn't been able to run for at least a year, but he doesn't seem to mind slowing down. He gets as excited about a quiet amble as he did when he ran on puppy legs.

At the Buchanan Shelter, talking with Blue Boy and Cracker Jack, I broached the topic of hiking alone. They both said they usually start hikes alone and end up with another hiker on the same trajectory who travels at about the same speed, which was how they ended up together. I thought about how hard it would be to find someone to buddy-up with when I hiked so slowly. It might be easier on the AT because there were more hikers.

I now had the answer to my question: Who is right about how difficult the LT is and whether it should be traveled alone? EVERYONE! It's a matter of opinion. My personal conclusion: If I know the trail and I'm comfortable with it, I enjoy hiking alone. If I don't know the trail and I'm worried about its difficulty, I should not hike alone. So there was the answer to the question I'd been afraid to ask myself: I was worried about the ledges and some of the other obstacles ahead, so I needed to find someone to hike with.

I came up with a plan; I would search for a hiking partner. It might not be easy to find the right person, but I wouldn't find anyone unless I let people know that I was looking. If I told enough people, I might end up meeting someone who didn't mind my slow pace.

I was vacillating between going it alone and pausing until I found a hiking partner, as I hiked from the Buchanan Shelter back to the main trail. The weather was good and I could have kept going, but if one little thing went wrong I'd be all by myself—and I didn't know the trail. I favored one choice and then the other for three-tenths of a mile, and still hadn't decided by the time I got to the LT. I set my pack down, ate part of a protein bar, drank some water, and weighed the issue. When I put on my pack, my body leaned north, but my boots turned south. I was going back to Bolton Notch Road to call Don and have him pick me up—again. Don't laugh, Wib, I'm not done yet.

Shortly after I started back toward Bolton Notch, I passed two NOBO thru-hikers and we stopped to chat. I asked them what they thought about hiking alone, and the older of the two, who was in his fifties, said, "Why do you ask?"

"I'm just wondering what you think. I'm trying to decide whether to continue alone or not."

His response: "If you're asking that question, then you've already made up your mind."

And so I had.

CHAPTER TWENTY-EIGHT

SCOOTER

The best remedy for those who are afraid,
lonely or unhappy is to go outside . . .
I firmly believe that nature brings solace in all troubles.
Anne Frank, "Diary of a Young Girl" [18]

After my Buchanan hike, I started telling anyone who would listen that I was looking for a hiking partner. I mentioned it to trainers, people at gyms in Vermont and Michigan, to online hiking groups, and people I met at the bookstore. And I contacted a person who wrote hiking articles for a local newspaper.

My quest for a hiking partner began in August, and by January I still hadn't found one. So I began confiding in friends that I was thinking about hiking alone again. Later that day, Sandy called to ask if I was planning to hike the LT that summer. We met a few days later for lunch, went over maps, and decided that we would head out from Jonesville, at the base of Bamforth Ridge, and go north for a week of hiking. We were both excited about getting back on the trail together. We set dates to do weekend training hikes, one in May and two in June, to be ready for the Long Trail in July.

When July came, Audrey dropped us off after a two-hour drive, and we set out from Jonesville at 9:30 a.m. All was well as we started to walk the first easy miles along Duxbury Road to the new Winooski Bridge, which had been dedicated a few weeks earlier and cut miles of road walking out of our journey. We stepped onto the bridge and I pointed to a bolt. "I contributed to the building of this bridge," I said. "I think my donation may have paid for that bolt."

We arrived at Buchanan Shelter at a little after 4 p.m. We'd been hiking for seven hours and I was glad to set my tent and restock my water. Sandy and I were alone at the shelter, preparing an early dinner, when we heard a call in the distance. Was it human or animal? As it neared, we heard a male voice calling out "Day-o" then, after a pause, another "Day-o," and then another, and another. He was getting close when I responded with a "Day-o" of my own. I heard a voice up the trail quietly say, "OK," and our hiker came into view.

Boot Lace had come upon a moose earlier in the day and they'd frightened one another, so he was warning moose or any other creature around that he was approaching. He was SOBO and complained that he needed a day off-trail, because he was killing himself. I wondered why he was pushing himself so hard. The three of us talked at the shelter's table, but when a light rain began to fall, Sandy and I retired to our tents. Wind and thunder soon followed, with heavy rain beating down.

I was glad to be in my tent, nibbling GORP and reading my nature guide. When the rain let up, I heard a female voice with Boot Lace. It sounded like Sandy had returned to the shelter. I thought about joining them, but it was still raining.

Over breakfast at the shelter table, I discovered that the female voice had been another hiker who'd come into camp in the rain. Snail was NOBO and said it had been a couple of days since she could fully straighten or bend her left leg. When Boot Lace shared problems with his feet and how many miles he had to put down in a day, I said: "You two should fire the person in charge of your schedule. If they're pushing you this hard, you might want to hire a more empathetic person."

They looked at me like I was from Mars and shook their heads, then we all went about preparing our individual breakfasts, chatting about food choices and where we hoped to camp that evening.

Sandy and I were the first to leave Buchanan. I was hoping to improve my speed from the day before, but the first miles changed my plan. The rocky descents required me to sit and scoot along the rough wet surface. I found

153

myself swearing, and not under my breath. I didn't think the rocks cared, but it felt good to vent my frustration. When I came to a flat stretch and was able to walk for a bit, my legs soothed me and the next challenging rock climb did not bring foul words.

I expected Snail to pass us, but it was afternoon before we saw her. Maybe she really was slow and that's how she got her name. Snail said her leg was slowing her down and she was planning to leave the trail at Nebraska Notch to give it a couple days' rest. I thought she might need more than a couple of days, but I kept that to myself.

Scooting on wet rocks left the bottom of my pack damp, even with my pack cover secure, but my clothing, sleeping bag, and other important items were tucked into their new water-tight bag within my pack—I'd learned that lesson, finally.

At our first break, we were talking about how many times I had to sit and scoot.

Sandy laughed. "Maybe your trail name should be Scoots-a-lot."

The tough terrain was making me scoot more than usual and late in the day, Sandy declared, "Your name is Scooter."

"I like it. Bent Bike requires too much explanation and the story sounds whiney. Scooter is easy to explain and it makes people chuckle. Short and simple—I am Scooter."

CHAPTER TWENTY-NINE

FOG MONSTERS

Adopt the pace of nature:
her secret is patience.
Ralph Waldo Emerson

It took us six hours to walk the 4.5 miles to Puffer Shelter, and we decided to stop there. At the rate we were traveling, we'd barely have gotten to Taylor Lodge before dark. When I read the description of the trail between Puffer and Taylor, I was certain we'd made the right choice. We discussed the possibility of hiking shelter-to-shelter for the rest of the week.

We ate a late lunch sitting on the edge of the shelter floor, gazing east to New Hampshire's White Mountains. The view was mesmerizing. Sandy seemed OK with the choice to stop there, as we set out our wet tents and rainflies to dry in the sunny breeze. We wouldn't have had the time to dry things out if we'd pushed on to Taylor.

Day hikers stopped for a break as we finished our lunch. A dad with two children were hiking from Route 108 to Bolton Notch Road. They were hiking in a single day the distance we hoped to cover in four or five. When they arrived at Puffer, perspiration was dripping from Dad's nose and the young man flopped down to drink from his water bottle. The girl looked fresh, like she'd just begun her day. She never sat down, removed her pack, drank water, or had a snack. She stood waiting for the guys to catch their breath and get their packs back on.

They'd begun a Long Trail thru-hike at the Massachusetts border, and when the trail became difficult, they decided to finish in day hikes. After they left, I was distracted from our fabulous vista by a flock of admiral butterflies, hovering inches from my feet. They flitted on the plants in front of the shelter like they were trying to entertain me.

Sandy was already asleep, snoring before her head hit her sleeping bag. How does she do that? I lay on my sleeping mat watching the butterflies and gaping at our overlook until I dropped off. When I woke, the scene had changed. The afternoon light transformed the vista, like dimming the lights on a theater set.

Sitting up, legs dangling off the sleeping deck, I made my journal entry. A sound that I knew but rarely heard pulled me from my writing. I looked up to see a crow flying at eye level a few yards away—I could see into his eyes. The sound of his wings moving against the wind was soft, like bare feet on a plush rug. The first time I heard the flight of a bird in a dense Michigan forest, I was amazed by the sound of wings on the wind. I'd assumed that I would look up to see a huge bird, an eagle or at least a hawk, and laughed in surprise at seeing a robin flitting by.

Hearing feathers singing on the wind is one of the things that draw me to the wilderness. Hearing the flight of a bird is a gift that does not come to you in the average backyard or park. It requires that you get away from all other sounds, sit quietly, and hear the forest.

Our northern vista was of Mount Mansfield. "We'll be walking over your summit in a few days," I told the mountain.

"You're talking to yourself out loud again." I hadn't realized that Sandy was awake.

"If you heard me, then I wasn't talking to myself."

"You were talking to a mountain." Sandy was sitting up.

"If the mountain answers, *then* we have something to worry about."

We discussed the next day's hike. The hike to Taylor Lodge was only 3.4 miles and that seemed short, even for me. The trail description sounded difficult, but the thought of hiking less than four miles in a day just felt lame. If we decided to go on to the Twin Brook Tenting Area, it would mean a two-mile hike to Butler Lodge the following day, or eight tough miles over the highest mountain in Vermont. I knew we'd want to spend time at the Mansfield summit, so that would mean an eleven or twelve hour day. We studied the map, trying to decide on a plan for the days ahead.

Sandy stayed in the shelter while I found a spot behind the building to set up my tent. I didn't know if other hikers would show up, but even if we were alone I preferred my tent.

The morning light was just a hint when I dragged my sleeping bag and mat to the shelter to watch the sun crest the White Mountains. Sandy was the lone shelter resident and she was asleep when I set myself up to watch and take pictures of a sunrise pouring over our panorama.

The low areas were filled with fog that appeared to be crawling along every depression, hunting for something. The early hints of light gave new life to the foggy dells. I was watching sea monsters moving through gorges beneath the surface of an expanse of water that flowed from my bird's-eye view to the wakening horizon. I was snorkeling and seeing an ocean floor that was four thousand feet deep.

The sun lifted itself above the Whites and the alteration in light changed the color and consistency of the sea monsters on the ocean floor, rising up in one area to dive deep into another. The sun not only changed their colors, it eventually caused my mammoth sea creatures to dissolve. Could that be how the Loch Ness monster eludes human eyes? Does she vanish? Is she a she, or a he? Nessie sounds like a she to me. The magic ebbed while we ate breakfast.

CHAPTER THIRTY

IT IS WHAT IT IS

One step at a time is good walking.
Chinese Proverb

The hike to Taylor Lodge was dismal; to hike less than four miles in a day seemed ridiculous, but it happened. I could tell that Sandy was disappointed. When I asked how she felt, she said, "It is what it is." I understand that to be a Buddhist tenet, but I interpreted her comment as far from positive.

I'd allowed the trail description to affect me. When I'd read the words "drop steeply over rugged terrain" followed by "descend through challenging ledges" to describe the route between Puffer and Taylor, I'd been daunted. Perhaps I shouldn't have read the guidebook at all, and allowed myself to be surprised. But that didn't seem wise either. Maybe I should have put on my big girl boots and walked.

We'd hiked down steep ledges with dense forest edging both sides. The rock was what you had to walk on, and in slippery places I'd scooted. There were moments when I felt like a child, holding a branch in my right hand to slide to the next branch that would allow me to slide again. I considered letting go and putting my hands up to squeal down a stone slide, but I didn't know how fast I would go or how I would stop. I scooted, wiggled, and pushed myself along until I found ground I could stand on. Sandy and I were both moving deliberately, but her long legs could reach steps that eluded me.

From Taylor Lodge, we thought about continuing on for the two miles to Twin Brooks Tenting Area, but I thought that would leave us too short a day to Butler, less than two miles, and too long a day over Mansfield to the Taft Lodge. So I settled for the shortest day of my distance-hiking career and hoped Sandy wasn't feeling suicidal or murderous.

I lay in my tent that night, thinking it would be a shame to summit Mansfield in the rain that was forecast to start after 4 p.m. the next day. I looked at the map, read the guidebook, and decided that if we started early, we could make the seven rugged miles over Mansfield to Taft Lodge the next day. It would be tough, but worth the effort to summit Mansfield in good weather. I decided to wake Sandy early to see if she agreed. As soon as I made that decision, I rolled over and got the best night's sleep I'd had since we began this stretch of the hike.

I came out of my tent at 5 a.m. as Sandy was returning from the privy. We talked briefly and were in agreement about getting to Taft that day. Moving quickly through our morning routine, we were on the trail by 6. If we made it to Butler by ten thirty, we could gawk at Mansfield's summit and make it to Taft before dark.

The sun was shining as we headed for Twin Brooks. The walk was easy by Long Trail standards and I was feeling good about our time. Based on our change of plan, getting to the tenting area the day before would have been a wise move. Hindsight can be cruel.

We slowed down heading to Butler and I'm not sure why. I had to butt-scoot in a few places, but the going was only slightly rougher than it had been to Twin Brooks. Even so, we arrived at Butler before 10 a.m., ahead of my 10:30 goal. We restocked our water, just in case, and set off for Mount Mansfield under sunny skies.

Sandy and I separated at the Forehead Bypass. The main trail leading up to the Forehead is described as "a steep rough climb over rocks and ledges, using ladders in some places." The Forehead Bypass is described as "the less exposed route to the summit in bad weather. It is also a better route for people with a fear of heights and for pets." That was all I needed to hear, but Sandy stayed on the true Long Trail, not taking the wimpy alternate route.

It had been sunny all morning, but as we began to ascend Mansfield, the rain moved in. The ledges I'd scooted down on Bolton Mountain the day before had been challenging, but moving up the same type of ledge soaked with rain created a new test— I couldn't butt-scoot up. The forested edge of a greasy gray slide was the only path available. If I started falling down that slide, I could build up some speed in the ten or fifteen yards I would cover before a bend in the trail would stop me. It wouldn't kill me, but it might make me wish I were dead.

I double-checked each handhold and tested every foothold before stepping forward. The forest was dense, with no alternate paths beyond the ledge. Tree branches poked and sometimes barred my forward progress like a bouncer's thick, folded arms. Moving to the opposite side of the ledge was *not* an option; the rock was too wide and slippery to cross safely.

Rain mixed with perspiration dripped from my hat brim. Branches blocked every avenue. The bouncer was winning. There had to be some way to keep moving—others had done it. With a solid hold on a sad hemlock, I tried a piece of stone that looked like it would work, but my foot slipped away and that hemlock became my best friend. I eased back a step, saw a soft mossy mass beneath the trees, and decided to crawl into that inviting space and make my way up to the next foothold at a crawl.

The moss was kind to my knees and I wished I had time to examine the ecosystem that lay in miniature beneath me. I was crawling between the bouncer's legs, feeling successful, when he noticed and dropped a dead tree across my path. I pressed it down, but it would not bow. I tried to stand to climb over it, but overhead branches (the bouncer's arms) held me in a crouch. I scrambled across the dead tree, but was forced to my knees again before inching to an opening along the ledge. That entire maneuver had gained me less than four feet of trail, but I felt like I'd secured access to the exclusive night club.

I was continuing at a one-step-at-a-time pace when my water bottle popped out of its pocket. I caught a glimpse of white as it came to rest on the moss at my feet. Grabbing the bottle, I eased to the next spot that would allow me to stand firmly. I couldn't reach the pocket the bottle had fallen from and couldn't remove my pack, so I loosened my pack belt, slid the bottle between my body and the belt, and tightened it snugly.

A few steps later, the bottle began to slip again, but I caught it before it hit the ground. The web strap on my belt caught my eye and I pushed the strap through the bottle's top loop. The strap was short and stiff, and I found myself talking to it, and not nicely.

With the bottle secured, I began to move handhold-to-handhold, foothold-to-foothold. I was gaining ground when I heard someone coming. Sandy was inching up behind me. She said that she was on open rock when the rain started, so she decided that the bad-weather approach was a better choice after all.

We found a dot of soil with enough space for both of us to stand. When I stopped to let Sandy pass, I asked her to put my water bottle back in its pocket. She waited while I struggled to untie the bottle from the uncompromising belt. This time, I didn't aim any foul language at the helpless strap; swearing at inanimate objects seems less sane when witnessed.

With everything firmly stowed, we inched upward. Sandy had just stepped out of sight when my left foot shot out from under me and my body turned, pulling my right arm from its tree branch. I was facing downhill on a steep slide when my hips slammed to the ground. I was sitting on the slide, my left arm grasping for a branch. Facing downhill on slippery rock, holding myself in place with one hand, I found my predicament almost laughable. Another branch had hooked itself into my backpack— or was it my pocket? Whatever it was, I was stuck. I tried to push myself up with my feet, but the rippled wet rock was like an oiled washboard.

I had nothing to grasp with my right hand. Gouging my nails into the stone did nothing. I pulled again with my left arm, but the grabby branch was in fact caught on my back pocket. I wondered if it was ripped and decided that I didn't care. I just wanted it to let go of me. I called out: "Sandy, I'm stuck!"

No response. What was she going to do, anyway, march down here and pick me up?

I clung to my handhold and rocked my hips. Nothing! Rocking more severely, to hell with the pocket, I felt the branch let go and pulled myself close enough to the mossy edge to right myself.

"Sandy, I'm heading your way." I wasn't sure if she could hear me.

"I didn't know how I was going to be able to help." She wasn't as far ahead as I'd thought.

We fumbled along the ledge until we came to a place where we could walk. We were nearing the summit; there was a difference in the air as the clouds moved off.

"We may have a view after all," I said. I wanted Sandy to get that view.

Every time I thought we were through with the ledge, it reappeared. When we walked onto a road, Sandy threw her arms up and I did a little dance. Like Killington, there were towers for TV, radio, and cell phones and there was a metal building humming with energy.

We walked roads and easy paths from the Forehead to the Nose, to the Chin and the best view. One moment we had a view, the next we didn't. We moved faster, trying to stay ahead of the rain. Sandy paused to take pictures when the clouds cleared, and I kept hoping for a 360-view on the open Chin.

Passing the Frenchman's Pile, a cairn erected to mark the spot where a French hiker had been killed by lightning, we were shrouded in dense cloud. There was little danger of lightning, but the clouds were thick and the rain intermittent.

At the Chin, the rain dropped onto us in earnest, the wind picked up, and we crouched among the rocks on the highest point in Vermont. There was no view, so we began our descent. Sandy had missed that stunning view after working so hard to get there. Don and I had day-hiked Mansfield on a lovely day, so I knew what she was missing.

The rocks Sandy and I were negotiating were irregular formations common on a summit, but thankfully, they were not slippery. We stepped from a surface sloping east to one sloping south to another sloping more severely west. The wind whipped at our rain jackets, our sticks clicked against the stone, and our feet found solid holds on each new tilted plane.

Sandy was leading when we came to a deep V among massive rock formations. The rock on the right side formed a wall straight and smooth, like a building tipped on its side. The left side was more slanted and just as smooth. There was a jumble of smaller stones in the cleft of the V and our white blazes were painted next to that groove. Sandy scooted down the cleft and came to a stop. She stretched and turned and then did it again. "I can't reach a step and can't find a handgrip."

"If you can't make that reach, I'm doomed."

Sandy removed her pack and handed it up to me. She scooted, then flipped onto her stomach, searching for a foothold. Her expression suddenly changed. "Got it."

"Now it's my turn." I slid her pack down to her and handed her mine. Then I scooted down to the point that had stopped her. I was about to flip to my stomach and reach for the next step when Sandy set her foot on her pack, allowing me to use her knee as a step. When my boots landed on the ground, I said, "Sandy I don't know what your problem is, that was easy."

"Next time you go first."

Getting to the top is optional. Getting down is mandatory.

Ed Viesturs[19]

In the next few miles, we found ourselves on level paths followed by the kind of wet ledge we'd experienced on the other side of the mountain. The ledge was slippery, but scooting down a greasy slide was easier than crawling up. The forested edges were helpful and we were quickly on level path again. At Taft Lodge we reviewed our options.

Sandy looked at the weather prediction on her phone and saw a forecast of rain for the rest of the day and much of the following. We decided to head for Route 108. It was 1.7 miles and all downhill, we hoped. It rained off and on as we reached a long area of rocky path followed by ledge, the path continuing back and forth from rock to ledge, until we could hear the cars on Route 108. A normal, rough trail appeared and a brightening sky made us feel like we were hiking again.

We called Audrey and asked her to pick us up in the morning. It would be a long drive for her and a lot to ask her to come get us that night. A fellow hiker named Willow had passed us on the summit and said there was a state park eight-tenths of a mile east of the LT/108 junction, so when we got to the road, we headed east. We were walking along smooth road, but it was uphill and we were getting tired. Sandy looked over her shoulder. "We've walked more than a mile already. I hope this park actually exists."

"Oh, don't say that. Willow talked like she knew."

"She also said eight-tenths of a mile, and we know that's not right."

I, too, was beginning to wonder if the park existed when we finally got to the entrance. We continued uphill into the park. It was more than eight-tenths of a mile from the road to the office.

The park employees were accustomed to LT hikers. They knew we were tired and gave us the closest campsite available. Sandy asked, "How far is it to the LT from here?"

"From the office to the trailhead is 3.1 miles." He'd answered that question before.

Our next priority was to walk to the nearby restroom—with flushing toilets—and use the quarters we'd gotten from the park ranger to take a shower. While Sandy took her shower, I looked through my stuff sack for the cleanest clothes I had. I ended up with unused rain pants and a shirt that didn't smell quite as bad as the one I was wearing.

Sandy walked out announcing, "That's the cleanest shower I've seen at a park."

The warm water created a stinging pain at the small of my back. I reached around and found the skin oozing in an area about the size and shape of a football. That hadn't happened before. When I'd put on my pack that morning, I could feel a little bulge at the very spot that was now slightly raw. I should have stopped and fixed the problem as soon as I noticed it: another lesson learned the hard way.

We'd walked for thirteen hours, twelve of them on the actual trail, but I was not hungry, just thirsty. We sat at our picnic table, heating up drinks and food by headlamp. Getting into my tent after my shower, I said, "Sandy, my tent stinks."

"Mine, too. There must be a skunk around here."

I pulled out my guidebook and reread the brief description of the bypass trail we'd taken up Mount Mansfield.

"What are you laughing at?" Sandy had heard me.

"Do you want to hear the guide's description of the bypass trail?"

I heard a grunt and assumed that was a yes. "Here it is: 'Although recommended in severe weather conditions, it, too, is rough and slippery when wet.'"

The dry response from Sandy's tent: "Really?"

I usually make my journal entry when I retire to my tent, but I was too tired to even think about sitting up one minute longer. I fell asleep quickly and woke a few hours later to the sound of rain.

CHAPTER THIRTY-ONE

ARACHNID RESEARCH

In all things of nature
there is something of the marvelous.
Aristotle

The sun was up, but rain still pelted our tents. Without leaving my tent, I heated some water for hot cocoa and ate a breakfast bar.

"I'm glad we're not hiking in this." Sandy's voice floated from her tent. "According to my phone the weather for the next few days is going to be great."

"Perfect." In order for Sandy to cover the sections of trail that I'd solo-hiked, we were taking separate routes the next day, so I was looking over my map as I spoke. "In two days, you should be able to cover the parts of the trail I walked on my sad solo hikes. Tomorrow, I can drop you at Hedgehog Brook, drive to the Monroe Trail, and meet you at Montclair Glen."

"Since I hike faster, shouldn't I drop you off?" Sandy was probably looking at her map.

"No way, you're doing Burnt Rock—that'll slow you down. My hikes will be easier and shorter on both days."

"The next day, I'm hiking up Bamforth Ridge to the top of Camel's Hump, right?" Sandy could see how steep Bamforth looked on the map.

"Yep. You said you'd rather go up that ridge than down. I'm glad you won't be doing it in the rain." Memories of my near-fall were still fresh. "I'll be waiting for you on Camel's Hump and we'll walk back on the Monroe together."

"We're ending both days in the same parking lot?" Maybe she didn't have her map out.

"To Montclair Glen, I'm hiking the Monroe Trail to the Dean Trail to the LT to Montclair. We'll walk back on the same path. On Camel's Hump, it's the Monroe almost to the summit, rock scramble on the LT to the top, and then back to the car. Both days, you're doing the hard part and I'm going for a walk."

I heard her map unfold and she was quiet for a few minutes. "I'm doing a lot more miles than you."

"That was my plan. In two day-hikes, you'll cover what I did on my solo hikes and we will both have completed the Long Trail from the Massachusetts border to Route 108."

All was quiet from Sandy's tent. I thought she was still looking over her map when I heard snoring. How does she do that?

I started my journal entry.

When my composition task was complete, I heard Sandy rustling around in her tent, so I asked, "When do you think Audrey will arrive?"

"She said she'd call from Waterbury. That should give us time to break camp and be ready."

I was getting bored, so I put everything I could into my pack to be ready to move quickly when Audrey called. I lay back on my sleeping bag and noticed that the sky was becoming brighter and the rain was letting up. I saw a daddy longlegs clinging to my tent wall and, out of boredom, I slowly moved my finger against the fabric toward the spider. It didn't move. I circled it with my finger, pressing against the wall it clung to, but it did not respond. I slowly moved my finger closer and closer until it came to one of the spider's legs. It pulled that leg up but still did not move; when I moved away the leg came back down. I moved my finger to another leg and got the same response. I shared this interesting information with Sandy, who said, "Stop tormenting the wildlife."

Then I spotted a slug moving up the outside of my tent, about eight inches from the ground. I performed the same experiment, and as my finger got close, its antennae retracted. I shared this with Sandy, who responded, "I didn't think you were into animal cruelty."

"This isn't cruelty. It's research."

"That's what Dow and Monsanto used to say."

"No animal was harmed during this research."

"I think they said that, too."

I repeated my experiment. No matter which direction I approached the slug from, it retracted its antennae from the same distance. "I can't sneak up on this guy." Sandy laughed. I think she was reading. The slug eventually decided to return to the ground; I was getting in the way of wherever it thought it was going.

I saw another daddy longlegs and tried my experiment again, but it didn't respond at all. I could move my finger all around it—up under its legs, directly under its body, and it did not react. I reported this news to Sandy, who did not respond. Was she sleeping or getting tired of my commentary? I looked around and saw many spiders, all daddy longlegs. Most of them were slightly larger than a quarter, body and legs. But, in one area, there were seven that were the size of a dime. "Sandy, it's training day for the spider family."

I heard a groan but couldn't stop: "There are seven little baby spiders over here. They are so cute and they don't seem to mind me moving around them at all. I wonder why that first one reacted and I wonder which one it was. There are so many now."

Silence from the other tent. "Wait a minute, there is one here that is bigger than the rest. This must be Dad. Hey big guy, you have a nice-looking family. I wonder if my hand moving toward you will make you move, or are you a tough guy?"

Another moan from Sandy's tent.

"Now, Sandy, I know you find this fascinating." No response.

"Is my boredom boring you?"

I heard her phone ring. "They're at the park entrance," she said.

We went into action. When I crawled from my tent, I had a cramp in my left calf, my right thigh was stiff, and my oozing back was stuck to my shirt. But I didn't care because the rain had stopped. We got our tents down and packed, with care taken to gently shake off young and old daddy longlegs. We were at the truck and stowing our gear when the sun came out. In the light, I noticed scrapes on my left leg and dried blood from a scrape on my right hand, but I didn't know how or when they'd occurred.

Audrey and her daughter Jill watched us throw all our gear in the back of the truck like it was a timed contest.

We told Audrey, "We got to take showers last night."

"I am ready for you. I have plastic sheeting, towels, and Fig Newtons."

Audrey knew how to greet distance hikers. We were lulled by the sunshine and the movement of the truck while we described where we'd been and what we'd seen.

"Do you two want to stop and get something to eat?" Audrey had heard us talk about how tired we got of trail food.

Sandy was asleep so I answered for both of us. "No, a few Fig Newtons will hold us until we get home. Our traditional post-hike meal is at the Long Trail Brewery."

Audrey and Jill were smiling. Sandy was awake again and Jill told us that she'd had surgery just a day or two before. We heard all of this, but were drifting in and out of sleep and it wasn't until we were nearly home that we were both fully awake and realized that Jill was becoming uncomfortable.

I was glad we'd declined the offer to stop for food. I didn't want Jill to take an extra minute getting home; every bump seemed to cause her pain. We were relieved when Jill got to her mother's house and could call her doctor to ask questions about the amount and type of pain she was experiencing. Audrey dropped us off and we thanked her profusely, giving her money for gas and sending well-wishes to Jill before Audrey hurried back to tend to her daughter.

Sandy and I began our post-hike routine. With our gear displayed in the sunshine, we cleaned up before heading for the brewery. At the table, we took out maps and discussed our next two days of serious day-hiking. My feeble solo hikes had messed up our hiking coordination and Sandy had to get over Camel's Hump and down Bamforth Ridge on her own.

We weren't going to review our hike, because it wasn't over yet.

CHAPTER THIRTY-TWO

HUMMINGBIRD

My heart leaps up when I behold
A rainbow in the sky:
So was it when my life began;
So is it now I am a man;
So be it when I shall grow old,
Or let me die!
William Wordsworth, "My Heart Leaps Up"

I dropped Sandy off at the Hedgehog Brook trailhead at 11 a.m. Sandy was picking up the Burnt Rock Mountain section that had hammered me so hard. I dawdled at the Monroe trailhead because I had a short easy hike and knew I'd have to wait for Sandy. The Monroe and Dean Trails were a pleasant stretch of the legs and it allowed me to get onto a couple of trails that I hadn't traveled before.

When I arrived at the Montclair Glen Shelter, Sandy had not yet arrived, so I sat down to read and wait. While I waited, I met the youngest thru-hiker I'd encountered. Hummingbird was a ten-year-old girl who'd been on the trail with her father, Goose, for thirteen days.

Hummingbird was not a poser. She was walking the walk, carrying a twenty-pound pack, wielding a pair of little trekking poles, and muddying-up her hiking boots. When I arrived at Montclair, she was returning from the water source humming a tune from *Annie*, having restocked their water bottles. We talked about her hiking experience, her age, and her school and when that conversation wound down she got out a book and sat on a boulder, immersed in *The Indian in the Cupboard*. I noticed her lips moving slightly, much as mine had at her age. It made me smile to see how comfortable she was with her place in the wilderness.

They said that "Mom" meets them at road crossings, so they don't have to carry much food, and I thought it probably also gave Mom a chance to make sure her daughter was still alive. Hummingbird set her book aside and was toying with a small box of candy.

"You should wait until after dinner for the chocolate." Goose spoke from the porch steps. "You are going to share with your dear old Dad, aren't you?"

"She brought you beer. The candy is for me." Hummingbird eyed the box, opened it, looked inside, then closed it and set it aside for later. I was sure she would share with Dad.

I was beginning to worry about Sandy. Had we crossed paths somehow, or was she having trouble? Another pair of hikers came in—a mother and daughter doing the LT in sections. When I voiced concern about Sandy, everyone agreed that one mile an hour was all that should be expected on Burnt Rock Mountain, so I sat back and waited. "According to the sign, the Monroe trailhead gates close at dark," I said, looking down the trail.

"No one is going to lock your car in," Goose declared with confidence.

I leaned back and tried to relax. "So you think it's an idle threat? I guess we have plenty of time. It doesn't get dark until eight, right?"

Shortly after that conversation, Sandy walked into camp. She'd covered 6.2 miles in six hours. Everyone agreed that Burnt Rock Mountain was brutal and we were glad to have that done. By the time Sandy and I were ready to head back to the car, Hummingbird had hung her socks on a line to dry, put on her pajamas, and was playing cards with Goose.

"They will remember these magic moments for years to come," I told Sandy as we walked away.

The walk down was easy, a stretch for Sandy's legs after a tough morning. We didn't talk much, even though there were no difficult rock areas between us and the car. The downhill proceeded with ease.

I touched base with Don and Audrey when we got back to our house, to tell them how our day had gone and where we were going to be hiking the next day. I was glad to hear that Jill was feeling better.

We took showers but did not eat dinner or even snacks before going to bed. I understood why Sandy was tired, but I'd barely walked four easy miles—I should have been fresh as a daisy, but I passed on dinner and went to bed early, just the same. I would have liked to reflect on our day, but Hummingbird's voice in my head got in just a few bars from *Annie* before I was out.

CHAPTER THIRTY-THREE

A STAR AMONG THE STARS

One touch of nature makes the whole world kin...
William Shakespeare "Troilus and Cressida"

The day was clear when Sandy started up Bamforth Ridge to the Camel's Hump summit. I planned to return to the Monroe Trail and we'd meet on Camel's Hump. Sandy's day would be 9.6 miles, much of it very steep; mine 7.8 miles up and down on the easiest access to Camel's Hump. I added a few miles to my day by hiking in with Sandy for an hour or so, to ensure I wouldn't get to the summit too early.

I dawdled at the Monroe Trail parking area, photographing the stone memorial commemorating a military plane that came down on Camel's Hump during a World War II training mission. Nine airmen lost their lives that day; James W. Wilson, gunner, was the sole survivor. I wondered how badly he'd been injured. In her book, *Unbroken*, Laura Hillenbrand indicated that there were more deaths and injuries on flight-training missions during World War II than occurred in the actual fighting. I was looking at a memorial that backed her claim.

I'd read that Mr. and Mrs. Monroe, for whom the trail was named, had a family cemetery near the parking area where they were buried, along with some of their dogs. At first sight I thought the commemorative plaque I'd found about the airmen had been their gravesite. When I walked back to the parking area to look for the family's cemetery, I discovered a path marked with a not-terribly-inviting wooden sign on a single wooden post: Monroe

Cemetery – No Toilet.

Katherine and Will Monroe must have loved their dogs, because there were seven headstones representing their pets. I thought about the two of them walking around the property they called Couching Lion Farm to select just the right location for their memorial. I imagined Will in a brown tweed jacket with elbow patches, a fedora on his head. I saw Katherine with dark hair in a stylish bob. She wore a green A-line skirt with a crisp white blouse. I pictured them burying Scottie, "a star among the stars," knowing that he would lie between them when their bodies were brought there for the last time.

The dogs' headstones bore words like: beloved, noble, devoted, worthy, and the one that made me smile, the jolly collie. What a lovely way to commemorate the life they'd shared with their animals.

After sufficient dawdling, I started for the summit. I watched a couple setting out ahead of me as I put on my boots, and passed them a short way into the hike when they stopped to listen to songbirds. When I got to the Monroe/Dean Trail junction, I met a couple from Indiana who were heading for the summit. He seemed gung-ho, but she was a little hesitant. I assured them that the view would be worth the effort. I kept my concern about their choice of footwear (sandals) to myself. They were already on their way, anyhow.

The Monroe Trail began easy and became more difficult as it neared the summit. I was perspiring heavily, which was no surprise, but I was struggling more than I should have been. What was going on? I could feel the summit getting closer when I *hit the wall.*

I *HAD* to stop, rest, eat a Clif Bar, and I had to do it *RIGHT NOW.* I'd been drinking plenty of water and had taken a brief break earlier, but I was stopped cold. The older couple that I'd passed near the parking area marched past me without a problem.

I was sapped on a dry, uncomplicated trail—what was wrong?

Then I remembered that neither Sandy nor I had eaten the night before. We'd purchased breakfast sandwiches at the Corners Store that morning, but that was all we'd eaten since a lunch of GORP and bars the day before. Our last real meal had been Thursday's breakfast. I was running on next to nothing; knowing that was reassuring. After a break, a bar, and some water, I was ready to head for the peak. I marched the last rocky miles without incident.

When I arrived at the summit, I looked for Sandy but didn't expect to see her for another hour. I sat down in the brilliant sunshine, basking in the fabulous view, ate some GORP and drank more water. Goose and Hummingbird sat down next to me to say hello. They'd removed their packs, shoes, and socks and were taking their lunch break. We chatted for a bit, and they told me they were heading to Bamforth Ridge for the night. I told them I was waiting for Sandy again. When they set off under full packs, Hummingbird looked like the perfect example of a miniature hiker.

I was a little bored and lay on my stomach looking closely at the tiny alpine plants among the rocks. On my snowshoe visit, there'd been no indication that these tiny living things existed under the mounds of snow and ice.

> *I like it when a flower or a little tuft of grass*
> *grows through a crack in the concrete.*
> *It's so fuckin' heroic.*

George Carlin

I decided to wait where I was until 3 p.m., which would be a pace of one mile an hour up the ridge for Sandy, and then I'd seek a shadier place to wait. There were plenty of trees just north of the summit, where a hotel once stood. From there, I'd see Sandy when she walked by. I was worried about how little she'd eaten before climbing Bamforth Ridge and wondered if she might be struggling. But when she arrived she was doing fine.

We chatted, ate, drank lots of water, and took a few pictures. The couple from Indiana walked up and the wife held her arms out, "I made it." After the four of us talked for a few minutes, I shared my doubts about hiking in sandals. My Indiana friend said, "We always hike in these." But I noticed she had blisters on both feet. Did she know she could hike without getting blisters?

Sandy and I were ready to head down, so we said goodbye. We'd not yet reached the Dean Trail when Sandy said, "This 3.4 miles of downhill seems endless."

She was tired.

On the way home, we ordered pizza, garlic knots, and a Greek salad. We went from no dinner one night, to more food than we could eat the next. Over dinner, we decided to make the next day easy. We would rent tubes and float down the White River for a few hours of effortless fun.

We were both tired and our bellies were full when we reviewed our hiking week. Sandy had hiked over forty-two miles and I'd done about thirty. We'd both completed every foot of the Long Trail from the Massachusetts border to Route 108, and were ready to head north from 108 the following year.

Sandy had picked up my pack at Puffer Shelter and said, "What're you carrying in here, bricks? Your pack is much heavier than mine."

I lifted both packs, and she was right, her pack was significantly lighter than mine. "Perhaps I should have left the anvil at home."

When we returned from our leisurely tube down the river, we got out our gear and went over every item. We weighed everything and removed three pounds from my pack. My empty pack weighed more than Sandy's. My tent weighted more than Sandy's, my sleeping bag was a few ounces heavier, and my sleeping mat was two ounces heavier. That adds up.

Sandy thought we could share a single water purifier, stove, fuel, and first-aid kit. She mentioned sharing a single tent but I said I'd rather carry the weight. I like being in my personal space and I sleep best sprawled out. I'd seen a couple of tents in Backpacker Magazine that were a bit lighter. A lighter tent could shave another two pounds from my gear. But I still carry too much food.

CHAPTER THIRTY-FOUR

SLOW BUT STEADY

Away from the tumult of motor and mill
I want to be care-free; I want to be still!
I'm weary of doing things; weary of words
I want to be one with the blossoms and birds.
Edgar A. Guest

As I shoveled the mid-January snow from our sidewalk, I thought of giving Sandy a call to see if she still wanted to hike this summer. When I walked into the house, the phone was ringing—it was Sandy with the same question. Two days later we met for lunch; we set hiking dates, looked over maps and began to get excited about a hike that was more than six months away. I couldn't help but wonder how I could get so wound up when I knew what kind of problems could be waiting?

I carried my old and new tents into the restaurant, eager to show Sandy how much smaller and lighter my new tent was. I'd lightened my pack by 6.3 pounds by getting a new pack, an Osprey Aura 50, and a new tent, a Big Agnes Fly Creek.

The first time I put up my new tent it took almost an hour; my learning curve on the Big Agnes was steep. On my second night out I was able to accomplish the same task in less than fifteen minutes, almost matching Sandy's pace. I'm constantly trying to keep up with her.

Sandy's flight came in without a hitch, it was not late, it did not rain, my car knew the way to the airport, and we were at my house for an early dinner.

We pored over maps and weighed our laden packs. This time, mine was three pounds lighter than Sandy's.

Early the next morning, I lay in bed listening to the rain and smiling into the darkness. The rain seemed like a sign that it was time to hike. At seven o'clock we threw our packs in the back of our blue Ford Explorer and Don drove us to Smuggler's Notch.

The rain had stopped but still threatened as we signed in at the trailhead wearing full rain gear. But it didn't rain again and the trail was dryer than we'd expected. The climb out of Smuggler's Notch was typical, with some tough areas of rock scramble. We stopped at Sterling Pond Shelter for lunch, four miles into our day, knowing we'd be pushing on to the Whiteface Shelter. There were a lot of people at Sterling Pond celebrating the Fourth of July weekend, but there was no one at the shelter where we ate and used the privy.

Sandy took a hard fall early in the day. She was using a small tree along an area of rock ledge to pull herself up, when the tree gave way and she landed in an awkward heap. She managed to hold onto the tree, which fell between her and the rocky surface, softening her landing and keeping her from sliding down the wet ledge. The little spruce had, at once, turned on her and saved her.

Hiking Madonna Peak was a struggle, but when we got to the summit, the clouds disappeared for a lovely view. As we began our descent, climbing backward much of the time, the clouds reappeared. We put down 7.8 miles on our first day and I was pleasantly tired.

By the time we got to the Whiteface Shelter the sky was clear. We ate dinner looking south to Mount Mansfield, where billowy clouds floated over its summit. I pointed south to the imposing mountain range. "We did that."

Sandy pointed north to the mountains waiting for us. "And we've got that left to do."

"I prefer to look back at what we've done at the end of the day. I'll look in the other direction in the morning."

Sandy's eyes scanned the southern horizon. "We are impressive, aren't we?"

"Aren't we just?"

Over dinner we planned to get to Roundtop the next day. It would be 10.8 miles, some of it on roads or logging trails; however, we knew the map could make the going look easier than it was. But the closest shelter, Bear Hollow, was 3.6 miles away and that seemed like a very short day. Perhaps we could cowboy somewhere between Bear Hollow and Roundtop.

Descending Madonna had been difficult, but moving down Whiteface was worse. Our new plan was to hike shelter-to-shelter due to the difficulty of the trail. We were both having trouble reaching handholds and footrests.

On Whiteface, even the small PUDs were challenging. In several areas, I couldn't reach up to the next level with my foot and had to kneel on the rock to pull myself up, crawling to a spot where I could again stand.

I climbed onto one such rock and got stuck. After crawling as far as I could, I found nothing to hold onto. I'd wriggled myself into a muddy trap. I couldn't pull myself to a standing position because of overhead branches, and I couldn't reach the handhold that taunted me, just out of reach. I knelt on inflexible rock, wondering if I'd have to climb down to find another route. My knees were already scraped and bleeding from earlier rock crawls, and I winced as I inched forward, trying to stretch to that elusive handhold.

Finally, I flipped over and sat on the muddy rock for a brief break, laughing out loud thinking about how my youthful walks had rid me of anger and pain. Looking at my muddy boots, I said, "Feet don't fail me now."

"Are you OK?" Sandy had heard me laughing and talking to my boots.

Hands splashing in the mud, I said, "I'm just great. I was thinking about making mud pies for lunch."

"I prefer cream pies, maybe lemon meringue." Sandy's voice was moving away, so I flipped back to my knees, looking for the handhold that had to be there somewhere. I spotted a scruffy, crooked pine tree and wriggled toward it, hoping it was solid. After testing to be sure it wouldn't fail me, I pulled myself to a standing position and inched along the mossy forest edge.

It took four hours to walk the 3.6 miles to Bear Hollow Shelter. I was glad to hear Sandy say, "I think we should stop here for the night."

In the Bear Hollow logbook, almost every entry mentioned how brutal Whiteface had been. We were the only people at the shelter that night, and there was no tenting area. We collapsed for a nap and as I sat making my journal entry, I heard Sandy deep in sleep. How could I be this leg-weary and yet unable to sleep?

I did fall asleep finally, and it must have been a sound sleep, because when I woke there was a father-daughter team setting up their sleeping mats and bags on the other side of the shelter. I usually wake up easily, but they'd been there for some time. Sandy continued to sleep while I talked to our roomies and discovered that they were section-hiking the LT SOBO. The young lady had done part of it with her mom and now she was hiking with Dad. I pointed out that starting at the Canadian border meant they were doing the most difficult part of the trail first and it might have been easier to start in the other direction. They'd heard that advice before, but they were already into their plan.

The mosquito problem at Bear Hollow, mentioned repeatedly in the shelter log, didn't nearly describe the thousands of little bombers that kept after us all night. We sprayed ourselves before bed and still fussed and wiggled, trying to free ourselves of their constant buzzing. After an uneasy night, our roommates were up by 5:30. The mosquitoes tormented us through breakfast and we were glad to get on the trail, just to be free of them.

There were 7.4 miles of trail between Bear Hollow and Roundtop, with some roadways and logging trails that should be easy, so we were in no hurry. We lolled at the Lamoille River crossing, sitting on the rocky bank in the sun for a leisurely morning break. We took another long break at Prospect Rock, and Sandy quickly dropped off to sleep. I leaned against my pack, mesmerized by two tractors working a farmer's field in the valley below. The Lamoille flowed through the scene like a stage prop.

I saw a horse trailer on the road below our perch and wondered where they were off to: a horse show, trail ride, or veterinary clinic. Horses used to fill my life. Their care took up much of my time with lessons to teach, horses to ride, and horse shows to take students to. I felt a pang of longing, but if I were still doing that, I wouldn't have been sitting on that fabulous roost. I closed my eyes and smiled, reflecting on old memories while creating new ones.

There were five people at Roundtop when we arrived, but I think we totaled more than twelve before nightfall. We had a physics teacher, a journalist/photographer, a high school student, and two middle school teachers, among others.

Hobblebush, our high school student, was twenty-three days into his thru-hike. He got his trail name because the hobblebush viburnum's leaves were his preferred toilet tissue. I shared with him that hobblebush was my preference in leaf, as well. He said he avoided the privies, always. Several people there told him that using the privy may be better for the forest and its woodland creatures, so he walked off toward the privy with a handful of round green leaves. When he returned I asked how the privy was, and he confessed quietly that he'd looked inside and headed for the trees. It's funny how personal our conversations got on the trail, even though we'd been strangers minutes before.

Another young man, Pinconning, shared a story about being in a shelter with a seventy-three-year-old female hiker who'd declared to the shelter at large: "If you don't want to see a seventy-three-year-old naked, you'd best look away."

"Pinconning, are you from Michigan?" I was surprised by the name.

"No, my dad's from Michigan and whenever we go there, we stop in Pinconning to get . . ."

Our voices twined together: ". . . cheese."

"I had some Pinconning cheese in my pack when I started the LT and no one had heard of it. It's in every store in Michigan, but I guess it stops at the Ohio border."

JourneyList asked, "What's special about Pinconning cheese?"

Sandy and I looked at one another. We were at a loss, but Pinconning offered, "It's somewhere between cheddar, jack, and Swiss." He'd clearly answered that question before.

Three SOBO hikers, new to the trail, asked about the shelters they'd encounter and accepted advice from the NOBOs who'd been on the trail for weeks. The SOBOs told us that Laraway Lookout has a great view and we should take time to appreciate it. They strongly recommended taking the two-tenths of a mile side trip on Mount Belvidere, saying, "Drop your pack and walk out to the summit tower. You will not be sorry."

NOBOs warned the SOBOs of the difficulties on Whiteface. We told them about Prospect Rock's great view and said that the Lamoille River was a great rest or meal stop. Over dinner, we discussed cookstove choices. Packhorse shared the difficulties he was having with his alcohol-fueled stove. He was going off-trail to resupply and wanted to get a PocketRocket.

As the sun approached the horizon, a few hikers planned to sit behind the shelter to see if they could spot distant fireworks displays. I was too tired to try to stay awake that long.

> *I look at my compass*
> *and it points north.*
> *It always does.*
> *That's where I'm going,*
> *moving toward Canada.*

Walking Home

I wonder what
my compass does
tucked into my pack.
Does it twist and turn
when it lies on its side?
Does it wonder why
I don't go faster
or wish I went south
to give it a break,
a change of pace?

But why would it care?
It's a compass.
It always points north.
It knows where north is
when I fall down, when
I fall behind, when I
fall asleep.
It's my trusty compass,
it always points north.

Celia Ryker

That's what happens when I tuck a Billy Collins poetry book into my pack. My hiking book has to be small because books weigh a lot, but Billy's tiny tome packs a punch. Like any good writer, he reconnects us to ourselves. He mentions hikers and then writes of Paris and planets, poems and piano lessons. He takes us to places we've never been while reminding us of places we can never forget.

CHAPTER THIRTY-FIVE

NIGHT SKY

The wandering man knows of certain ancients, far gone in years,
who have staved off infirmities and dissolution by earnest walking.
Charles Dickens

O n day four, my back was stiff in the morning, as it often is at this point
in my life. I stretched and attempted to find relief, reminded of one of
Fay's favorite laments:

Old age sucks, and then . . . you die.

It didn't hurt much and I could usually walk it off, so I stretched a bit,
popped an Advil, and was on my way. Carrying my pack and walking was
no problem, but bending forward, even slightly, was painful. I took another
Advil at noon and again at four when we got into camp, which eased the pain
only slightly. A single capsule usually did the trick for the day, but on this day,
bending forward from the waist was agony. It was different from my usual
back pain and I wondered what sleeping in my tent would do for it.

Everything else worked so well that day, the back pain was a minor issue.
The trail wasn't as grueling and we stopped at a lovely cascade early in the day
to restock our water, as we were drinking a lot. Sitting with our feet in the
water was a pleasant break from the heat, and taking our time didn't seem to
be bothering Sandy.

At Laraway Lookout, we took another break to enjoy the view. The physics
teacher from the night before was there when we arrived and I asked him
about his personal hiking style. He didn't use trekking poles, which was

unusual but not unheard of, but he had two jackets: a raincoat and a light, quilted jacket, tied around his waist. He had a standard backpack, but he carried his food bag cradled in both arms in front of him. As we chatted about trails we'd hiked, where we lived, and what kind of food we carried, I asked, "Is there some physics law we don't understand that explains jackets tied around your waist and carrying your food like that?"

He laughed. "It's not that scientific—I just can't get all this crap into my pack."

I tipped my head. "When you go up and down the steep areas, what do you do with your food bag to free your hands?"

"The same thing you do with your poles. You have to either carry them in one hand or set them down somewhere, and that's what I do with my food bag."

He'd been asked that question before.

We walked into Corliss Shelter at 2:30, and even with all the stops to smell the spruce along the way we'd covered 8.2 miles in eight hours. The day had gone well, other than my nagging back pain. It was nice to be able to walk upright like a human for a change. I'd hoped the easy trail would help my back, but it didn't. The slightest incline forward was still painful, and in fact, it was getting worse.

I crawled on hands and knees to set my ground cloth and tent in place. Still in a kneeling position, I aligned the metal tent poles and moved to the corners to create the tension required to support my tent. I clipped my tent to the poles, barely able to reach the topmost hangers, then crawled to a tree to pull myself to standing. I set the rainfly in place, double-checking everything before dropping to the ground to inch around, securing the corners. With that chore complete, I crawled to another tree to drag myself up and leaned my sweaty body against its trunk.

The break didn't last long because I still had to restock my water supply. I carried bladder and bottles to the water pump indicated at the shelter, thinking the pump would be easier than using our water filter at a creek or pond. But I was wrong. The pump head was two feet high, which meant bending at an agonizing angle. I filled a bottle and stretched. I poured the water into the bladder and stretched again. I filled another bottle, stretched, poured, stretched, and kept this up until I'd filled my water bottles and CamelBak. I crouched to pick up my water containers, pulled myself straight with a tree branch, and hobbled back to camp.

I was nearly asleep when I noticed that one corner of my tent was sagging—I must have missed a tent stake. I wriggled painfully into the night and easily remedied the problem from my prone position. When I pulled myself across an area of rich, soft grass, I lay down to stretch. Rolling onto my back, I looked up at the stars and the image took me to a starlit night long ago.

My friend Jeff and I were nine years old and well into winter activities—ice skating on the canal and sledding on our favorite hills, when we decided to try something new. There was a long steep hill from the road to the canal and a smaller, more challenging hill on the tiny island in the canal that we liked to sled down. The hill on the island wasn't as high as the one from the road, but the ground was uneven and there were trees in the way. Jeff and I decided we should each start on opposite hills and high-five as we passed each other on the ice of the canal.

Getting the timing right took some doing. I was coming down the bigger hill and Jeff had to calculate where I was on my hill to determine when he should start down his. We tried it a few times when the other kids were around, but they became bored with our failures and went home. We tried a few more times after the others left, and were about to give up when it happened. As my sled dropped off the bank, the metal runners slammed onto the ice and I heard Jeff's sled hit the ice simultaneously. We'd done it!

My joy vanished when I realized we hadn't decided which side to high-five on. I was right-handed, Jeff was left-handed, and our trajectory was wrong. We were about to meet forehead-to-forehead.

With seconds to respond, I slammed one foot into my sled's steering lever and Jeff did the same. I turned left, Jeff turned right. We were not going to meet head-on, but we were definitely going to meet, *Right Now!*

When I regained consciousness, I was looking up at a sky much like the one I saw above my tent. It was inky black, making the stars seem brighter, and I lay there for a few moments wondering what most people wonder as they come to: "Where am I?"

The stars didn't give me a clue, so I lay there trying to figure out what happened when suddenly it hit me. Jeff—where's Jeff?

I sat up. Jeff was gone, his sled was gone, and my sled lay beside me with a few broken pieces of wood on the ice next to its bent metal front. I was alone and darkness was not approaching—it was here, deep and quiet.

I stood up, grabbed the rope on the front of what was left of my sled, and started up the hill toward the road. The snow lit my path but the dark sky pressed down on me as I got to the road, and for reasons I could not explain, I wanted to cry. I fought back tears as I walked the half block to our back door and tucked my sled next to the porch, out of sight. I didn't want to get in trouble for breaking it. I walked in the back door like nothing had happened.

Mom was at the sink and didn't look up. "Where have you been?"

I stopped, trying to think of an answer. She looked at me and dropped what she was doing. With her hands on my shoulders, eyes looking into mine, she asked, "Are you OK? What happened?"

The tears came; they'd been waiting during my walk home and they were primed to fly. I don't remember what was said or done after that, I don't remember a headache, or any pain at all, but I couldn't stop crying. I wondered if my back pain decades later could have originated on that icy canal in 1958.

The next morning when I saw Jeff at the bus stop, he was relieved to see me. "I thought you were dead." We both knew that killing someone would get you in big trouble, so he'd gone home. I understood. I probably would have done the same thing. I wasn't dead and the bus was there, so we lifted our slush-covered feet to the slush-covered step.

On the soft grass next to my tent, the starry night soothed my heart and mind, if not my back. I crawled into my warm tent and dropped off to sleep thinking of a winter night long ago.

CHAPTER THIRTY-SIX

THE MANTRA

My rainfly faded to a lighter shade of green as the sun came up, and I realized that my back was feeling better. Then I moved and discovered the truth. Getting my socks on was almost impossible.

Crawling to take down my tent was quicker and easier than putting it up had been. It was so much easier, I thought I'd be able to hike under my pack, but I was wrong. My back ached with every step. That hadn't happened before. I walked slower than usual, reciting a mantra to myself:

> Don't think about it.
> Right foot
> Do not
> Left foot
> think about it.
> Right foot
> Do not
> Left foot
> think about it.
> Right foot

That didn't take long to bore me and it wasn't working, so I changed my mantra:

> Just walk,

> look at the trees,
> take a deep breath,
> listen to the birds,
> feel your feet move
> across the ground.

My back throbbed as I tried a new mental trip:

> Walk
> look at trees
> breathe
> listen to birds
> feel your footsteps
> Walk
> look
> breathe
> listen
> feel.

By our first morning break, my back no longer hurt. Had the forest cured me or should I give some credit to the Advil and stretching exercises? But they hadn't worked when I'd been in less pain. I wasn't feeling less pain when we stopped—I was feeling NO pain. None! I couldn't believe it. After two days of agony, I felt great!

By LT standards, the day was easy. We walked over Bowen Mountain and its three peaks. It was over ninety degrees and the humidity was high. Walking in the woods, we felt the heat but when we ventured into an open area, the blistering sunshine, heavy with moisture, slapped us in the face. Fortunately, open areas were few.

Spruce Ledge Shelter's water source was at the trail turn-off. Sandy had finished pumping her water by the time I arrived, so she handed me the water filter and headed to camp. I sat on a rock and pumped water with ease. I could pick up my bottles without pain—I could straighten my legs and touch my toes.

"What a difference a day makes." I could almost hear the music coming from the green plastic radio on top of Gramma's china cabinet. I felt great.

Spruce Ledge had a picnic table under its own roof and I sat there to make my journal entry. The day was closing, the birdcalls quieter—no harsh jays or raucous crows, like the birds knew it was time to slow down. I was listening to the night approaching.

Sandy and I took a walk before dinner and found an overlook to the north. "That's Belvidere Mountain, our first summit next year," I commented. It looked like a pile of gray slag halfway up, and was huge. There must be some kind of mining going on over there, I wondered if we would walk near it.

"That is a mountain of slag, it must be a big operation. I hope we don't hike past that." Sandy had heard what I was thinking.

There was a young couple from Chicago in camp when we returned to the shelter. They were hiking the Long Trail during a break between college and their grown-up lives. They were young and healthy and traveling at the same speed we traveled. Bookworm said she was glad they'd changed their hiking plan. "We tried putting down ten-mile days, but that wasn't for us. We want to look around, see where we're going, enjoy the view, and relax in the evening playing cards and reading."

They were young and fit, and hiking at my speed—on purpose. I felt validated.

Our final day on the trail began without a hint of back pain. We had a three-mile hike to Route 118, where Don would meet us. We set out into a sunny day that promised a ride home, a shower, and real food.

Devil's Gulch was at once beautiful and daunting. Huge boulders made up the path with ample irregular spaces between them to lose trekking poles into—we were vigilant not to drop them, or anything else. We had to watch each step, some of the rocks wobbled.

I took one bad step and my boot caught between two rocks. I couldn't lift it straight up or turn it to either side. I tried every angle, but it was locked in place. I sat down to remove my boot, worried about losing it into that hole. But before I touched the laces, my foot popped out like it'd been pushed from below. I looked into the hole like I might see a hand down there. I felt like I was being watched and walked away looking over my shoulder.

We walked at the base of a cliff that was two or three stories tall and consisted of one huge rock that leaned above our path like a forest-version of the Leaning Tower of Pisa. Blazes were few and were painted on the rock path. I scooted a few times as the trail eased from nearly impossible to merely improbable.

"Who thought to make this the trail?" My voice echoed.

"Look around, where else could it go?"

We walked through a cave created by two gargantuan slabs of boulder leaning into one another. The light shone from both ends of the cave and there were tiny rays of light overhead, like rugged track-lighting.

Beyond the gulch was easy going. We stopped to enjoy the view at Ritterbush Lookout, and made it to Route 118 by 10 a.m. I'd told Don two days earlier that we'd be coming off-trail on Route 118 on the seventh at about 10. How's that for accurate?

We waited for Don on the shady side of the road. It was another hot day and sitting in the harsh sun was not a friendly option. Someone had painted huge white bigfoot-like footprints across the road, and I thought Don would easily see them as he drove up.

Sandy and I were chatting about our hike and how long it might take to finish up the following year, when I saw our car drive past and then it was gone. Don had not seen the footprints.

We picked up our gear and walked fifty yards west on 118 to the trailhead parking area on the north side of the road. Don was not there, and I wondered where he'd gone. We walked back to the road and sat near the parking area sign, keeping an eye out for a blue Explorer. I was beginning to wonder if I had seen our car or one just like it, when Don drove up from the west. When he didn't find us at the LT trailhead, he'd driven to Belvidere Pond, thinking he had time to kill before we'd be ready for him.

We were ready.

CHAPTER THIRTY-SEVEN

CANADA OR BUST

Now I see the secret of the making of the best persons,
It is to grow in the open air and to eat and sleep with the earth.
Walt Whitman, "Song of the Open Road, 6"

I arrived in Vermont a week before Sandy, to train in the mountains with Don and the dogs as my training partners. Ringer went happily to the meadow, then we'd take him back to the house—his old legs were too weak for mountain hiking. Don, Flurry, and I walked every trail on our property. I also hiked the Deer Leap and Sherburne Trails, putting down miles on relatively easy mountain paths, meeting day- and thru-hikers on each excursion. Moleskin was heading into her last five hundred miles on the AT. She had a tattoo I recognized along the inside of her forearm: a thin line with little squiggles along the way. It was a tattoo of the Appalachian Trail, with Georgia just above her wrist and Katahden below the crook of her elbow.

Sandy's plane arrived in Manchester at 10:30 p.m. I had time as I drove to reminisce about the first time I followed my GPS to that airport. There was no rain or lightening show on this drive, but I was more anxious than I'd been before our first venture onto the Long Trail. I thought about our first LT steps on the Pine Cobble Trail. Blue Jay had been at our first shelter and told us he was SOBO and would be finishing the LT the next day. It had taken him seven years to finish. I'd thought at the time that we wouldn't take nearly that long, yet there I was eight years later, preparing to finish a trail that had both challenged and thrilled me.

Sandy's flight came in without a hitch and there was no looking back during our drive home. We were talking about our gear and the four days we thought it would take us to get to Canada. The anxiety drifted from my mind, melting into excitement.

When we walked into the house, Sandy saw my gear spread over half the sofa, leaving room for hers. Don and I had brought Sandy's pack with us when we drove from Michigan, so she wouldn't have to fly with it. She'd packed it two weeks before and I was sure she'd want to look it over one more time, but she decided to wait until morning.

Everyone was up early. Sandy sorted through her kit and we were packed and ready to hit the road before seven. We picked up breakfast sandwiches on the way and ate as we began the two-hour drive to the trailhead on Route 118.

Don took pictures of us signing the logbook, and we walked onto the shaded trail at a few minutes after nine, eager to see what lay ahead for us. We walked in silence, feeling eager and anxious. I was glad to know that we'd get to our first summit, Mount Belvidere, on a clear day.

In spite of the sun overhead, the trail was wet and tough. I was disappointed in our speed, but relieved each time Sandy wanted to take a break. The trail was made trickier by blow-downs (fallen trees). In many places, the trail was so overgrown we couldn't see the path. My boot discovered the ground I couldn't see, with glancing steps onto rocks and roots.

We learned from other hikers that the light-gray mound on Mount Belvidere we'd seen from Spruce Ledge Shelter the year before, was from asbestos mining. Sandy and I had both thought that asbestos was a man-made product, not an ore mined from the bowels of a mountain.

As my boots felt for the next step, I found myself thinking about Dan Fogelberg's song, "The Sand and the Foam." Why was my mind playing bits of that album as I walked?

I wasn't tired and the trail was not tough enough to feel the need for musical inspiration, but Fogelberg's voice seemed to be living in the woodland mist and his guitar riffled through the leaves. The guitar measures played in the background as the words rattled in my ears, like a Saturday memory on a sunlit porch step, waiting for the clock to cut me loose.

We hoped to get to Canada by Friday, but if the trail continued to be that tough, we might not finish until Saturday. Don had offered that option, but I knew he'd prefer to get home a day or two before he had to begin work.

On a dry slope, I took my first fall. My left foot shot out from under me, my right foot twisted back, and I felt like I was sliding downhill into second base. I skidded to a halt, my left boot resting against a fallen log and my right boot next to my hip. Sandy turned as I came to a halt. "Are you OK?"

"Yeah, just embarrassed to fall on the surest footing we've seen all day."

We arrived at Tillotson Shelter at three thirty, having done 5.8 miles in 6.5 hours. I reminded myself that it was our first day. I reminded myself, too, of the young couple who'd chosen a slow pace last year. This was not a contest.

There were a couple of male hikers at the Tillotson Shelter; Gray Beard was about my age and Pesto was closer to Sandy's. They brought up the poor trail conditions, wondering why the blow-downs—many of them quite old—had not been addressed by maintenance crews.

"The trails are in better shape where the rich people live," Gray Beard announced.

But I had a different theory: "I don't think its wealth, I think its population. There are more volunteers there. There are fewer people living in the Northeast Kingdom, either hiking or wanting to work on trail crews."

Pesto looked a little sheepish. "I live close enough to come out and do this work. I hike these trails and complain, but I haven't done anything about it—and I'm a Green Mountain Club member." That ended the talk of trail conditions.

Sandy and I looked over our map at the table in the shelter. We planned to get to Hazen's Notch by 1 p.m. the next day, which we could do if we got out of camp by 7 a.m. We could find a place to cowboy near Bruce Peak or Domey's Dome, making it easy for us to get to Laura Woodward Camp on Thursday and to Journey's End on Friday.

Sandy chuckled reading through the notes left in the shelter's logbook. Most of them mentioned an aggressive red squirrel. We discussed blow-downs and pored over maps with that little squirrel constantly at the window, on the table, or hanging off the wall. He seemed to be everywhere. Maybe it was not him (or her), but *them*. I don't know if one squirrel could have been that persistent.

Looking into his little eyes, I told Sandy, "Squirrels rarely live alone. There must be a family here somewhere." But we never saw more than one squirrel. He appeared to be alone, fast, and persistent. And we were glad to not be staying in the shelter itself, as our little friend would probably get into everything, his tiny paws keen on thievery. Unsure of gender, I decided to call our pest Little Paws.

Little Paws was buzzing around our tents as we broke camp in the morning. We hadn't seen a squirrel near the tenting area the night before, Paws had been exclusively at the shelter. People taking down tents must be an easy target, because that rodent was everywhere. Little Paws's persistence was annoyingly cute, but it didn't score a single peanut from our stores. Once our packs were ready, there was no sign of a squirrel. He knew the game.

We walked into the early morning forest with Dan Fogelberg wafting through my mind again.

Looking at the map, we assumed our next mountain, Tillotson Peak, would be about the same as Belvidere but shorter, with less than a mile to the summit. Fogelberg made the walk a little easier.

Ascending Haystack Mountain seemed endless. We were glad to feel the breeze around us as we neared the summit, but the descent was rough. Clam Digger, a NOBO end-to-ender, passed us during our slog and we chatted a bit about nearing the end of our journey. He was thru-hiking and had been on the trail for weeks, but he was enthused for us all to be nearing our destination.

We mentioned the number of blow-downs and overgrown trees and shrubs along the trail, and he said, "Some south-bound guys back at Tillotson were talking about that, but it hasn't bothered me at all, I've hardly noticed it. But Haystack was wicked-tough, don't you think?"

When we crossed Route 58, we took a short break with 1.5 miles left before Hazen's Notch Shelter. There were fewer blow-downs and cloying branches, but it didn't improve our time. Sandy had to stop and drop her pack three times. The second time she stopped, her face was ashen and I asked, "Are you OK?"

Sitting on her pack, her pale face wet with perspiration, she said, "I feel like my legs are drunk. I have to think about every step."

Sandy looked like she needed more rest when she picked up her pack, so I said, "We can rest longer if you want."

She settled her pack on her shoulders. "No, I'm good. Why don't you go ahead and I'll catch up. We don't have far to go."

"I don't think so. You look like you're about to melt and I don't want to have to walk back down here to sop up your puddle." We walked on, but she had to stop and drop her pack one more time. Her coloring wasn't any worse, but it wasn't any better.

"You can go ahead. I'll catch up." Her lips were pale.

"That is not going to happen. We can rest as long as you want, but I'm not leaving you for a minute."

Sandy didn't take off her pack after that, but she had to stop often, about every twenty steps. I counted. She'd stand with both hands on her poles, catching her breath, before she could walk another twenty steps. We all do momentary rests in difficult spots, but not that often. When she stopped I stopped. I thought about what I might do if she reached the point where she just couldn't go on, or worse, if she passed out. I was worried. There were enough people on the trail that day that I could send another hiker for help while I stayed with Sandy. If I had to, I could leave Sandy with a SOAP note and head back to Route 58 myself, without my pack, to get help.

The SOAP note was one of the things I'd added to my pack after my weekend of wilderness first-aid training. SOAP stands for Subjective Objective Assessment Plan, and it allows me to record time and vital signs: heart rate, respiration, etc. If I left a SOAP note with Sandy, anyone who came upon her would know what her condition had been at a specific time. I hoped I wouldn't have to leave Sandy or a note, but I was giving thought to these possibilities as she struggled.

During her next pause, I offered, "We can stop for a bit. I'm good with that."

"I'll be fine if I keep moving."

"You passed fine an hour ago." We now walked without musical accompaniment; Fogelberg knew when to shut up.

When Hazen's Notch Shelter came into view, I hoped Sandy would feel invigorated, seeing how close we were, but she stopped three more times, hands on poles, sweating and breathing deep, saying, "My legs feel drunk."

I envisioned runners I'd seen collapsing at the end of a long race, their legs like rubber as they crashed to the ground. "I'm just out of energy and I don't know why."

When we got to the shelter, we both dropped our packs and I told Sandy to eat something right away. She made up a freeze-dried meal and gulped it down. The transformation was immediate—her color improved and she appeared to be back to normal within the hour. That hour was 4:30 p.m. It had taken almost nine hours for us to walk 6.2 miles. I said, "I hope you're not planning to go on, 'cause I'm beat."

She laughed. "I think we could make Domey's Dome . . . or not."

The trail had been the usual degree of difficulty, with lots of ups and downs on rocks. Sandy had shown great determination and when I mentioned that, she said, "What choice did I have?"

We set up our tents and dove inside for a much deserved nap. Later, over dinner, we discussed our updated plan: coming off the trail on Saturday, rather than Friday. I was able to get a call out to Don and he was fine with picking us up on Saturday.

Don also shared during that conversation that Ringer had pipeline diarrhea and was not eating. Our aging friend had always been a fussy eater and often skipped meals, even as a pup, and in his old age he was prone to digestive upset, so either incident alone would not be cause to worry. But he'd been so wobbly the day before I left, he was standing still when he tipped over. He got back up, but I'd never seen him fall like that. I was worried about my old friend.

That conversation reminded me of the day my father stopped eating. It was as if he'd forgotten how to swallow. He would endlessly chew the tiny bit of food deposited in his mouth, but he couldn't swallow. The look in his eyes was sad and confused. Dad had been ill and we knew the end was coming, but when he stopped eating it hit us hard. He went into hospice where they took great care of him, but he was soon unconscious, never to wake up. He had many visitors and we still talked to him as if he could hear and understand every word, just in case.

I gave Don the go-ahead to make whatever decision regarding Ringer that he thought was appropriate. I didn't want Ringer to suffer just so I could come home and say goodbye. Don didn't think we were at that point yet and I hoped he was right, but Ringer's condition rattled in my head as Sandy ate her second dinner.

CHAPTER THIRTY-EIGHT

TO OZ

I firmly believe that nature brings solace in all troubles.
Anne Frank, "Diary of a Young Girl"

On day three, the trail was as tough as we'd expected. Sandy was walking nearly as fast as usual, but she stopped for breaks more often. She'd eaten two dinners the night before and a good breakfast in the morning, and we were both munching at each break.

While walking Jay Loop toward the Jay Camp Shelter, Sandy suggested that we keep going and camp on Jay Peak. A family I met during my training week had told me they'd camped there. I'd been thinking about that possibility, but hadn't said anything; I was afraid Sandy might agree whether she was feeling up to it or not. We restocked our water supply and moved on.

Jay Peak was as steep as it looked on the map, but our legs were ready and Sandy was doing fine. Several SOBO hikers had mentioned that Doll Peak was going to be especially difficult, worse than Jay, so we knew the next day was going to be tough. Each time I struggled for a handgrip or stretched to reach a toehold, I thought about how much more challenging Doll Peak would be.

When we got to Jay's pinnacle, the afternoon was clear and we could see forever. The building housing the ski lift and restaurant marred the view in one direction, but it felt good to have another summit under our belts.

As we walked past the ski lift building, we read a sign indicating that the gondola was running until 5 p.m., but nothing else was open. That explained the people walking around in flip-flops with small children at their sides. We scouted around for the best campsite and decided on an area near the Long Trail sign that would lead us off the mountain in the morning. It had a view in one direction. We took a break, waiting until after the gondola closed to set up our tents. We weren't sure if we were allowed to camp there. Leaning against our packs, we chatted with tourists.

I hadn't mentioned Ringer or his health problems all day, but Sandy brought it up and I had to admit I'd been thinking about the old guy during much of our walk.

We talked about how attached we get to our dogs and how they complicate our lives while adding so much to them.

I leaned on my pack, gazing into a clear sky. "My dogs have made me a better person. They don't worry about unimportant things, they don't care what you look like or how you're dressed, and as they age they do as much as they can for as long as they can. They don't fret about things in the past or worry about what might be coming."

Sandy was about to share her dog-owner philosophy when a family stopped for a chat about hiking. The husband picked up my pack. "This must weigh thirty pounds."

"With a week's food and no water, it weighs 24.6 pounds," I said.

His wife asked, "You weigh it?"

Sandy added, "We weigh everything."

They would have asked more questions, but their kids were antsy—they didn't care what my pack weighed.

A pleasant breeze ruffled the pages as I began my journal entry, but by the time I finished, I was struggling to hold the paper down. A steady wind had developed and we dove into our fluttering tents for a nap before dinner. When I came out to start my stove, Sandy was resetting her tent. A couple of stakes had been pulled up by the wind and she pounded them in with a rock. Following suit, I used another rock to get my stakes as deep as I could.

I wanted to leave my door open for air and to appreciate the view, but the gusts were so strong I feared my tent would become a giant windsock. We talked over dinner about feeling good and being glad that we'd taken two miles off our goal for the next day. On the map, the next day looked like a simple 5.4 miles, but six SOBO hikers had mentioned how difficult Doll Peak had been and two of the men said the mud-covered rocks coming out of Shooting Star Shelter had been brutal. We would be going down that slope instead of up, which could make it easier, but there was the chance that backing down steep greasy rocks would actually be more difficult. We were prepared for day four to be harrowing.

The wind speed changed as night fell, and not for the better. It blasted harder than anything my tent had yet endured. It rattled every corner, making me wonder how much the fabric could take. Then the wind would stop dead, no hint of movement. I could hear the wind in the distance, coming closer, the sound increasing until it was all around my tent, shaking its taut skin and then stopping without a hint of a breeze. This happened over and over.

The moon shone so bright outside my tent, I thought a utility light was left on. I peeked out and discovered a brilliant full moon and unzipped my tent. Holding on as the door flap snapped in the wind, I scooted out in a seated position, facing into the tent. I could hold onto my unzipped door and view the moon glowing in the night sky. Leaning to the left, I looked down the side of my tent and saw Sandy's tent a few feet away. Beyond her tent, the view opened into an expanse that stretched further than it had during the daylight hours. How could I see further in the dark than I had in the daylight? I was so mesmerized by that wonder, even the harsh wind couldn't move me. Eventually, a blast of wind that would not be ignored drove me back inside. I wriggled back into my tent like a snail pulling into its shell. With everything snugly zipped, I lay in the darkness smiling at the next gust of wind, thinking about the look on Dad's face when I'd shared my hiking plan with him. He'd told me that I would create life-long memories. And he was right. I'll never forget that magic, frightening, moonlit night.

I crawled from my tent in the morning, pleased that the wind had died to almost nothing. I stood facing Sandy's tent on a bright calm morning, but her tent was gone. I looked behind me; had she moved it in the night? There was no sign of her at all, except for a tent stake where her tent had been. When I picked up the stake, I saw another a few yards down-wind. Crouching for the second stake, I saw a third stake, high in a tree where the mountain dropped off into the distance. Sandy and her tent had evidently been picked up, like a bounce house lifted into the air dribbling children as it rose skyward. Sandy was gone.

I jolted myself awake and lay in the darkness wondering if that could happen. Why not? Bounce houses take flight. We were in the midst of another deceiving calm, the wind audible in the distance preparing another attack. My tent rattled and swayed, and when the calm descended again I decided to check on Sandy, just in case. But as I reached for the door zipper, I heard snoring drifting from the direction of Sandy's tent. I laughed and thought for the hundredth time, how can she sleep like that?

My inflatable mattress had deflated again. I blew it back up, knowing it wouldn't last long. I wouldn't be getting much sleep anyway. Could we really blow off the mountain? I'd read that the highest wind velocities ever recorded on the planet Earth had been on New Hampshire's Mount Washington, and wondered what Jay Peak's record was. I had visions of Dorothy's house lifted by a twister, with Dorothy, Toto, and our tents swirling off to the Land of Oz.

CHAPTER THIRTY-NINE

SHOOTING STAR

We knew the 5.8 miles to the Shooting Star Shelter would be grueling, based on reports from SOBO hikers. Sandy announced from her tent, "The forecast calls for rain by 4 p.m."

"OK, we should get out of here after breakfast."

I heated up some cocoa and unwrapped a protein bar. At 5:15, Sandy reported, "The weather forecast now calls for thunder storms by 11 a.m."

We pulled on our packs at 5:50. I'd never eaten breakfast and broken camp so fast.

The trail to Laura Woodward was the usual LT difficulty, but Doll Peak was waiting for us and we were glad to get started up her slope before the rain started. At the summit, we looked at one another. "What were those people talking about?" I asked.

"Maybe the descent is brutal." Sandy was ready for it.

I was still dreading what lay ahead when we walked into an open area with a sign for Shooting Star Shelter.

Sandy stood at the shelter sign. "That was it?"

"Doll Peak was easy and the hike to Shooting Star was nothing." I was shaking my head.

"Maybe it was easier NOBO than SOBO." Sandy was trying to defend them.

"They are SOBO, just getting started. They have no idea how difficult this hike is going to be."

Sandy agreed. "Haystack and Whiteface are waiting for them."

We were in camp by 12:30 and I thought about heading for Journey's End that day, but Sandy was content to stay. So we set our tents on opposite sides of the shelter, in the only available flat spots. Sandy dropped for a nap and I sat at the shelter making my journal entry.

I was almost finished when a family arrived: Mom, Dad, two girls, one boy, and a chocolate Labrador retriever. As soon as their packs were off, Dad and one daughter went for water, while Mom and the other two scouted for tenting sites. I warned them that there wasn't much around. They found no tenting area, so they spread out in the shelter. Mom announced, "We try to stay out of shelters, because we take up so much space."

Sandy joined us for dinner. Dad's trail name was Woodpile. He'd hiked the Appalachian Trail as a teenager. He found a saw early on that hike, and left stacks of firewood and kindling from Georgia to Maine. Now he was sharing part of that experience with his family. At Shooting Star, Woodpile found and cut wood, leaving kindling and fire logs neatly stacked beneath a bench near the shelter.

The young boy was called Slug Sock, because he'd put on his boot one morning with a slug inside. He had a moose antler attached to his pack. No one would complain about the extra weight of that priceless find. An antler shed is a gift from nature.

We were all heading for Journey's End. Haystack was discussed and all agreed that Doll Peak had been easier. I noticed a fresh, nearly bleeding scrape on my leg and looked around at our group. Every leg was scraped, bug-bitten, and mud-smudged.

Mom read the description of the hike from Route 105 to Journey's End: "This is a gentle and scenic hike to the northern end of the Long Trail at the Canadian border." She continued, with a description of a ". . . stroll to Carlton Mountain."

That gave me a twinge of guilt, that we could have hiked out that day and given Don an extra day at home before work. But we all agreed that the description may not be accurate. We were discussing that when cold raindrops sent me to my tent. I'd been dry all day and wanted to stay that way.

I lay in my tent on a sleeping mat that would no longer inflate and listened to the rain. Sleep would not come—it was too early, but I wanted to stay dry. I worried about Ringer for a little while and then my mind strayed.

As a kid, I easily walked off anger, frustration, and disappointments, but sorrow was a different story. The day Vena died, I tried to walk her death out of my mind.

I remember leaving the house before Mom could finish the sentence, slamming the gate as hard as I could and walking as fast as my legs would go. I didn't run, because I didn't want to stop to catch my breath. I wanted my heart to thump right out of my chest, I wanted my lungs to burst, but most of all, I wanted my dog! I charged up the hill behind our house, into the woods, and when I got to the swamp behind the high school, I stomped right through it. I didn't care about anything; getting wet, muddy, or covered with swamp scum meant nothing to me. I was sad and angry, and I was trying to walk away from the worst sorrow of my young life. I was through the swamp and into the deepest of our woods when I began to slow slightly, calling out to the forest, "My dog is dead!"

I slowed and called out even louder. "My dog . . . is dead!"

Slower still, allowing each step to coincide with a word, my voice raised in octave and decibel level. "My—dog—is—dead!"

I slumped down next to a tree trunk and cried. I cried like a baby, with my entire body. I don't know how long I was there, but after a while the sobbing eased to mere tears, then ragged breathing and nose wiping.

I had to charge into the woods to be free to cry that hard. I could never do that in front of anyone. People who cared would reach out, hug me, and say things like "I understand" or "It will be all right." But it wasn't all right and they didn't understand and I couldn't explain it, so there was no hope of making them understand. I didn't want to be hugged, I didn't want to be consoled, I wanted to be alone, preferably in the woods. I wanted to lament my loss without interference.

I was also angry. Vena had been ill, we all knew it. She was so old that her black muzzle had gone white. I knew she couldn't live forever, but when Mom told me that Dad had taken her to the vet and they'd decided the best thing would be to put her to sleep, I exploded. I could not comprehend how they could've thought that was a good idea. They killed Vena. They killed my dog. She was MY dog and the people I loved most had murdered her.

The gray sky was descending to twilight as I walked home with unhurried steps. When I got to the swamp, I slowly walked around its wettest areas. Earlier, as my tears had eased, I'd pulled a leach from my leg and I didn't care to invite others onboard. I took the longest, most time-consuming route home. I needed a sedate mournful return, thinking about how many times Vena and I had walked past this bog or that tree. I was saying goodbye to my dearest friend.

When I got back to the house, my tears had dried and Mom took me outside where she and I convened for a heart-to-heart at the picnic table. We sat in the darkness as she explained in detail what had been wrong with Vena, and that a dog as old as she was would not be able to recover. She asked questions like: "Would you want her to die slowly, in pain?"

"Of course not," I snapped

Mom tried to explain. "Sometimes the best thing to do is not the easiest. Your father and I made the decision because we thought it was best for Vena."

"But why didn't you ask me? I didn't have a chance to say goodbye, and that's not fair. You should have asked me."

She sighed. "Because you are too young to make a decision like this. We could not put that responsibility on you. Your father and I loved Vena, too, but we love you more and we decided this was the best way for everyone. Someday you will understand."

I jumped to my feet. "I will never understand." I stomped off to my room.

Later that night, I was beginning to comprehend what they'd done. I didn't have to like it, but I knew they were doing what they thought was best. I listened to the quiet beyond my bedroom door; no one downstairs was watching TV, arguing, singing, or playing. The house was in mourning. When I realized how sad everyone else was, I felt bad for being so mean to Mom. I was eleven years old and I should be able to handle this. She was a great dog, but Vena was our dog, not just mine. She'd never been MY dog, but in my pain I couldn't see anyone else.

When I opened the door, the quiet enveloped me. What were they doing down there? When I descended the stairs, I found everyone reading or quietly talking, the way they do at a funeral home. I went into the kitchen and gave Mom a hug. I didn't want her to feel worse because I was so sad. We both cried a little and Mom got out a dish she'd set aside for me. I didn't like it, but I would learn to live with their decision. I sat looking at the puckered peas on my plate. Vena loved peas. I would never again sneak unwanted food to her. I cried as I ate disgusting green raisins in her name.

I fell asleep in my tent thinking about the dogs that had filled my life.

CHAPTER FORTY

BRING IT ON

I took a walk in the woods and came out taller than the trees.
Henry David Thoreau

We left Shooting Star at 6 a.m. under menacing skies. The family in the shelter was beginning to stir as we quietly departed. It was a half-mile to the summit of Burnt Mountain and then we would descend 1.2 miles to Route 105, where we could begin the "stroll" up Carlton. Burnt and Carlton Mountains were relatively easy, except for the mud. We put our poles into the muck to steady our bodies as we inched along the slippery the rock. In some areas, the muck was three inches deep, in others, three feet. If we slipped, we might land in mud to our thighs.

I called out as we walked, "This is the Sandy I remember hiking with."

For the first time on that trip, she was walking the way she usually did—I couldn't keep up with her. The trail was easier and there were strolling moments. A warm rain set in at Carlton peak and we decided to travel without our ponchos. When the rain turned cold, I stopped to put on my rain gear and saw Sandy doing the same up ahead. Shortly after that, we got to the sign we'd been looking for, and it was huge.

We'd walked from the Massachusetts border to Canada. The rain let up and we started taking pictures. We got pictures of Sandy at the sign, me at the sign, the sign from this angle, the sign from that angle, and selfies in front of the sign. We walked out to the border-line post and did the same thing. We felt like tourists visiting Niagara Falls for the first time. We took pictures of each other at the border-line, of our backpacks near the marker post, and of Canada's Sutton Mountains in the distance. The U.S.–Canada border was marked by a wide mowed swath that disappeared into the distance. Every time we thought we were done, we'd stop for more pictures.

Sandy joked, "I hope I don't run out of film."

I asked, "Can you imagine carrying film canisters and loading our cameras when we used up our sixteen or thirty-two shots?"

Sandy added, "The young people at Shooting Star know nothing about using film."

We passed a young couple just getting onto the trail. Their plan was to hike the entire LT SOBO, and we gave them a pep talk about how challenging and beautiful it was. After they were out of ear-shot I asked Sandy, "Do you think they'll make it to the Mass border?"

"Why not?"

"Did you see how they were dressed? They looked like they were going to the mall."

"But they're young and strong, and if they really want to do this, they probably will." Sandy defended them.

"But she was wearing makeup, earrings, a necklace, and two bracelets, and their clothing looked like if it got wet it would take forever to dry. And it *will* get wet—soon." I was dubious.

Sandy laughed. "Then this will be a learning experience for them."

"They don't have trail names yet. She could be Max Factor or Laurie-L. He could be Mall Walker or Wet Denim."

"I wonder what they have in those packs." Sandy was still laughing.

That was the conversation that followed us to Journey's End Shelter, where we stopped at the symbol of our expedition's conclusion. We took more pictures and signed the last logbook of our journey. The shelter was tidy and I wondered how many people actually used it. It was 1.9 miles to the parking area—what SOBO would want to stop that early in their hike and what NOBO would want to stop when they were that close to a ride home? We walked the park-like path to the road, the sun popped out to match our mood, and I announced, "Now, this is a stroll."

We were not reminiscing about our hike as we raced toward the parking area. Instead, our conversation turned to the need for a hamburger, fries, and a cold drink. We'd taken our first off-trail meal after each section hike at the Long Trail Brewery, but we didn't think we'd be able to wait through the two- to three-hour drive. There would be restaurants everywhere. I was salivating just thinking about a warm, juicy burger in a soft, tasty bun.

We walked into the parking area at 10:35. It had taken us 4.5 hours to walk 5.7 miles, but we'd dawdled and taken as many pictures on our last day on the trail as we had in our first week. Sandy suggested we walk to the end of Journey's End Road, rather than sitting there for an hour and a half. When we got to the end of the road, we plopped down on the edge of a driveway to wait for our ride.

Sandy leaned back against her pack and I thought she might fall asleep. I sat on the butt of my pack with the belt splayed off to the side. "I'll sit up and keep an eye out for Don."

The thought of him driving past without seeing us kept me alert. We seemed conspicuous sitting by the side of the road, but Don might miss us. I was hell-bent on preventing that.

We'd switched to our crocks while we waited. I saw a car coming, but it was white. Then I saw another, but it was red. There was another that was too small, and I got bored and took a couple of pictures of my muddy feet. Then I took a picture of my boots, with socks and gators draped to dry.

I kept my vehicle vigil, but it was boring, so I began announcing each car: "Car . . . too light."

"Car . . . too small."

"Car . . . this might be it—no, too Jeep."

"Car . . . Ford—but the wrong Ford."

I interspersed my narrative with things like "Do you want to know what my hat's made of?"

No answer. "100% cotton."

No response.

"Whoa, have you smelled your socks at the end of a hike?" Still, no response.

"The fragrance defies description." Nothing.

"Here, take a whiff."

Comes a sound from Sandy somewhere between a moan and a grunt. "Well, at least I know you're awake."

Silence.

"Am I keeping you awake?" No response.

"I can be quiet. It's not easy, but I can do it."

Less than thirty seconds later: "See, I CAN be quiet, it's just boring."

After another twenty or thirty noise-free seconds: "Really boring." More silence.

"Really, incredibly boring."

Sandy sat up. We both sat on our packs watching for cars, so I didn't have to announce them.

As my watch clicked over to twelve, I announced, "OK, he's officially late."

"At one minute late I don't think we should consider firing him," Sandy responded.

"Yeah, he's pretty good most of the time."

Sitting on my pack, I fastened the seat belt across my lap. "Look, Sandy, I have a seat."

Sandy glanced over and cracked a smile.

I snapped and unsnapped my new seat belt until that got boring. With it snapped in place, I said, "Do you think wearing my belt like this would keep me from falling off a mountain?"

Sandy shook her head.

With my hand muffling my speech: "Ladies and gentlemen, for your safety, we recommend that you keep your seat belts fastened throughout the flight. We have a novice co-pilot at the wheel, the captain's asleep, and the navigator's drunk. Your host and hostess crew have donned their parachutes and are about to leap to safety. In the meantime, we want you to stay in your seats, trays up, seat belts fastened and we thank you for flying HAVA—Hire A Vagrant Airline. And as we say in our commercials, HAVA nice day."

We both chuckled and I told Sandy, "I'm beginning to worry about Don."

My mind had wandered to accidents, Don going to the wrong parking area, and Ringer taking a turn for the worse. I consoled myself with the hope that the GPS had misdirected him, he'd figured it out, and would be there any minute.

There was a car coming, and it looked right. It was Don but he was looking at a map as he began to turn onto Journey's End Road. I looked at Sandy, "He doesn't see us."

Then I yelled, as loud as I could—and I can be loud: "DON!"

Don stopped partway around the corner. We grabbed our gear and hobbled over as he opened up the rear hatch. He helped us stow our gear and we clambered into the car. Don popped open a cooler with oranges, cherries, soda, and beer and our stories, coupled with Don's questions, began. Don asked, "Do you want to stop and get some lunch on the way back?"

Almost simultaneously, we said, "Yeah, we're starving."

Don told us that Ringer was doing better: eating, passing solid stool, and acting like a normal crippled old dog. We told Don about the tough parts of the trail, the people we'd met, the mountain views, taking a million pictures at the Journey's End signs, the Canadian border marker, and Journey's End Shelter. Don spotted a General Store that had a deli counter. "Do you want to stop here?"

In unison, Sandy and I said, "Nah, we can wait until we get back."

With a cold drink and chilled fruit, we were content. We shared oranges and conversation for two and a half hours. At the house, our post-hike tradition began for the last time.

I took a shower while Sandy aired her gear, then she showered while I cleaned up my gear. I'd purchased a couple of T-shirts that our friends Mary and David recommended, and I placed Sandy's on her bed while she was in the shower. It was a green shirt with a black hiking-boot footprint on the front, and in white lettering it said, "Hiked it, Liked it, Vermont." Within the boot tread were the words "Bring It On," and that is what Sandy said as she walked onto the porch wearing her new shirt.

CHAPTER FORTY-ONE

WALK ON

My grandmother started walking five miles a day
when she was sixty. She's ninety-seven now,
and we don't know where the hell she is.
Ellen DeGeneres [20]

My tale of decision, adventure, setbacks, and triumphs reminds me of a story an exchange student once shared with me. Rikke, an aspiring veterinary student, had come to us from Denmark. She hoped to use her time working with Don in his veterinary practice to benefit her vet school application.

Rikke's story was about sailing as a cadet on the tall ship *Danmark*. During her voyage between Copenhagen and New York City, a crew from *National Geographic* was on board filming a documentary. We were sitting down to watch the film when Rikke said, "You won't see me much. They made it about the ones who were seasick or afraid to climb into the rigging. If I'd been throwing up or crying, I could have been a star." She held her hand to her chest and threw her head back.

We saw her only briefly in the film; her biggest scene was joking with U.S. sailors, trying to teach them proper Danish pronunciation of words that defy the American tongue. She was not the subject of a storyline, but she was fearless, climbing on rope rigging to the top of the tallest mast. But this did not provide *National Geographic* with a story we normal people could identify with.

Her voyage had been one of the stormiest the *Danmark's* captain could recall, and when I asked Rikke how she climbed into the rigging during storms, she said, "When the mast comes toward you, you hold on very tight, and when it moves away from you, you climb very fast." It was so simple to her.

I'd seen that aptitude in many of the hikers I met on the trail. I'd struggled where they walked with ease. Terrain that challenged them left me crawling and scooting. If I could hike like Rikke could climb, my story would have been short:

I decided to go for a hike.
I bought some gear.
I went for a hike.
It was nice.
The End.

During my days of hiking, I was surprised by how often I thought of people from my past. Some of the people who rattled around in my head were cousins who I rarely saw; BJ and Jennifer showed up in surprising places. But most of the people I thought about were dead. Memories of family and friends who'd passed away followed me, and the number of people on that list increased with each passing year. I watched my parents lose friends, relatives, movie stars, and politicians of their era. When Dad was in his eighties, I realized that all of his old friends were gone. He'd outlived his wife, one of his sons, his three sisters, his lifetime friends Barney and Joe, and all but one of our relatives of his generation. His new friends were around his age, but they hadn't been with him since his youth. I bet he thought of his old friends often, but he didn't talk to me about it. He knew I wouldn't understand.

When Aunt June died, I was struck by the fact that she was the last member of that generation in our family. My parents and all of their siblings and siblings' spouses were gone. That made our generation next in line for that sobering milestone. Gramma died when I was six years old. She'd introduced me to the wonders of nature and I knew she would have approved of my hike.

My ghosts did not haunt me, they kept me company.

But I had one more ghost to visit.

I asked Audrey if we could go to the cemetery, so I could tell Wib that I'd finished the Long Trail.

"He's in the dining room." She pointed to the urn.

"Can I talk to him? I think he's expecting me." She held out her arm toward the doorway.

As I walked into the dining room, Audrey stepped away. I guess she thought I might have something personal to say. I addressed the urn: "Well, you old fart, I did it. I finished the Long Trail and you weren't there to make snide comments about how long it took. I thought I would be talking to you at the cemetery. I was going to stomp on your grave, just to show you I could. But there you are all dressed up with no place to go. If Audrey weren't here I would give you a good shake."

I looked into the next room and thought about it but I'd feel awful if Audrey caught me. I'd feel even worse if the urn fell open and I threw Wib all over the room.

"You would do that to me, wouldn't you?"

I could hear his laugh.

Death ends a life, not a relationship.

Morrie Schwartz, "Tuesdays with Morrie" [21]

I'm sitting in our screen room now, a space that evolved from a happy accident, completing my first book. A soft summer breeze reminds me how nice it is outside.

I was at Fay's house on trash day, the week after she replaced the windows in her vintage Victorian home, and the old windows were leaning against garbage cans. Looking through the aging panes, I thought about the craftsmen who'd built them so many years ago and wondered where and when the rippling glass had been manufactured. I reflected on the first family to move into this lovely house. When they'd looked out these windows, what had they seen? Where there are now paved streets, curbs, and sidewalks, there was probably a gravel road or a two-track lane through an open field. Where the neighbors' homes now stood, there may have been a pasture for the horse or two that lived in the little barn that is now a garage. How many times had these windows been painted and by whom; were the painters young or old, happy or sad? Were they the homeowners or hired help? As I sorted through the windows, I decided that some of them had too much life left in them to be thrown away. Those that were beyond repair, I left for the garbage truck, but I drove home with a backseat filled with windows wrapped in blankets.

Don saw me moving the windows to my garden shed and asked, "What new project is this?"

"I'm not sure yet. They just seemed too nice to throw away."

Don tipped one for a better view. "They look like they've seen better days."

"These are still quite solid. I left the ones that were shaky. Think about the man who built them, how he chose the wood for each window, measured, cut, pinioned the joints, glazed the glass, and carefully painted each frame."

Don tipped the window again. "It doesn't look like the recent painters have been all that careful."

"I can scrape that with a razor blade. Look at the ripples in the glass. They don't make glass like that anymore."

Shaking his head, he said, "There may be a good reason for that." Smiling, he added, "Do I get any input on this project?"

"I'll clear the drawings with you before I start anything, but I have no idea what I'm going to do with them."

Ringer walked back and forth with us as we stacked the windows in the shed that day. He sniffed at them as if he knew who'd built them or where they'd been. He was probably sniffing out Fay's two collies, but his interest persisted long after he should have given up on the scent of dogs he knew so well. I expected him to take off on his usual flights around the yard in rutted tracks worn deep by his excess energy; his neurological condition affected his walking stride, but at a run you'd never guess he was disabled. But he didn't give up sniffing at the windows until I was ready to close up the shed. When the door snapped shut, Ringer disappeared as if he'd been shot from a gun.

Our salvaged windows found a new home in this screen room, a free-standing enclosed porch with the windows dictating its design. Since we already had such a room in Michigan, the windows traveled to Vermont. Each half of a double-hung window became a window unto itself, hinged at the top and suspended by chains to allow full air circulation. The angled windows reflect the ferns and shrubs around the building and bring the outdoors into the space.

We eat most of our meals here, come out to read, entertain guests, and sometimes spend the night in the tiny sleeping loft. Ringer declared his approval of our little house before construction was complete, hopping onto the sofa to supervise the window installation. Ten years later, it was still a favorite spot for him to hang out, although he can't get up on the sofa anymore.

Ringer and I have changed. His face is almost as gray as my hair, but we still love our screen room. When Don and I need to keep Ringer back while we go for long walks, he is satisfied if we wander around the meadow and contented to wait for us on his cushy dog bed in the corner. He's sleeping on that bed now, and I pause long enough to be sure he is still breathing. He's sixteen years old and becoming fragile; he can no longer run at all and his wobbly walk fails him occasionally. His breathing is fine, but I know he won't be with us much longer. I hope he will quietly take one last breath and drift away peacefully, but I know there may come a time when his legs fail altogether and we will have to do what's best. Don and I joke about our old friend "circling the drain," thinking that humor makes this time less sad, but there will be no joy in Mudville when Ringer stops barking.

I wonder if, or should I say when, I can no longer hike, will I be as happy as Ringer to waddle around the meadow and fall asleep in the screen room? He gets excited each time we take him for a short stroll. Does he wonder why we don't take him up the hill anymore? Does he care? Will I care when I can no longer go up the hill? I hope I'm as happy as Ringer appears to be with the bits of his old life that he can still take part in. He has the same happy bark (with a deep old-man tenor), the same body vibrating with excitement. His face is gray and his stride falters, but when I look into his eyes there's a joyful spark.

I'm not delusional. I know how old I am and I know that age changes things. Many of my friends have passed on, and each day moves me closer to that moment. People have asked me who I'm trying to impress with this geriatric hiking. My goal is to follow Ringer's example and stay as active as I can for as long as I can.

There is no magic wand to ward off age or death, but Ringer's acceptance and grace are my model. He's not embarrassed by his current state, he doesn't worry about what's coming, and his glowing eyes make my eyes glisten. I hope that when I'm sitting in the screen room instead of walking up the hill, I will be soothed by pleasant memories.

Walking the lakeshore with Mom, I knew she was trying to explain death. At six years old, I'd seen dead animals before so I had some idea what it meant.

Mom was using gentle words to tell me what had happened to Gramma. I knew I wouldn't see her again and that Mom and Dad were very sad. I was sad, too, but I wasn't sure why. As we approached the cottage, Mom asked, "Can you be a good girl and play with the toys on the porch while I help Aunt Thelma in the kitchen?"

I nodded. I could see through the windows that there were a lot of people in Gramma's house. Mom guided me through the door and the maze of mourners within. I saw few faces that I recognized, but Dad patted my head as we walked by.

I looked around. "Mom, where did all these people come from?"

"They're Gramma's friends."

I kept looking for familiar faces. "Where were they when we came to see Gramma?"

Mom smiled and squeezed my hand.

When we got to the screened porch, I headed for my favorite spot—the white wicker sofa with soft green cushions. When we stayed at Gramma's, I slept on that sofa, and if I needed a nap on a long summer afternoon, that was where I'd go. Mom took my hand. "No, honey, save those seats for the grown-ups. Why don't you sit near the toy box?"

I sat on the floor next to the wooden crate full of toys, listening to people talking about Gramma. I'd pulled out some Lincoln Logs, thinking about what I might build, when a woman loomed in the porch doorway. I'd seen her once before, but not in this house. I knew Gramma didn't like her. She shouldn't have been there. The tone in Gramma's voice when she spoke to this woman was one that I'd never heard her use. Gramma's words that day, as the big woman walked away, were, "She looks like a sack-a-potatoes wearing a belt."

As Sack-a-potatoes lumbered toward the wicker sofa, the floorboards moaned beneath her and the wicker screeched as she sat down. A tiny woman followed her out. Her stick-thin legs skittered below her skirt, reminding me of a bird—a sandpiper, darting on the beach. The floorboards did not notice her and the sofa cushion barely dented when she sat.

Sack-a-potatoes said, "Augusta was a strong woman."

Sandpiper replied, "Yes, and she was so kind."

215

Sack-a-potatoes cleared her throat.

Sandpiper went on, "She was strong and kind."

Sack-a-potatoes groaned, and people nearby glared. They knew she shouldn't be there.

Sack-a-potatoes struggled to think of something nice to say. "It's so sad. She'd just signed up for dance classes with Arthur Murray."

Who was Arthur Murray? I'd heard that name before. Was he there somewhere? Sandpiper added, "And she had three new dresses in her closet."

"That's so sad." Sack-a-potatoes didn't sound sad.

A man leaned casually in the porch doorway, gazing out at the lake. His eyes scanned the water. "I don't think it's sad. I think it's beautiful. She lived until she died."

Decades later, in a philosophical discussion, I was asked what I would like people to say about me at my funeral and I heard Sandpiper's voice. I repeated her comment about strength and kindness like I'd been planning it for years.

As I approach the end of my life, I realize that hiking, writing, and living until I die are engrained in my personal philosophy.

Also, I hope I die with new dresses in my closet.

Endnotes

1. Harrison, J. (2008). *The Woman Lit by Fireflies* (Reprint ed.). Grove Press.
2. de Graaf, J. (2017, January 14). A Backpacker's Theory of Life. *Sierra: The National Magazine of the Sierra Club.* https://contentdev.sierraclub.org/www/sierra/green-life/backpacker-s-theory-life
3. Demetri Martin is an American comedian, actor, director, cartoonist and musician (demetrimartin.myshopify.com).
4. Doiron, P. (2013). *Massacre Pond: A Novel.* Minotaur Books.
5. Abbey, E. (1990). *Desert Solitaire.* Touchstone.
6. Doiron, P. (2013). *Massacre Pond: A Novel.* Minotaur Books.
7. Mabe, C. (1989, November 18). Alice Walker Through The Looking Glass. *Sun Sentinel.* https://www.sun-sentinel.com/news/fl-xpm-1989-11-18-8902100502-story.html
8. Seuss, D. (1990). *Oh, the Places You'll Go!* Random House Books for Young Readers.
9. Carson, R. (1964). *Silent Spring* (Mass Paperback Edition). Crest Books.
10. Muir, J. (2018). *Our National Parks* (First Edition). Gibbs Smith.
11. Abbey, E. (1977). *The Journey Home* (1st ed.). Dutton Adult.
12. Gibran, K. (2003). *The Prophet.* Rupa (Educa Books).
13. Howe, N. (2009). *Not Without Peril: 150 Years Of Misadventure On The Presidential Range Of New Hampshire.* Appalachian Mountain Club Books.
14. Hillary, E. (2000). *View from the Summit: The Remarkable Memoir by the First Person to Conquer Everest* (Illustrated ed.). Gallery Books.
15. L. (2015, June 15). Kierkegaard on how "if one just keeps on walking, everything will be all right." Tolstoy Therapy. https://www.tolstoytherapy.com/kierkegaard-on-how-if-one-just-keeps-on/

16. Muir, J., & Anderson, T. (2018). *The Mountains of California*. CreateSpace Independent Publishing Platform.
17. Guillemets, T. (n.d.). The Quote Garden - Quotes, Sayings, Quotations, Verses. The Quote Garden. Retrieved February 25, 2021, from https://www.quotegarden.com
18. Frank, A. (1994). *Anne Frank: The Diary of a Young Girl By Anne Frank*. Bantam Dell.
19. Viesturs, E., & Roberts, D. (2007). *No Shortcuts to the Top: Climbing the World's 14 Highest Peaks* (Reprint ed.). Crown.
20. Ellen DeGeneres Quotes. (n.d.). BrainyQuote. Retrieved February 23, 2021, from https://www.brainyquote.com/quotes/ellen_degeneres_131597
21. Albom, M. (2002). *Tuesdays with Morrie: An Old Man, a Young Man, and Life's Greatest Lesson*, 20th Anniversary Edition (Anniversary, Reprint ed.). Crown.

ACKNOWLEDGMENTS

If I mentioned everyone who helped me along the trail of bringing *Walking Home* to publication it would require another book. There were so many of you; some who didn't know they were assisting me.

I must begin my appreciations with Sandy Evans, who hiked the Long Trail with me. Audrey and Wib Putnam, who dropped us off and picked us up when my husband was not available; Ewa who led me through my weekend training hikes in Michigan; every hiker who offered assistance or advice along the way.

I would like to thank my early readers; Fay Kozlowski, Mary Drewek and Lois Robbins. One of Lois' questions still makes me laugh: "Are you allergic to hyphens?"

Many members of the League of Vermont Writers offered encouragement and advice. It was at an LVW seminar where I heard two agents tell us: "If you're not working with a writer's group you're working at a disadvantage."

I participated in many workshops at the Writer's Center of White River Junction, Vermont, led by Joni B. Cole and Kim Gifford. In these groups we learned much from the instructor and from each other.

Stephen McArthur and Samantha Kolber, at Rootstock Publishing guided me through the publishing maze with kindness and understanding. My editors Courtney Jenkins and Deborah Heimann were also considerate and helpful.

Mentioned last, but first in my heart, is my husband Don. He balances the arc between honest criticism and encouragement.

ABOUT THE AUTHOR

Celia Ryker's first career was training horses, teaching and campaigning students on southeast Michigan's local hunter jumper circuit. After thirty years she went back to school and switched to gardening and landscape design. When she began distance hiking her husband said, "She got to H in the alphabet and stopped. She went from horses, to horticulture, to hiking." Beyond all of those, she writes. She has been writing all of her life and is now an author. Her first book Walking Home is a memoir about hiking Vermont's Long Trail. It is a series of short stories brought together by a difficult hike. Celia and her husband Don live between Vermont and Michigan with their border collie, Flurry. Visit her website, celiaryker.com.

In Memoriam

Ringer, 2002-2019

 **Also Available from Rootstock Publishing:**

The Atomic Bomb on My Back
Taniguchi Sumiteru

Blue Desert
Celia Jeffries

*China in Another
Time: A Personal Story*
Claire Malcolm Lintilhac

An Everyday Cult
Gerette Buglion

*Fly with A Murder of Crows:
A Memoir*
Tuvia Feldman

The Inland Sea: A Mystery
Sam Clark

Junkyard at No Town
J.C. Myers

*The Language of Liberty:
A Citizen's Vocabulary*
Edwin C. Hagenstein

A Lawyer's Life to Live
Kimberly B. Cheney

The Lost Grip: Poems
Eva Zimet

Lucy Dancer
Story and Illustrations by Eva
Zimet

Nobody Hitchhikes Anymore
Ed Griffin-Nolan

*Preaching Happiness:
Creating a Just and Joyful World*
Ginny Sassaman

*Red Scare in the Green Mountains:
Vermont in the McCarthy Era
1946-1960*
Rick Winston

Safe as Lightning: Poems
Scudder H. Parker

Street of Storytellers
Doug Wilhelm

*Tales of Bialystok:
A Jewish Journey from
Czarist Russia to America*
Charles Zachariah Goldberg

*To the Man in the Red Suit:
Poems*
Christina Fulton

*Uncivil Liberties:
A Novel*
Bernie Lambek

The Violin Family
Melissa Perley;
Illustrated by Fiona Lee Maclean

Wave of the Day: Collected Poems
Mary Elizabeth Winn

*Whole Worlds Could Pass Away:
Collected Stories*
Rickey Gard Diamond

*You Have a Hammer:
Building Grant Proposals for
Social Justice*
Barbara Floersch

CPSIA information can be obtained
at www.ICGtesting.com
Printed in the USA
BVHW050537050921
616040BV00005B/15

9 781578 690534